Living & working in
South Africa

Living & Working in
South Africa

Survive and thrive
in the new South Africa

MATTHEW SEAL

How To Books

Published by How To Books Ltd,
3 Newtec Place, Magdalen Road,
Oxford OX4 1RE. United Kingdom.
Tel: (01865) 793806. Fax: (01865) 248780.
email: info@howtobooks.co.uk
http://www.howtobooks.co.uk

British Library Cataloguing in Publication Data.
A catalogue record for this book is available from
the British Library.

Edited by Julie Nelson
Cover design by Shireen Nathoo Design
Cover image by PhotoDisc
Cover copy by Sallyann Sheridan

Produced for How To Books by Deer Park Productions
Typeset by PDQ Typesetting, Newcastle-under-Lyme, Staffs.
Printed and bound by Cromwell Press, Trowbridge, Wiltshire

NOTE: The material contained in this book is set out in good
faith for general guidance and no liability can be accepted
for loss or expense incurred as a result of relying in particular
circumstances on statements made in the book. Laws and
regulations are complex and liable to change, and readers should
check the current position with the relevant authorities before
making personal arrangements.

Contents

List of Illustrations

Preface

If you ask me what's special about South Africa, I wouldn't say the Big Five, Sun City or the Cape Winelands. Shopping in Sandton City, going up the cable car on Table Mountain and surfing off Durban aren't the real thing either. Nor is it the cheap prices in the shops or the chance to own a millionaire's mansion for the cost of an English semi.

It's hard to pin down, but South Africa's attraction definitely has something to do with the weather. Which Brit could not be charmed by over 300 days of sunshine a year in Johannesburg? It's also partly the big skies, the ancient red earth, the bougainvillea and jacaranda flowering pale purple in October.

Nature in South Africa is elemental, exciting, dangerous. Now come to the people – perhaps the same three adjectives could apply equally! Whatever else it is, South Africa is alive, dramatic, quick-changing, and so are its people.

It is remarkable that despite years of apartheid, repression and dehumanisation, the notion of *ubuntu*, of getting along with others, of trying to see the humanity even in your oppressor, was never lost. It was Nelson Mandela's wisdom and greatness to harness this quality of forgiveness and reconciliation – given concrete expression in the heart-rending and searing accusations and confessions of the Truth and Reconciliation Commission – into a unique political settlement that saw the country's first democratic elections, the most liberal constitution in the world and the rebirth of the country as the 'new' South Africa.

Yet for years Mandela, and everybody else in the African National Congress and SA Communist Party in prison or in exile, were shadowy, demonised figures, who could not be quoted or photo-graphed. Apartheid did this, separating people and families, judging some as good and others bad, saying some could work or be educated and have decent health care while others had to live in fictitious 'homelands' in the heat and dust because they were labelled black or coloured.

Apartheid was a criminal system, and rightly condemned as sinful by the United Nations, yet its perpetrators were given a hearing at the TRC hearings or allowed to continue to enjoy their lavish state pensions. They were not put to death or stripped of their ill-gotten gains, as would surely have happened elsewhere in Africa.

Living through this process, from the dark days of P. W. Botha's last-ditch defence of 'grand apartheid', the years of struggle and eventual democratic triumph of the ANC, has been an exhilarating and anxious ride. The overwhelming personal impression, though, in this most politicised of nations, hasn't been political. Rather it has been something more basic, more of human size. It's to do with watching and sharing in a process of survival and hope, getting through life happily against all the odds and retaining dignity and optimism.

Time magazine reported in July 1999 a global survey by the Angus Reid Group, in which people were asked how they felt about the future. Their answers formed a 'hope index'. The survey found pessimism reigned supreme in Europe, with Germany (gross national product of $28,000 a head) scoring 18 per cent and France ($26,000) only 17 per cent. South Africa ($3,500) by contrast, scored 42 per cent and Brazil ($4,400) registered 64 per cent on the hope index. Having so little materially, the average South African, Mr Dube and Mrs Van der Merwe, Professor Naidoo and Mrs Radebe, Dr Jacobs and Miss Smith, can still keep smiling. And to think they speak English too.

Exploring the family connections

I arrived in South Africa in 1982, at the time of the Falklands War and a British economy in recession. Apart from a jingoistic blip in the national mood during this contrived 'war', the hope index in England was low, and my own was even lower. A vivacious blonde South African girl I'd met in Cambridge in the horrible winter of 1981–82 pulled me out of my Brit pessimism and persuaded me to try my luck in Johannesburg. I lost the girl, as it happened, but I never regretted the chance to start afresh under African skies.

I relate in Chapter 5, on working for a living, how after my initial contact had petered out I was lucky enough to find a job and a company to sponsor me as a temporary and later a permanent resident. I'd suggest you try something a little less chancy and plan your own work prospects more carefully. Chapter 3, on moving to South Africa, gives an idea of how the process happens these days.

Some time after I had emigrated, my mother told me there had already been some sort of family connection with South Africa. Her mother's elder brother, Fred Harwood, was a regular soldier in the British army in India. I have a sepia picture from G. W. Lawrie, 'artists and photographers' in Lucknow, of my blond-haired, blue-eyed, dimple-chinned great uncle, probably from the 1890s. The faded photo shows a man in full vigour and with two arms. Fred Harwood was to lose his right arm at the shoulder in one of the battles in the South African (Anglo-Boer) War, and always hoped to return, but never did. His brother-in-law and my maternal grand-father, Fred Hale, was a compositor and printer. Impressed by Fred Harwood's stories of the beautiful African land, Fred Hale nearly settled with his family in South Africa around the time of Union in 1910, but illness prevented him. Strange to think my mother and I might both have been born in the country I later came to live in and learn to love.

Opportunities and risks

While this book addresses the anticipated concerns of the would-be or new immigrant to South Africa in chapters on immigration, settling in, work and tax, retirement, health and education, social life, leisure and transport, South Africa's unique circumstances also demand some special treatment here. The long introduction, a chapter on the new and the old South Africa and another on the national scourges of crime and HIV/Aids reflect other priorities that merit your attention. I have tried to be objective about the dangers posed by alarmingly high crime rates and the even more frightening spectre of Aids killing a quarter of the population within ten years, but if you are unlucky enough to become a crime or Aids statistic the matter suddenly becomes personal and very meaningful.

You must balance for yourself the opportunities and risks involved in moving to South Africa. Try and do a cold-blooded cost-benefit analysis of your own. Speak to as many South Africans as you can, whether these are people who have fled the country (thus contribut-ing to the skills shortage you may be helping to fill) or are on holiday in Europe.

Above all, take a chance to visit the country on holiday, feel its drumbeat and give yourself time to experience its rhythms. Package trips are relatively cheap in pounds and dollars, and if it's February in the depths of a British winter don't you deserve some sunshine, cricket and the beach? But be warned, there's something hypnotic and beguiling about the southern tip of Africa, something special and pulling about the skies, soil and people that never leaves you, despite the harshness of its everyday life.

Great in geological age, Africa is new in human terms, especially South Africa, which after all was only reborn in 1994. There is so much to contribute in the nation-building that was always Nelson Mandela's favourite theme. As the Roman writer Pliny said some two thousand years ago, 'Africa always brings something new'. Maybe it's your turn to find it.

A note on conversions

Following South African practice, the metric system is used for expressing distance, size, weight and so on, and temperatures are given in degrees Celsius. South African time is either one or two hours ahead of Greenwich Mean Time (in the British summer and winter, respectively). Telephone and fax numbers are given as from within South Africa, with the 011 prefix for Johannesburg, 021 for Cape Town, and so on. Dialling from the UK, the international code is 00 27, followed by a two-digit place code (e.g. 11 for Johannesburg, 21 for Cape Town), and usually a seven-digit telephone number. During the writing of this book the rand was at between R9.30 and R10 to the pound and R6 to R6.50 to the dollar.

Matthew Seal
Johannesburg and Norwich

Acknowledgements

This book is largely based on research conducted in the archives of *The Star* and The South African Institute of Race Relations, both in Johannesburg. Without the helpful advice of the librarians and staff of these institutions the book could not have been completed, and grateful thanks are offered both to Independent Newspapers and the SAIRR.

Other documentary and printed sources referred to are listed in the section on further reading. Perhaps surprisingly, considering the long tradition of Brit and Boer meeting in South Africa, there seems to be no other directly comparable and up-to-date book on settling, living and working in the country. So this one may well have something of a 'trekking' spirit about it, of pioneering and perhaps colonising a new area of research.

Tom Killoran gave specific advice on the retirement chapter and Annemie Dover on the immigration chapter, for which I am grateful. My colleagues Pat Lucas, Margie King and Roberta Hunte spared time from their subediting duties at *Business Report* to comment on some of the chapters and help with the research. Thanks for all the help and encouragement. I alone remain responsible for the content and opinions expressed.

Thanks also to Jack Rubin for making the initial suggestion that I approach my publisher.

I am indebted to Giles Lewis, Nikki Read and Ros Loten of How To Books for taking me on and helping an old hand at subbing finish his first book. It was disconcerting to find myself repeating the same faults as the writers I had worked with over the years, but my publishers allowed me an author's foibles while still getting their own way on the things that mattered.

My biggest thanks must be reserved for my wife Julie, to whom I dedicate this book. We met in the same week that the book was commissioned and were married just one week after the typescript and disk were delivered to Oxford. Julie has been the perfect partner, pushing, prompting or threatening me as the need arose, but always with humour and good sense. This is truly a joint project, and she is its other parent. She also drew the maps. *Baie dankie, Julie!*

1

Introducing South Africa

We will begin this book fairly traditionally, with an overview in this chapter of South Africa's geography, history, politics, economy, society and law, followed by a second chapter which takes up the theme of the 'new' South Africa, its prospects and challenges.

While this first chapter will necessarily be descriptive and scene-setting, the second will be more argumentative, reflecting on the big issues for survival and prosperity, not only in South Africa but in many senses in the larger southern African region too.

UNDERSTANDING THE GEOGRAPHY

Big, beautiful and surprising

South Africa often surprises newcomers with its **size** and diversity. At about 1.2 million square kilometres it is as big as Germany, France, Italy and the Benelux countries combined, or, in American terms, as large as Texas and California together. Cape Town is on the same latitude south as Sydney and Johannesburg as Brisbane.

The **population** was estimated to be some 43 million at the start of the millennium, with scattered large cities and townships in a heartland of largely dry farmland, sparsely peopled in the dry north and west but with a denser rural population in the more fertile east and south-east. Outside the cities the impression is of big skies, space and an ancient land with a huge potential.

In terms of **area** the country stretches some 2,000 kilometres from the Limpopo river in the north to Cape Agulhas in the south (with the good roads you can just about drive this in a day), and almost 1,500 kilometres from Port Nolloth in the west to Durban in the east.

Flanked by cold and warm seas

Situated at the southern foot of the African continent (an obvious fact of geography many South Africans are only just rediscovering now that the new South Africa has opened up unprecedented contacts everywhere), the country sits between the cold but nutrient-rich **Benguela current** to the west and the warm **Mozambique-Agulhas current** to the east.

The Benguela current brings Antarctic cool to the western seaboard, but a multitude of fish; it lowers temperatures as well as reducing rainfall. The current to the east flows from the Indian Ocean southward, supporting lush subtropical vegetation at the KwaZulu-Natal coast. Durban is usually at least 6 degrees Celsius warmer than Port Nolloth and receives 16 times more rainfall, at 1,000 mm a year.

The **coastline** is a long 2,954 kilometres, with considerable areas of unspoilt beach and a small number of working harbours, including Saldanha Bay, Cape Town, East London, Port Elizabeth, Durban and Richards Bay.

Highveld, lowveld and semi-desert

The country is often divided into **three main geographical zones**: a central interior plateau (the highveld), a narrow coastal plain (lowveld) and the north-western desert (Kalahari basin).

The divide between highveld and lowveld is marked by dramatic mountain escarpments, including the Drakensberg in the east and other ranges in the southern and western Cape. The coastal strip varies from some 60 km wide in the west to about 220 km in the east.

The lowveld generally has more fertile soils and more rainfall than the highveld, while much of the country from the Karoo north is semi-desert, with hot days and cool nights and scant rainfall. The interior is essentially a dry plateau at about 1,200 metres above sea level.

Looking below ground, the country is blessed with an abundance of precious **minerals**, including diamonds and gold, but also coal and iron ore. According to the Minerals Bureau, South Africa has 40 per cent or more of proven world reserves of chromium, gold, manganese, platinum group metals and vanadium. The only significant shortfall is in oil, and even here synthetic oil-from-coal producer Sasol meets nearly half the country's needs.

On the other hand, there are no commercially navigable rivers or lakes in the country, and many rivers only flow in the rainy season. The combined run-off of all the country's rivers is estimated at half that of the Zambezi to the north.

A generally benign climate

For all its problems as the so-called crime capital of the world,

Johannesburg unarguably enjoys one of its best climates. Situated not far south of the Tropic of Capricorn, but inland at an altitude of some 1,700 metres, it records well over 300 days of sunshine a year. It has predictable warm and windless summer (October to April) days, typified by afternoon thunderstorms, and clear, bright and crisp winters. Heavy hailstorms in summer and frosts and static electricity in the winter are about as extreme as it gets.

Cape Town has a more Mediterranean and variable weather pattern, with cool and wet winters and hot, dry summers; high winds can happen at any time.

The **southern coast** along the Garden Route is temperate and pleasant, while **Durban** has both heat and humidity at most times of the year, becoming almost unbearably hot in summer. In the central interior, **Bloemfontein** has what Europeans call a continental climate with more extremes, typified by cold winters and hot summers.

Overall, the country is considered a **dry zone**, with an average rainfall of 464 mm, just over half of the world average. Two-thirds of South Africa has under 500 mm of rain, which puts it below the norm for dry crop farming and into the pastoral arena. The implication is that the region is prone to drought, with periodic water shortages.

An environment with few natural disasters

However, South Africa is essentially free of floods, tidal waves, typhoons, monsoons and other forms of climatic affliction. By the same token, earthquakes are rare (although in mining areas there are often rockfalls and incidents of subsidence), and there are no active volcanoes.

The natural environment here is hard, no doubt, but seldom severe – although Voortrekkers in a winter snowstorm in the Drakensberg in the 1830s or shipwrecked sailors on the Skeleton Coast would disagree. What has been unique in the world is the way South Africa has made and remade its human environment.

UNDERSTANDING THE HISTORY

Rather than a potted chronological history of South Africa, which you can find easily elsewhere, there may be more benefit in highlighting certain historical themes that still have a resonance today.

Ancient land, modern history

Say you are reading these words in Johannesburg in the year 2000. You are in a city only 115 years old and in a country that has been fully democratic for under a decade. Yet the land below your feet was once part of the ancient super-continent of Gondwanaland, before the southern continents we recognise today split apart some 65 million years ago and Africa came into being.

The peoples of southern Africa, apart from the San and Khoi hunter-gatherers (once called Bushmen and Hottentots, respectively, and collectively known as the Khoisan), are actually all immigrants within the last two thousand years, which is a flea bite considering the age of the land itself.

An original home of humankind?

The imprint of modern humanity was late in arriving in southern Africa, yet there is a strong case that humankind itself developed here. Evidence is rapidly accumulating to show occupation by human-like creatures for at least three million years. Little remains of most of that human occupation, with only fragments of skulls and bones to tantalise scientists. Yet it is probably because settled occupation has been so recent that so many remnants of far earlier human beings still exist and can be found.

And in another twist of the very ancient and the very new that characterises so much of living in South Africa today, there is a recent boom in palaeotourism, with well-organised trips for ecotourists to sites of early humanity.

No empty interior in southern Africa

It was an invention of Afrikaner mythology that the interior of southern Africa was unpeopled and available for settlement by the next oxwagon train of Boers (farmers) that trekked through the highveld.

There are known to have been two broad migrations of peoples into this region from the north in historic times. To the west of the country bands of Khoisan, at about the start of the Christian era, moved into the western Cape, tending their cattle and oxen, and scavenging on the shoreline.

By about the third century, to the east, Bantu-speaking groups from central Africa were settling in present-day KwaZulu-Natal. These peoples were pastoralists but also grew grain. Historians believe it was the lack of regular rainfall in the western interior, which made farming unproductive, that kept these Bantu-speaking peoples in the east.

The two migrating groups did, however, intermingle to some degree, which accounts for the introduction of Khoisan 'clicks' into the Bantu languages. By the fifteenth century, most of the eastern side of the country was settled, with sophisticated iron smelting and mining of precious metals that was far in advance of contemporary Europe.

South African history didn't start in 1652

Thankfully, the history syllabus in new South African schools no longer has a place for the National Party nonsense that the country's 'real' history began in 1652, when the Dutch East India Company far-sightedly set up a permanent trading post in Table Bay, which would become the 'Mother City', Cape Town, and launch a glorious white supremacy in southern Africa. Historians now know it was a series of fortuitous good harvests and some skulduggery in cheating the local Khoisan that would lead to the first Dutch settler-farmers (a mere 120 of them) deciding they wanted to stay; they also needed more labour for the farms.

The leader of the group, Jan van Riebeeck – an ordinary soldier and administrator, not some prototype Afrikaner superman – decided by 1660 to grant property rights to the farmers and arranged for some 200 black slaves to be brought in. Van Riebeeck had followed orders in planting gardens to supply the settlement but also put in a long hedge to separate the Khoisan from the Europeans. These three decisions – to promote permanent white settlement, guarantee that settlement by forced black labour and segregate white and black – were an early precursor of the country's subsequent racially scarred history.

Slavery continued until its abolition in the British colonies in 1833, and Slave House, the former slave auction building, in central Cape Town, is today a poignant reminder of the actual origin of the Cape's prosperity.

However, there was no grand plan, no foreknowledge by the Dutch that their experiment of setting up a victualling station in Table Bay to provision ships passing through to the East Indies would lead to a white, Afrikaner South Africa.

A nation of successive streams of immigrants

South Africa's immigrants include the victims of religious persecution (like the 200 **Huguenots**, who fled France in the 1680s and settled in the Cape, becoming its leading grape farmers and winemakers), economic refugees (like the impoverished 5,000 **1820**

Settlers from England, who moved into the eastern Cape) or **get-rich-quick miners** (a cosmopolitan crowd which flocked to the diamond rush around Kimberley in the 1870s and the even bigger gold rush in Johannesburg from 1885).

Other streams of immigrants came as indentured labour, notably sugar workers from south and later western **India**, who in the 1860s and later settled on the cane farms of Natal, and the **Chinese** mineworkers, who from 1904 to 1907 kept the mines of the Witwatersrand going as the British strove to revive the gold industry after the ending of the second South African War in 1902.

In addition, we should not forget the continuing streams of **migrant labourers** who for a century have come on contract from what are now Mozambique, Lesotho and Zimbabwe to work the South African gold and coal mines. Without their labour – and exploitation – there could be no continuing South African mining industry.

Each of these groups found more reason to stay than return to their places of origin, and all added their rich culture to the evolving country, as well as influencing its settlement geography.

Forced migrations add to the population mix

Let us take three examples of another kind of population movement in South Africa, where it was less a matter of choice than desperation or necessity that led to a decision to move on.

- What prompted the **Great Trek** of 1834 to 1836, when hundreds of Boer farmers, in what dissolved into a number of rival groups of 'Voortrekkers', ventured with their wagons and families into the unknown east and north of the country? The Voortrekker leaders claimed they had been forced into it by unbearable demands of the British government of the Cape, by a 'charter of liberties' granted to the Khoisan and by pressure from the new influx of English settlers. Whatever the objective merits of their case, they knew they were risking clashes with the British but more likely all-out war with Shaka Zulu.

- Shaka, the warlord of the Zulu, and his successor Dingane were the cause of a second great migration. Known as the 'African Napoleon', Shaka was a military genius who welded separate groups into a formidable unified fighting force, which drove all before it. The **Mfecane** of the late 1810s and 1820s is the graphic term, meaning 'crushing', which describes the violent upheavals among the peaceful, agricultural black kingdoms of eastern South Africa. It was effectively the end of settled tribal life in the old sense. To join Shaka, fight him or flee were stark options. Many chose the last, and some groups relocated hundreds of kilometres to the north to avoid the Zulu *impi* (armed bands). Numerically, it was the biggest movement of the population then seen, and the dispersal of settled kingdoms would later be reflected in the patchwork of black communities in apartheid's 'homelands'. A Sotho group took refuge in the mountains of what is now Lesotho, and another group, the Swazi, settled in the east. Both survived to nationhood after long periods of 'protection' from the British.

- A third example of enforced migration is all too vivid within living memory, with the **forced removals of apartheid**, as established mixed communities were broken up and obliged to relocate in designated segregated 'group' areas. The destruction of such communities as District Six in Cape Town and Sophiatown in Johannesburg was to become emblematic of the wholesale dehumanisation of the non-white population that apartheid stood for.

Two hundred years of British and Boer mistrust

Any superficial reading of South African history must reflect the old antagonism of British and Dutch (later Boer and later again Afrikaner) in a power struggle for the Cape, the central interior and for a while Natal. It is a dynamic which has echoes even today.

After Dutch rule since 1652, in 1795 the British annexed the Cape, which reverted to Dutch rule briefly under the Batavian Republic but became British again in 1806 and would remain so until Union in 1910.

The rivalry would continue in the era of the Boer republics through the nineteenth century, over exploitation of the discovery of diamonds and gold, and above all in the two Anglo-Boer wars. These wars (now more accurately called the South African wars of 1880–81 and 1899–1902 to reflect the involvement of black and coloured Africans, along with other nationalities) were to leave a bitter legacy of mistrust against the British that still continues in some Afrikaner families in the new South Africa.

Unable to end the second of these wars quickly, the British military commander, Lord Kitchener, ordered Boer women and children to be detained in 'concentration camps', while Boer homes and land were destroyed in a 'scorched earth' policy. About 25,000 Boer prisoners died from malnutrition and disease in the camps (while, unlamented, at least 14,000 Africans died in other British camps). These events of a century ago not only revolutionised the tactics of modern war (and we might note that 'khaki', 'commando' and 'boy scout' also made their appearance) but also laid the groundwork for this century's fraught relationships between Briton and Afrikaner in industry and commerce as well as political power.

It remains true in South Africa that, along with a remarkable tolerance and 'getting on' that *ubuntu* signifies, there is also a hard strain of lack of forgiveness and inhumanity, seen not only in Kitchener's camps but also in apartheid's death squads and the modern-day hijackers who think nothing of killing the driver of a car they want to take.

A hollow and divisive union

The Union of 1910 effectively redrew the map of South Africa following the victory of the British in the war and the Peace of Vereeniging on 1902. The country became officially a self-governing dominion within the British Empire. The country's four provinces – Cape Province, Transvaal, Natal and the Orange Free State – would remain until the new South Africa, albeit with apartheid overlays of 'independent states' and 'homelands'. All the provinces got something in 1910, with Cape Town named as political capital, Pretoria (Transvaal) as administrative capital and Bloemfontein (Orange Free State) as seat of the supreme court. Pietermaritzburg in Natal received financial compensation.

So why call it 'hollow'? Because the majority of the population, black, coloured and Indian, had virtually no part in the lengthy deliberations before Union and were excluded from its provisions (except that coloured people in the Cape did have some minimal voting rights). Bitter disappointment and anger at this rejection was strengthened as the post-Union Boer coalition government laid down a raft of repressive legislation. Black workers could not strike, skilled jobs were reserved for whites, and pass laws, restricting black freedom of movement, were rapidly passed.

The process went further, in 1913, when the first of the Native Land Acts restricted black landholding to no more than 7.5 per cent of the country's area (and black people comprised 70 per cent or more of the population), with specific 'reserves'. Many squatters were forcibly removed from farms designated as white.

The foundations of modern apartheid

The foundations of modern apartheid were thus well and truly laid in the years between 1910 and the First World War in 1914. The main players were also in place, with the National Party (NP) of General Barry Hertzog being formed in 1914 and the South African Native National Congress in 1912. From 1923 this organisation would be known as the African National Congress (ANC). Add in the Afrikaner Broederbond (or band of brothers), the Afrikaners' behind-the-scenes power base for nearly 70 years, founded secretly in 1918, and the South African Indian Congress, an important ally for the ANC, established in 1920, and you have a depth of political culture, on both sides of the spectrum, which would endure with a surprising degree of continuity and polarity.

Historians of apartheid would often go further and say it was not the politics of Union that paved the way for the system of apartheid. Its real origins, they say, should be placed right back in van Riebeeck's decisions of 1660 (see above), and in subsequent Dutch and British settlement and administrative history in which racial discrimination was practised unthinkingly and routinely.

What was to change was that after 1948 the NP's form of racial discrimination would become a legally enforced process of racial dehumanisation and restriction unknown otherwise in history, except for the Holocaust.

UNDERSTANDING THE POLITICS

A brand-new system of government

What is so special about the democratic constitution of South Africa that the world holds up as a model of enlightened reform? Partly it is a matter of wonder that it exists at all. Was not South Africa the pariah among nations, the most repressive of police states, where what the United Nations called the sin of apartheid was given scriptural sanction by the Dutch Reformed Church? And to go within five years from P. W. Botha to Nelson Mandela as president? Such is the stuff of dreams and legends.

Make no mistake, the final constitution signed into power by President Mandela at Sharpeville on 10 December 1996 – on the site of the Sharpeville shootings in 1960 in which 69 pass law protesters were shot down and killed – was not easily won. It took hard negotiations at Codesa (the Convention for a Democratic South Africa) from December 1991 to December 1993, with significant crises and breaks in between, for the temporary constitution to become law and formally end apartheid. The Constitutional Assembly then met from August 1994, after the country's first democratic elections in April, thrashing out issues until the final constitution was approved at Sharpeville.

Unparalleled entrenched rights
The new dispensation creates a constitutional democracy with universal adult suffrage. It entrenches separation of powers and a extremely wide Bill of Rights.

The **Bill of Rights** guarantees equality before the law and outlaws discrimination based, in the words of the document, on 'race, gender, sex, pregnancy, marital status, ethnic or social origin, colour, sexual orientation, age, disability, religion, conscience, belief, culture, language or birth'. It guarantees freedom of conscience, religion, thought, belief and opinion, and the right to assemble, demonstrate and strike. It outlaws detention without trial, torture and forced labour or servitude.

What is rare, if not unique, is that these fundamental rights are protected in one law against both individual and government abuse. It is also unusual for socio-economic rights, like housing, health care, access to food and water, social security and basic education, to be constitutionally protected, as here.

The courts, through common law, are expected to explore and decide on what is fair for the individual in the matter of overlapping rights and expectations, particularly in the 'second-degree' socio-economic sphere.

Three tiers of government
Power to legislate and enforce laws is vested in national, provincial and local governments:

- The **national government** consists of executive, legislative and judicial branches, all subject to the constitution, and the three Union capitals of Pretoria, Cape Town and Bloemfontein respectively have been retained as centres of the three branches.

- Nine **provincial governments** were recognised, namely Western Cape, Northern Cape, Eastern Cape, KwaZulu-Natal, Free State, North West, Gauteng, Mpumalanga and Northern Province. The provincial governments each have a premier, legislature and cabinet. They have limited financial powers, and their budgets are heavily dependent on transfers from central government. Provincial legislatures consist of between 30 and 80 members, who are elected by the voting public in the general election.

- At the **local government** level, local councils combine executive and legislative functions. There are six **metropolitan councils**, with four in Gauteng, and one each in greater Durban and greater Cape Town. **Metropolitan local councils** function within the metropolitan councils, with a network of **district councils**, **transitional local councils** and **rural municipalities** in the rest of the country. Unlike the national and provincial levels, where political parties are allocated seats in proportion to the votes cast for a party list, at local government level there is a mix of proportional representation and constituency representation.

A mixed style of parliamentary government
There are two houses: a National Assembly of 400 seats and a National Council of Provinces (NCOP) of 90 members. The NCOP was a new body, which replaced the former Senate.

- Members of the National Assembly are elected directly by the proportional representation method (there are no parliamentary constituencies). Members of the NCOP are appointed by the provincial legislatures, each province having 10 members.

- The head of state is the president and is elected by the National Assembly, rather than by the people. There is no prime minister as such, although the president has more in common with a Westminster-type prime minister than an American president. On the other hand, he/she is head of the armed forces and has other executive powers denied to most prime ministers.

- Parliament functions through an extensive system of multi-party committees, which review bills of new legislation.

- National elections take place every five years.

Provision for traditional leaders
In addition to its western-style democracy, South Africa has a body for traditional leaders, the Council of Traditional Leaders, which meets to consider all legislation on indigenous law, traditions or customs.

At provincial level, in provinces with recognised traditional authorities (that is, all except for Gauteng, Western Cape and Northern Cape), a House of Traditional Leaders will be established.

Majority power used for vastly different ends

It is strange to think that you would need to be at least 60 years old to remember a time in South African politics when the ruling party did not enjoy a huge majority.

When D. F. Malan won the 1948 general election for the National Party (NP), defeating war hero and elder statesman Field Marshal Jan Smuts, it was as much a surprise locally as Winston Churchill losing the 1945 British election to Clement Atlee. Few gave the NP much chance of survival in 1948, after winning 70 of the 150 seats and taking power only in coalition with the Afrikaner Party, which had nine seats. Yet the 'Nats' were to hold power in ensuing elections, with crushing majorities, until the country's first democratic election of 1994.

In both the 1994 and 1999 elections the ANC also won resounding landslides (with 63 per cent and 67 per cent of the votes respectively) that left the tiny opposition with little real power but that of annoyance – which was the ANC charge, vigorously rebutted by Democratic Party (DP) leader Tony Leon, before the 1999 election that the DP were 'chihuahuas'.

The lack of a substantial parliamentary opposition does worry some commentators, who regret there are insufficient 'checks and balances' on the authority and potential authoritarianism of the ruling party. But what a difference the new is from the old South Africa, when such matters were purely theoretical! Now the party in power – which could be the ANC for many years as things look at the millennium – will be judged by the electorate on matters such as delivery of services like education and health, on unemployment and ongoing crime and corruption.

Although small, the opposition of the DP, Inkatha Freedom Party, the New National Party, United Democratic Movement, Freedom Front and others will do their best to keep Thabo Mbeki's parliamentarians honest and responsible.

Indeed, cry the beloved country

Numerical power is perhaps the only way one could possibly compare the ruling parties in the old and the new South Africa. Reread Alan Paton's classic novel of 1948, *Cry, the Beloved Country* (which is far more interesting than most school set books!) and get a feeling for the huge disaster which apartheid was to be in both national and individual terms.

As everyone knows, the NP was a racist regime, voted in by a minority of whites (in a window-dressing exercise in 1983 the NP brought Indians and part of the coloured population into the process), while the ANC won power in a free and fair election with universal franchise under the auspices of a new constitution that was among the most democratic and transparent anywhere.

If it's extremes you like, there could be nothing further opposed in South African political history than the old, unreformed NP of P. W. Botha at the end of the 1980s and the ANC before it took power. Botha's NP had essentially become a rubber stamp for an undemocratic and right-wing police state run by shadowy 'securocrats', a blend of military, police and intelligence mandarins, nearly all members of the Broederbond, and the President's Council, a non-elected team of top-level advisers. The Cabinet and ordinary MPs were denied a real say in the country's affairs, and the president wielded almost absolute power.

With a state of emergency from 1985, up to 30,000 people detained without trial, troops in the townships and endless political killings, plus a continuing campaign by the ANC and 'civics' to make the townships 'ungovernable', sanctions, rampant inflation and a falling rand, South Africa in the late 1980s was a desperate and insecure place for all its citizens. Botha's grudging reform concession in lifting the pass laws and anti-mixed marriage laws would never be enough to stem the tide of popular protest and support for the liberation struggle being directed from the townships and from the ANC's bases in Lusaka and elsewhere.

A demonised, shadowy organisation

When the ANC was unbanned in February 1990 it was indistinctly known to most South Africans, thanks to years of news blackout and demonisation of its activities, policies and leaders. When Nelson Mandela was released that month nobody even knew what he looked like, because no photograph had been published for many years – and few really knew what he would do.

Some doughty white businessmen and politicians had dared to meet ANC officials secretly overseas in the 1980s and began a remarkable underground reform dialogue that the general public knew little of but which set the agenda for a possible change of power.

As 1990 dawned, given its alliance with the SA Communist Party (SACP) and the trade unions (the tripartite alliance), its avowal of nationalisation, including the banks, and redistribution of wealth and land, most observers saw in the ANC a doctrinaire Marxist liberation movement that espoused armed struggle and stood far to the left politically.

Last-ditch reform to avoid disaster

It makes it all the more remarkable that new NP leader F. W. De Klerk, then considered an ultra-conservative, could promise to undo the legal structure of apartheid, unban the ANC, SACP and Pan Africanist Congress, and release Mandela. This was in February 1990, soon after De Klerk took office, on P. W. Botha's retirement on grounds of ill health.

Did De Klerk jump or was he pushed? In the manner of such things, the ex-Nat leader has vociferously claimed it was his pragmatism and accommodation that made the transition possible; the USA and other countries said it was their sanctions that brought South Africa to its knees economically and forced the political changes; economists pointed to the collapse of the rand dictating political events after foreign banks refused to roll over loans; and the ANC, both within the country and in exile outside, insisted its mass following and that of the United Democratic Movement had made such self-destruction by the NP inevitable.

Almost as remarkable as the NP's transition, in effectively saving the country but losing its own reason to exist, was that of the ANC. As its evolving policies since 1994 have borne out, it has managed its own transformation from liberation movement to democratic governing party, even if not without defections and rebels in the ranks. It has shown flexibility in being able to jettison nationalisation (though the tripartite alliance creaks on) and embrace privatisation of certain state institutions. It has guaranteed the Reserve Bank's independence and honours the country's overseas loans, including a massive apartheid debt of some R40 billion. Its interventionist initiatives under the Reconstruction and Development Programme in education, housing, health and welfare, as discussed in later chapters, are socialist and populist, but the private sector is still functioning strongly in each sector.

A weakening of political extremes

South Africa is a much calmer place in 2000 than it was in 1990 or 1980. One reason, apart from the need to recover after dramatic years of repression and release, could be that political activity, by common consent, seems to have come to rest around a broad centre, with only a few crackpots manning the barricades to the left or *laagers* (protective circle of oxwagons) to the right. In a remarkable transition both left and right, which were as far apart as Stalinists and advocates of a *volkstaat* (people's state) could be, in a mere five or six years have lost their edge and threat, even their newsworthiness.

It was a far different story in April 1993 when two members of the organised right wing, one a Conservative MP, shot down the icon of the left, Chris Hani, in his driveway. With negotiations at Codesa on a knife edge, this was South Africa's moment of truth, when the choice of further endlessly stalled negotiations or armed uprising was stark and immediate. By a whisker, with Mandela's calming authority perhaps tipping the balance, the country decided to keep on talking.

Eugene Terre'Blanche, leader of the AWB (Afrikaner Weerstandsbeweging), a neo-Nazi *volks* party, is today an irrelevancy and a curiosity, but only a few years back his threats of wrecking negotiations by armed force were seriously meant and taken.

If Terre'Blanche and the Afrikaner far right have gone farming or are languishing in jail, the far left, even more strangely, appears to have taken to capitalism and the role of captains of industry. Marcel Golding, former deputy in the National Union of Mineworkers, is today a magnate in financial planning circles, while Cyril Ramaphosa is the highest-profile union and ANC stalwart to exchange T-shirt with slogan for Gucci suit. And if black youth in April 1999 disappointed their parents by preferring a *kwaito* (township fusion music) party to a political party and stayed away from the polls, saying politics was boring, what better implicit praise for and acceptance of the South African miracle?

Barring the unexpected, it seems politics has become normal and mundane, a matter of competition for the middle, and even twitchy foreign institutional investors have started praising South Africa as the most politically stable of the emerging market nations.

UNDERSTANDING THE ECONOMY

Unquestionably Africa's superpower

For all its economic woes, which South Africans are all too quick to lament, it shouldn't be forgotten that the country is by far Africa's largest and most advanced economy.

- South Africa accounts for fully half of the electricity produced in Africa, 40 per cent of its industrial output, nearly half of its mining production and is by far the largest agricultural exporter.

- The province of Gauteng is South Africa's smallest, but has some two-thirds of the country's gross domestic product (GDP) and no less than a quarter of the whole continent's GDP.

- The country's economic infrastructure and financial system at their best are First World, with a well-developed road and rail network and modern ports that link the whole southern Africa region with the wider world.

- South Africa has the means and appears to be developing the self-belief and will to lead the Southern African Development Community as a significant regional trading bloc.

Staggering inequalities remain

As a personal aside to introduce this section, I was working on a financial weekly in the late 1980s and had to edit a story on the declining gold price (there's nothing new in Africa!). For the illustration of liquid gold being fed into the ingot moulds I devised the caption 'Rich pour'. It seemed to convey the dependence on gold and unholy mix of wealth and poverty, First World and Third, that the country exhibits so sharply.

In global inequality indexes, South Africa scores consistently in the top three, often with Brazil and Indonesia, as having the most skewed wealth distribution anywhere. South Africa has had four strikes against it in terms of historic inequality:

- It has been and still is largely an extractive economy, in minerals, fishing and agriculture, which almost invariably means rich exploiter and poor exploited.

- Secondly, it has been colonial, whether Dutch or British, with wealth shipped in various forms to the mother country, which again maintains an entrenched inequality.

- Thirdly, apartheid made racial inequality the institutional basis of over forty years of misrule. The non-white majority had to be kept separate, poor, illiterate, unskilled and powerless if the system was to survive.

- Fourthly, in the words of a 1999 report by the International Labour Organisation, globalisation favours the skilled. To be so poorly skilled as South Africa's majority population, and with so little access to global networks and networking, adds a new twist to a trend of increasing inequality between the techno-haves and have-nots.

It will take years of 'affirmative action' by the ANC and business, through new laws and the downward percolation of wealth, through job creation and economic growth, for those at the bottom to attain and exceed minimum wage levels. Meanwhile those at the top complain of being overtaxed and of not being able to take all their wealth out of the country (at the time of writing, exchange controls still remain in a reduced form).

There is even the scary prospect of the inequality gap growing larger as the black middle class expands and the newly promoted affirmative action executives enter the taxpaying élite, while the pool of long-term unemployed continues to expand.

New directions in wealth creation

In Chapter 5 on work and employment, we refer to the changing South African economy and the opportunities for starting one's own business, in sectors like franchising, the Internet, tourism and leisure, and outsourcing.

While it remains extremely difficult to start a business and make even one job for somebody else as an employee, it appears to be alarmingly easy for large employers, like the mines, steelworks and railways, to shed staff as company profitability drops or as global changes lead to 'downsizing' or 'rightsizing', those modern euphemisms for firing staff. The South African economy is currently shedding more jobs than it is making, and there is still far too much red tape involved in setting up a business, not to mention the difficulty of obtaining start-up capital.

In an era of worldwide competition, where service counts and information is gathered and shared on the Net, governments, including South Africa's, will have to learn to be far more positive and entrepreneurial – proactive rather than reactive, as the jargon goes – if the shift from large, lumbering and backward-looking product-manufacturing to small, nimble and innovative service-rendering business is to happen.

Most would agree with Clem Sunter, the futures scenario guru at leading industrial conglomerate Anglo American, that fostering small, informal and entrepreneurial business is the quickest route to wealth and job creation.

Government moves into GEAR

President Mbeki admitted soon after assuming office in 1999 that his administration would be judged on its record in job creation, as well as the critical big issues of crime, HIV/Aids, education and other social services. Some of the business and labour measures taken by Mbeki and his illustrious predecessor are outlined in Chapter 5. The overall macroeconomic policy is **GEAR**, meaning **growth, employment and redistribution**.

Among other policies the ANC has pursued is industrial development in geographical areas of need. Its cross-national initiative, the **Maputo Corridor**, connecting Mpumalanga and Mozambique, and **spatial development initiatives**, including in the eastern Cape near Port Elizabeth (Coega) and on the west coast close to Saldanha Bay, are on track and promise much. New transport connections, high-tech and heavy industry and rural job creation are some of the planks of GEAR in industrial policy.

Heavy industry in sectors where South Africa has special skills and competitive clout has been promoted in regional centres like Richards Bay (the Alusaf aluminium smelter, the largest of its kind in the world) and Mpumalanga (with the Columbus stainless steel development, also a world leader in its category).

Unfortunately, uncontrollable global events like the emerging markets collapse of October 1997, which knocked South Africa, although not as badly as Southeast Asia and Brazil, the fall in the gold price to crisis levels of $250 an ounce in 1998 and 1999 and the inability of the economy to grow at even 2 per cent a year (when a figure of 6 per cent to 8 per cent is needed), have made GEAR's goals look utopian. With low growth and negative employment trends, the redistribution aspect of GEAR's triple policy has hardly even begun to take effect.

On the other hand, the ANC is taking positive strides with GEAR-related targets of reduced inflation and interest rates and a lower budget deficit, further relaxation of exchange controls, the effective maintenance of the rand value, trade reform, more privatisation, improved exports (for instance, South Africa is now a car-exporting nation) and greater fixed investment locally as well as more overseas fixed investment in the country.

Two key constituencies in the new economy

Although the **trade unions**, both individually and as members of the largest union umbrella, Cosatu (the Congress of South African Trades Unions), are an integral part of the triple alliance with the ANC and SACP, this does not mean an easy ride for the unions if their aims conflict with GEAR or other policy grails of the government.

This fact came out in several strikes in 1999. As expected, Cosatu backed the combined public service unions in wage and retrenchment talks with the government and also supported the National

A Silicon Valley for South Africa?

In 1999 Cape Town came up with a plan to brand itself as South Africa's Silicon Valley, using the local alternative name 'Silicon Bay'. The idea is to promote and link a number of business, high technology and academic initiatives in making Cape Town the nexus of an ultra-modern, high-tech region.

Among recent successful developments are:

- two technoparks (the Stellenbosch Technopark and newer Capricorn Science and Technology Park)

- long-standing scientific and medical research facilities at tertiary education institutions

- aeronautical infrastructure with Sunsat, the country's first satellite, being assembled at Stellenbosch

- a variety of high-level information technology innovations

- over R2 billion investment in the area by Vodacom, one of the country's two cellular phone providers

- the building of Africa's first 'intelligent city' at Century City, near Milnerton.

Union of Mineworkers in its annual wage talks. The government, however, made clear its insistence that fiscal rectitude and sticking to wage settlements in line with or below current inflation rates of around 8 per cent was non-negotiable. Hard as it was, it appeared that the government was prepared to separate and favour national ahead of sectional interests, even when those interests were very close to its own heart.

In general, however, the ANC government has put the demands of those already in work ahead of the millions who want work, and it has failed to deliver on job creation. Its 1994 election manifesto of 'jobs for all' must rank as one of its implementation failures.

The other constituency with growing economic power in the new South Africa and enjoying the limited fruits of affirmative action is the **black middle class**, along with women, both black and white, and the disabled.

Affirmative action is nothing new in itself in South Africa. The British in colonial days favoured their own, and the Afrikaners certainly did in their industrial and commercial expansion in the

1930s, not to mention during full-on apartheid after 1948.

New laws, as described in Chapter 5, and the Employment Equity Act in particular, embed affirmative action and equity goals in legislation, in confirmation of provisions in the constitution. Some commentators noted with alarm that regulating social and economic policy through strict laws was how the inequities of apartheid were perpetuated. Others were worried that Mbeki had hardened the government stance on affirmative action and that he meant business.

In practice, at the turn of the millennium, affirmative action had not gone very far or deep. A clutch of new 'black chip' companies had been launched on the Johannesburg Stock Exchange; key directorial appointments at the top of formerly white listed companies had gone to blacks, both male and female; most foreign direct investment had sought black partnerships; and some black labour unions had entered the stock market in consortiums, with investments in growth companies in the media, telecommunications and financial services. However, it appeared that rather than a broadening down of wealth, the small, emergent black middle class was creaming the best of the rewards for itself.

UNDERSTANDING THE SOCIETY

It was, if memory serves, Archbishop Tutu who in the 1980s first coined the expressive term '**rainbow nation**' for South Africa's melting pot of culturally diverse peoples. The term has stuck, allowing the more optimistic newspaper headline writers to talk of 'pots of gold' and the more gloomy to hint at 'over the rainbow'.

Across the spectrum of the rainbow nation

Who are the 43.05 million people who inhabit the new South Africa? The figure is a mid-1999 official estimate, but is probably a considerable underestimate, as 5 million illegal immigrants, by some counts, are already living in the country.

Given the liberalism of the present constitution and its ending forever of official racism, it seems anomalous if not perverse to use the old **racial classifications** in describing new South Africans. However, this remains how the statistics are presented (if only for the sake of historical comparison), and some presentation of the figures is needed, even if it might appear to be perpetuating a discredited ideology.

- The statistics indicate a **mid-1999 population** of some 33 million black people (about 76.7 per cent of the total), about 5 million white people (10.9 per cent), 3.5 million coloured people (8.9 per cent) and over a million of Asian, particularly Indian, descent (2.6 per cent).

- The **black** population was split by 1930s anthropologists into nine ethnic groups, a division which the apartheid planners abused in their homelands superstructure. There had been no correlation between tribal groups and their traditional lands ever since Shaka Zulu had scattered the black populations over a century before (see page 20), but NP planners went ahead with their elaborate fictions anyway. The grand, preposterous plan was to designate geographical areas to specific groups and move the black population physically to fit into their so-called homeland area. So all the Zulus were to be settled in KwaZulu-Natal, the Xhosa in Transkei and Ciskei, the Pedi in Lebowa, and so on.

  As already mentioned, forced removals went some way to making this nightmare a reality, and large numbers of black people have remained in places where they had been relocated, still leading lives of desperate poverty. The new South Africa can have brought precious few benefits – perhaps a water pipe and far-distant electricity pylons, and a rural clinic a long bus ride away – to these long-term victims of apartheid's racial geography. Just ask the people living on R100 a month within sight of the Sun City complex in the former Bophutatswana.

- The most significant rivalry between black peoples, which precedes Shaka and still continues, is that between the two most populous and historically powerful of the groups, the **Zulu** and the **Xhosa**. Generalising baldly, large numbers of ANC followers are Xhosas, while for many Zulus their allegiance is to their ruling monarch, King Goodwill Zwelithini and the Inkatha Freedom Party (IFP) of Chief Mangosotho Buthelezi. The story of Zulu and Xhosa competing for political power in KwaZulu-Natal and the townships of Gauteng in the 1980s and during negotiations in the 1990s is beyond the scope of this book, but it is a twisting tale of passionate and often deadly political rivalry which led to thousands of deaths among supporters and standby victims alike.

The striving for political superiority has not ended, even though the IFP is in government and Buthelezi remained at his post of home affairs minister from Mandela's administration into Mbeki's (though Buthelezi declined to stay on as deputy president in 1999). Not quite as entrenched as Catholic and Protestant hatred in Northern Ireland, the power struggle between Zulu and Xhosa nonetheless remains a worrying dynamic in the new South Africa.

• Among the **white** population, perhaps 60 per cent is Afrikaner and 40 per cent of British and other European origin. Expect to find a majority of Afrikaners in much of Gauteng, Northern Province, Mpumalanaga, Free State and North West. The British-European group has a concentration within KwaZulu-Natal (popularly known as 'the last outpost' of the British empire), and the Western and Eastern Cape. The Afrikaner population is often rural while the British-European group tends to be urban.

  There are significant minorities of Jewish people (about 130,000), Portuguese (35,000), many of them refugees from Mozambique and Angola following independence in the 1970s, and smaller communities of Germans, Dutch, Italians, Greeks, French and Chinese.

• The **coloured** population had its early origins in the Cape, from liaisons (more rarely marriages) between imported slaves, the Khoisan and Dutch settlers. It is a largely Afrikaans-speaking population, concentrated in the Northern Cape and Western Cape, and suffered forced removals under apartheid, especially to the desolate Cape Flats from inner-city areas of Cape Town. In a bitter reference to the old racial classifications, some coloured writers describe themselves as 'so-calleds', hinting at the formal description of 'so-called coloureds'. They are vocal about their continued exclusion in the new South Africa, saying they were too black for apartheid and now appear to be too white for affirmative action.

• The **Indian** group has remained in KwaZulu-Natal, where the former segregated townships of Chatsworth now comprise a prosperous city, but also has concentrations in Johannesburg, Pretoria and other cities across the country. Without Indian shopkeepers opening for long hours, many mining areas and older cities would have no access to everyday goods.

No less than 11 official languages

It is strange, perhaps, that the constitution recognises the nine ethnic groups of apartheid racial geography by entrenching their languages as official, plus English and Afrikaans.

The South African population divided by home language shows Zulu and Xhosa as the most numerous, Venda and Ndebele as the least. The actual percentages, as recorded by the relevant government office, Statistics South Africa, are: Zulu (22.4), Xhosa (17.5), Afrikaans (15.1), Pedi (9.8), English (9.1), Tswana (7.2), Sotho (6.9), Tsonga (4.2), Swazi (2.6), Venda (1.7), Ndebele (1.5) and other (including Gujarati and European languages, 2.0).

This does not yet mean, thankfully, that every TV or radio programme is broadcast in 11 languages one after the other, though each of them has a proportion of airtime allocated to it. Government notices and legislation are printed in the leading languages, but in the streets most signs are still in English and Afrikaans, as before. Despite the show of democratic magnanimity to other languages, the ANC government knows well that **English** is the language of international commerce and business and has been wise in not pushing languages, including **Afrikaans**, that have no standing on the international stage.

It is to President Mandela's credit that as well as going out of his way to greet and be photographed with apartheid icons like Mrs Betsie Verwoerd, widow of one of the architects of the system, Hendrik Verwoerd, he would speak to them in Afrikaans and also give portions of his state messages in the language of his oppressor. Such sensitive appreciation of **symbolism**, as with the handling of the issues of the two anthems and new national flag, and his actions at the 1995 Rugby World Cup (see Chapter 11), was characteristic of Mandela's personal understanding of the emotive importance of language in nation-building.

If you are monolingual European coming fresh to South Africa, be prepared to shamed by the numbers of people, mainly black but often white too nowadays, who speak three, five or more languages. One black journalist I worked with in Johannesburg could speak all 11, with differing degrees of fluency ('Venda was the hardest,' she said, 'and I can't write them all.').

Admittedly, the languages do have much in common, but it still takes considerable effort to commit so much vocabulary to memory. Given the poor quality of education on offer in the old South Africa, and even now in the new, it is remarkable that there are so many self-taught language experts about.

A country with no official religion

Perhaps it's a sign of the new national tolerance to human rights matters, but South Africa's constitution does not proclaim any one religion over others.

- The country is nominally **Christian**, but this does not mean it pursues a mainstream line. Far from it, there is actually a huge **diversity** of Christian fellowship. Among African indigenous churches there are said to be maybe 4,000 different groupings.

- The Afrikaans-speaking **Dutch Reformed Church** has also been prone to schismatic splits, including on the issue of whether to support apartheid formally.

- The **African indigenous churches** can still be broadly traced back to an Ethiopian stream, which broke with the early Methodist missions, and the Zionist stream, which grew out of American pentecostal missions early this century.

- The **Zion Christian Church** (ZCC) is by far the largest religious group in the country, if not Africa, with adherents variously numbered at 3 or 7 million. Wearing a silver Star of David against a green and black ribbon, ZCC members are respected as solid workers, who do not drink or gamble and maintain old-fashioned moral codes. The Easter weekend finds millions of ZCC followers taking minibus taxis and chartered buses to Moria, near Tzaneen in the Northern Province, for a huge celebration. This produces the most spectacular traffic snarl-ups on South Africa's dangerous roads, but the occasion itself is notably free of crime and trouble.

- The **Anglican Church of South Africa** has had a strong record of opposition to apartheid, and it was secretly involved in sanctions-breaking and in keeping ANC communications supply lines going.

- There is a strong following of **Muslims** in the urban centres, and many of the Cape Malays have followed this faith for three hundred years.

- **Hindus** predominate in the Indian community.

- At the **alternative** end of the religious spectrum, all the well-known groups from Anthroposophists to Zen Buddhists have small but committed followings, and with a bit of effort (including on the Internet) you can find almost any religious network of your choice.

- **Ancestor worship** as such is not widely practised, but it does form a component of some of the hybrid mix of religious beliefs found in black communities around the country.

- **Secularism** has long been associated with leftist social movements in South Africa, as elsewhere, and there are many people who are proud to call themselves communists and atheists. Indeed, the SA Communist Party still has doctrinaire elements said to be found rarely outside places like Albania and North Korea. At the same time you do find people, including President Mbeki, who see nothing contradictory in describing themselves as both communist and Christian. Such is the ever-surprising nature of South Africa's belief systems.

UNDERSTANDING THE LAW

The structure of legal administration

In the old days it used to be a sick joke or oxymoron to refer to the South African minister of justice. The modern equivalent is a reference to the minister of safety and security, where these qualities are seemingly as rare as justice used to be.

The 1996 constitution established the **Constitutional Court** as the watchdog of the law and ultimate protector of the country's human rights. The novel principle of the constitution, still perhaps to be widely understood in the country, is that the same law is binding on citizens, government, the police and all courts.

The other judicial institutions entrenched in the final constitution are the **Supreme Court of Appeal**, **high courts** and **magistrate's courts**. At the local level a number of **small claims courts** deal with minor cases of up to about R3,000. A court official hears claimants and counter-claimants directly and decides on the case. A small fee is charged to bring a case to this court.

The constitution also set up a number of **institutions** to support its principles. These bodies are independent but report to parliament once a year on their use of the budget granted to them. They consist of:

- Public Protector
- Human Rights Commission
- Commission for the Promotion and Protection of the Rights of

Cultural, Religious and Linguistic Communities
- Commission on Gender Equality
- Auditor-General
- Independent Electoral Commission
- Independent Broadcasting Authority.

The constitution in practice

The world has hailed the degree of personal liberty guaranteed in South Africa's negotiated constitution. In practice, a problem, ironically, has been that the guarantees have seemed to favour criminal rights at the expense of victims' rights. In a period of criminal lawlessness unparalleled in the country's history, bail is granted to dangerous repeat offenders, many sentences are cut short by prison authorities, an alarming number of state cases are thrown out of court because of inadequate prosecution paperwork, and on top of this the escape rate from jails is high.

The government has been taking legislative steps to tighten up the criminal justice administration, but until more money is released into the system and into policing in general, the crime wave seems to roll on unhindered, and to crime victims many of the fine flourishes of the constitution seem hollow and another sick joke.

A changing profile in the judiciary

In one area, that of recruiting to the courts people from previously disadvantaged groups, there has been a measure of progress. In April 1994, there was one black judge and no females among the country's 186 judges. Three years later there were 28 black male judges and three black females. In the magistrate's courts the number of new black recruits rose in the same period from 39 to 453 out of a corps of nearly 1,400.

Capital punishment outlawed

From being a country with an extremely high rate of executions in apartheid days (over 100 hangings a year through the 1980s), the new South Africa has determinedly set its face against the death sentence. In 1995 the Constitutional Court decided that capital punishment was incompatible with the constitution and banned the practice outright. Nelson Mandela, himself almost a victim of the hangman, has always said he and the ANC would oppose the death sentence at all costs.

These principled stands run against much current opinion in the country, which regards the threat and reality of capital punishment as a strong deterrent to criminals. It appears that this contention will go untested for the time being.

The Truth and Reconciliation Commission (TRC)

This commission, chaired for most of its tenure by Archbishop Desmond Tutu, was set up after 1994 to examine crimes of the apartheid era. Its work has been gruelling and heart-rending, but also contentious, with its methods criticised by some human rights observers as lacking precision and fairness.

The TRC is widely regarded as one of the new South Africa's finest and bravest innovations. In setting its terms of reference, comparison was often made with the Nuremberg trials of Nazis following the Second World War, and assertions about the need for the truth about apartheid to be exposed before national reconciliation was possible. Tutu held that 'without forgiveness there is no future, but without confession there can be no forgiveness'.

The TRC heard accounts from both perpetrators and victims, with accepted confession by the guilty resulting in full amnesty. The understanding was that those choosing not to appear before the commission would face criminal prosecution later. P. W. Botha was the most high profile of those refusing to accept the TRC's good faith; he was found guilty and sentenced to a fine and jail term, but on a suspended basis in consideration of his advanced age.

Critics of the TRC process within the country have complained that altogether too many apartheid collaborators have been given full amnesty for lesser crimes than they committed, that criminals were being absolved after claiming political motivations and that the ANC has erred in stretching the amnesty period for political crimes from 1960 to 1994. On the other hand, without the public process of accusation and forgiveness for the experience of apartheid, how would the majority of the population be able to move on and face other harsh realities of life in the new South Africa?

Most would agree with the description by journalist John Carlin of the TRC's final report, published in October 1998, which used a million words to tell the harrowing story of 31,000 cases of human rights abuse during apartheid, as 'one of the century's exemplary documents'.

Corruption still a burning issue

In an international corruption index published in July 1997, South Africa was placed 33rd out of 52 countries, nine places down from the previous year. Denmark was found to be least corrupt of the countries surveyed, Nigeria the most.

Without begging questions of how the corruption index had been compiled and its criteria for most and least corrupt, it is clear that South Africa's fabled transparency in government has its murky side. The public was nonetheless shocked soon after the 1999 elections when the new ANC premier of Mpumalanga went on record as saying it was all right for politicians to lie in public.

Provincial administrations have been dogged by accusations of misconduct, fraud and mismanagement in the new South Africa. Partly it could be a matter of too much wealth passing through the hands of newly appointed bureaucrats who cannot resist dipping into the till. However, it is possibly more to do with a remarkable tradition of a **lack of public accountability** by Cabinet and other ministers, who can seemingly waste or divert millions of rand, mislead the voting public and still only receive a rap on the knuckles by the party leader. A notorious example is President Mandela's continued support for his health minister, Nkosazana Zuma, during the *Sarafina 2* affair (see Chapter 9 below).

Yet let an offender criticise party policy, whether in the old NP or the ANC, and out he or she goes, without a second thought. It is a strange continuity from old South Africa to new that party loyalty is esteemed far higher than public accountability, even though the parties, as we have seen, have had overwhelming numerical majorities in parliament.

At less rarified levels, this acceptance of slack public morality, although fiercely condemned by both Mandela and Mbeki, pervades people's everyday dealing with authority, whether at the police station, in the waiting list for subsidised housing or in car licence departments. In each of these three instances, among other examples in the late 1990s, the press reported significant scams or rackets, not to mention the international money-laundering the big crime syndicates have been carrying out in South Africa. It appears the country is not yet ready for a moral crusade along the lines of that promoted in the UK by a John Major or Tony Blair.

So what is the new South Africa ready for and what does it stand for? This forms the subject of the next chapter.

2

The New and the Old South Africa

SOUTH AFRICA'S RAINBOW: MYTH OR REALITY?

A snap verdict on the new South Africa

In a newspaper supplement published in May, just before the 1999 national elections, the second in a democratic South Africa, eight voters were canvassed for their opinions on whether things had changed for the better or worse since 1994 and what their hopes were for the future of the country.

In a way, these eight random voters, who ranged from a white male Afrikaner trade union official to a black female social worker, were being asked for a verdict on the 'new' South Africa. What did they say?

- Five of the eight were positive, believing things had definitely improved.

- The white Afrikaner thought things had definitely got worse. ('The ANC's affirmative action policy makes it impossible for my people to enter the labour market and get promotion. We've changed from a government that focused only on the minority to one focusing only on the majority.')

- A female psychologist from Krugersdorp sat on the fence, saying 'since 1994 we've been on honeymoon, going through changes and getting used to the idea of freedom'.

- Another critic, a female insurance agent from Maitland in Cape Town, said education and health 'have really gone down into the dumps'.

- Among the five who were optimistic, each settled on a different reason to be cheerful: one said it was a more moral society than before; one that 'Africans used to be treated as second-class citizens, now they are recognised as belonging'; another stressed more freedom of thought and movement; the social worker highlighted better health care, water and housing; and the fifth, a

43

young black graphic designer, instanced better communication, since 'we are now more exposed to all races than ever before'.

- On their **hopes for the future**, the reactions were equally diverse. Tackling crime and building a strong economy were the priorities for a black advocate in the sample; a black personnel officer said his concern was for the rural areas; a female Muslim doctor wanted equality for women in practice and more focus on Aids; the social worker was most interested in housing; the trade unionist wanted self-determination for the Afrikaner; and the psychologist was articulate about reconciliation and forgiveness to make the country work.

New slogans for the new South Africa

What do these opinions prove? Certainly something about cultural diversity and, following this, the huge challenge for any South African government in meeting such wide expectations.

Over and above, though, is the confidence to admit a passion for the new dispensation, despite its many shortcomings. It is an almost naive delight in patriotism and a proper pride in the distance already travelled, plus a willingness to forget the past and move on that is intoxicating to the majority of South Africans.

At key moments this sense of national unity and shared hope is palpable – on Mandela's release from jail in 1990, on election day 1994, on the day in 1995 when the Springboks won the Rugby World Cup and in the next year when Bafana Bafana became African soccer champions. In each case Nelson Mandela was there to give focus to the nation's happiness. On such days South Africa is the best place in the world to be – exuberant, noisy, *toyi-toying*, loving, undivided, with diverse peoples in harmony, celebrating *because of* their shared diversity. On such days Archbishop Tutu's '**rainbow nation**' seems an immodest description because it doesn't claim enough.

A rainbow nation in one family

Tokyo Sexwale was an ANC prisoner on Robben Island and a former premier of Gauteng. He is now involved in black economic empowerment schemes. His wife Judy is white.

Sexwale recently described his family version of the rainbow nation: 'If blacks get hurt, I get hurt; if whites get hurt, that's my wife; and if you harm coloured children, you're looking at my children. Your unity embodies who I am.'

It is on such heady days that President Mbeki's own slogan of an '**African renaissance**' seems fully appropriate, with South Africa taking on the leadership – political, economic, financial and even intellectual – of a revived continent in the new millennium.

A last slogan must be mentioned here, the '**new' South Africa** itself. Although used so many times that it has since become meaningless, the phrase began life as a National Party invention of the late 1980s when the Nats decided to embrace limited reform while trying to keep the reins of real power. However, like the genie released from the bottle, the Nats let loose far more of the new than they could control, and ended by talking away 45 years of power. By December 1993, with the interim constitution being adopted, the structure of apartheid had crumbled and the way to democratic elections in a unified country was opened up.

Ironically, perhaps, the now much-reduced rump of the NP decided, after F. W. de Klerk retired in 1997, to relaunch itself under leader Marthinus van Schalkwyk as the New National Party, as though the word 'new' had not done enough damage to its cause already.

P. W. Botha had unwittingly composed the epitaph for his party and apartheid itself when he said in the 1980s 'we must adapt or die'. But apartheid could not be adapted; it could only be kept going by force or be overthrown. The final means of its overthrow – and this was the miracle of the new South Africa – was to be not guns but negotiations.

Leaders prepared to talk it through

How was it possible for a South Africa on the brink of an armed, racial confrontation that could so easily become all-out civil war to sit down in the Codesa meetings at Kempton Park and negotiate its way into a new distribution of power and reject apartheid for ever?

Perhaps with Botha stepping down the Nats had reached a point of no return, and De Klerk and a coterie of reformists were prepared for the boldest gamble any new political leader could make, to concede the trappings of power in order to maintain its reality. Or perhaps De Klerk was a genuine peacemaker and statesman behind the party political trappings?

Meanwhile international sanctions had bitten deep, the economy was running down and the outlook for recovery and growth was bleak.

Then again, the world at the end of the 1980s was in a phase of unprecedented reform, symbolised by Gorbachev dismembering the old Soviet Union and the Berlin Wall coming down in late 1989.

The Nats of 1990 were faced with a team of ANC leaders, now newly unbanned and entitled to return to South Africa from Robben Island or from exile overseas, who were an extremely able and committed group of negotiators.

While such factors might account for a limited transfer of real power, there must be another reason for the sheer magnitude of South Africa's unique transformation – and this can only be the Mandela factor. The Nobel Prize committee was impressed enough in 1993 to award Mandela and De Klerk the peace price for their efforts. Tutu had been awarded the same prize back in 1984. So the world has recognised something special in these South African peacemakers.

The Mandela magic

If there is one reason above all why the country was able to move from 'old' to 'new' in relative peace, it was the incredible good fortune of having **Nelson Mandela** to lead the negotiations. Vitally, it was Mandela's huge moral authority, earned in 27 years as a political prisoner, that persuaded black South Africans to parley with their white oppressors.

Read *Long Walk to Freedom*, Mandela's autobiography, published in 1994, and learn first-hand of his deep conviction that any problem can and must be talked through rather than settled by guns. It is both a personal and a political article of faith. The African credo of *ubuntu*, the search for and experience of harmony between people, preceded Mandela and the ANC he served all his adult life, but seldom has a personal philosophy been so faithfully carried into the public spotlight. Then too, Mandela's personal magnetism was such that he could persuade any opponent, by charm, intellectual argument or force of character, that there were loyalties higher than political party or sectional interest.

Mandela's highest goal was for a unified, democratic South Africa with a new liberal constitution. The magic was that he could convince others that this nation-building he constantly spoke of was their highest good too. Somehow he and his team were able to draw the potential poison of an armed and angry white right wing, equally armed and angry Zulu nationalists, diehard Nats and firebrand 'civics' in the townships. Negotiations continued, in those danger years of 1990 to 1993, not only in Codesa but in many other forums. And all the talking was done under Mandela's dominant shadow and often in his name.

It was another mark of Mandela's stature that he could bow out of public life, as he had promised, after the 1999 election. He had left much of the day-to-day running of the country to Thabo Mbeki for a couple of years before this, but how many presidents, especially in Africa, resign peacefully on the appointed day without a backward look? Only someone exceptional.

THE OLD SOUTH AFRICA LIVES ON

Racism remains the great divide

Yet not every day can have rainbows, and much of the old South Africa remains to haunt the new. Years of colonial racism followed by apartheid racism have left scars that even the Mandela magic cannot fully heal.

A survey of some 3,000 people by Independent Newspapers just before the 1999 election found that 81 per cent of those interviewed said the media should stop talking about race because 'we are all just people'. Despite being 'raw from the racist past', in the words of Nadine Gordimer (South Africa's first Nobel Laureate for Literature in 1991), the overwhelming majority in the sample wanted to build a new nation on the basis of non-racism.

Yet whites are still the haves, blacks the have-nots. Whites have the jobs, status, houses and cars blacks want, and they can enjoy private education, health care, holiday homes and overseas travel in ways denied to all but the black élite.

Many South Africans – often disappointed whites, coloureds and Indians – are not so hopeful as the newspaper sample. They say the ANC is building a new racism or a new élite through the reverse discrimination of affirmative action. Every institution, so the argument goes, is forced into the Procrustean bed of race quotas, where the first question concerns race, not qualifications. New legislation positively discriminates in favour of blacks and women.

As *Time* magazine commented in an insightful article on the state of South Africa's race relations in 1999, both perceptions and realities in the new South Africa inevitably still come down to racial attitudes. The long-serving South Africa bureau chief Peter Hawthorne wrote:

'Under the rainbow there are people who still think racist and cry racism. But, unlike Europeans, they don't go to war about it. They have accepted the legacy of Nelson Mandela, one of the world's great reconciliators.'

'Precarious though its transition may continue to be, there is a bond, a strong glue that somehow holds it all together,' the magazine concluded.

Ignorance is a continuing enemy

Many of South Africa's problems caused by racial stereotyping are a direct result of ignorance of its component cultures. It is hardly surprising. The legacy of apartheid's partial success in forcefully separating peoples, even families, geographically and in perceptions, together with its denial of adequate education to non-whites, has meant many South Africans understand each other only super-ficially.

Take these examples of cultural ignorance, with some specific incidents and some more general causes of misunderstanding:

- A black Grade 10 pupil is expelled from school for shaving his head following his grandfather's death. Removing hair is a sign of respect in African cultures but is seen in Western society as a fashion trend or youthful rebellion.

- A Muslim girl is not admitted to a school in Ladysmith because according to her religion she must wear a headscarf, which the school says is not its policy.

- A Hindu girl is banned in Chatsworth for wearing the sacred black dot, which, remarkably, the school says clashes with its rules.

- A black man should precede a lady into a lift, since only cowards try to avoid danger by letting women go first.

- Not making eye contact when addressing a person is respectful in African cultures, but offensive and negative in Western societies.

- It is also rude in African society to speak quietly as this can be construed as gossiping. Hence the misperception among whites that black people 'shout'.

- 'Liberated' white or Indian men help with the washing up, household chores and childcare in ways that black males still find awkward and unmanly.

Note: Some critics believe the biggest challenge in South African society is to alter black men's self-perceptions. They suggest that until black men are liberated from their burden of stereotypes, black women too cannot achieve their potential. This could be the equivalent of a view that sees one of the hidden gains of the new South Africa and 1994 as the liberation of whites from apartheid, their own nemesis.

The legacy of the homelands lives on

In an article in a Sunday newspaper in mid-1999, referred to above, author Nadine Gordimer makes the important point that things were not better in apartheid days, they were better hidden. Street children are now in the cities, not tucked away in the homelands.

Unemployment and crime are strongly linked, Gordimer argues. Unemployment, that 'social disease', was once quarantined out of sight in the back of beyond, but has now 'burst from its inhuman confines of the past'. If there are no jobs, people will turn to crime to stay alive.

The fact that was obvious to the outside world all along was that the 'independent homelands' were never independent nor home; and nor were the 'self-governing' states anything but Pretoria's puppets.

The West reacted then with sanctions, which were needed to defeat apartheid. If that limited South Africa's industrial development in the years of struggle, globalisation is limiting it further now.

The black unemployed in South Africa are suffering on both counts, with the added burden of having been denied education and skills for an increasingly technological labour market. Legal equality, Gordimer adds, has been achieved, but economic equality is a harder goal that must be worked for. Overall, it will take years to overcome the backlog caused by '40 lost years' of Nat rule. The homelands have been reabsorbed into the Republic but as pauperised, badly administered and ill-equipped for the challenges of the millennium.

Building a new national identity

Gordimer emphasises something South Africans are waking up to discover: that South Africa is an African country, not an outpost of the West nor an extension of Europe.

It is an exciting time to be in the country, with the dead weight of the past visibly lessening. Cellular phones (mobiles), satellite TV, legalised casinos, McDonald's, 24-hour petrol stations, a national lottery, rave clubs, gay marches and the Internet were unguessed at in the last years of the old regime; now the new one has also answered simpler basic needs in bringing water, electricity and telephones to many in the old homelands, townships and countryside.

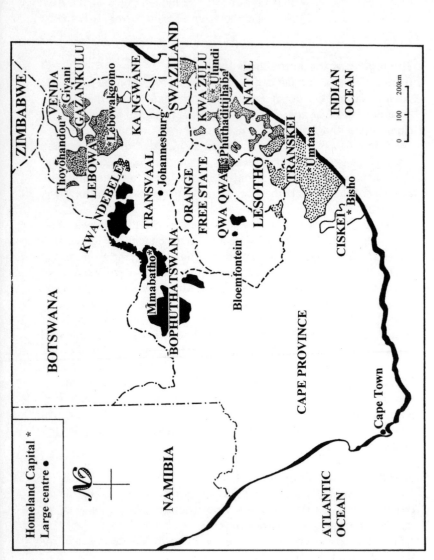

Fig. 1. Map of the 'old' South Africa.

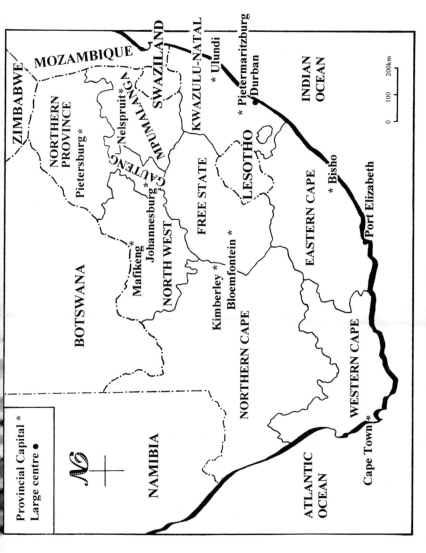

Fig. 2. Map of the 'new' South Africa.

51

Links with Africa and the wider Indian Ocean community, at diplomatic, trade, political and cultural level, have never been closer, and are poised to reach new heights of acceptability and friendship. As host of the Non-Aligned Movement's global meeting in 1998, bidder for the 2004 Olympics and potential host of the 2006 World Cup for soccer, South Africa also has a starring role on the biggest international stage.

The Mandela magic, known as the 'Mandela teflon' in some quarters, has given the fledgling rainbow nation and Thabo Mbeki – with an unassailable parliamentary majority, the support of business at home and political allies and financiers overseas – the unexpected chance to strive for the leadership his dream of the African renaissance calls for.

This is the exciting nation in the making you can be a part of and contribute to if you feel Africa's drumbeat inside. Let's examine now how you should go about it and what you can expect.

3

Moving to South Africa

BACKGROUND TO IMMIGRATION

Before we examine the actual process of immigration to South Africa – the rules and the paperwork, the things to do and to avoid – let us begin with some general background and set the scene for a would-be immigrant at the turn of the millennium and shortly thereafter.

We will look first at issues like the traditional South African migrant worker, illegal immigration, a recent and ugly rise in xenophobia (the dislike and persecution of foreigners), legal immigration, what the government figures do not reveal and the existence of a brain drain and its cost to the country. Such specifically local issues are important to bear in mind when making an individual decision to emigrate to South Africa, in addition, of course, to all the other personal factors you must consider.

The need for migrant workers

South Africa has been using migrant labour in its fields and mines for over a century, and still today most of the workers in the mines come from neighbouring countries, like Lesotho and Mozambique. It's a two-way street, for as much as South Africa needs this pool of willing labour, so do these poor countries rely on the regular inflow of funds from migrant workers to their families at home.

The flow of migrant workers on short-term renewable contracts goes on independently of the formal immigration and emigration process, and the figures involved dwarf the few thousand, mainly professional people who come into or leave South Africa each year.

The Department of Home Affairs, for example, reported that over 175,000 people were granted permanent residence in 1997 (up from 90,000 the year before). It was an exceptionally high figure, for of that total 124,000 were people belonging to the Southern African Development Community (SADC) of neighbouring countries who had been granted special leave that year to upgrade their status from migrant worker to permanent residence.

A flood of illegal immigration

Many people living in South Africa remark on the irony that entry barriers raised by the Department of Home Affairs for legal immigrants are high and difficult to cross while at the same time the country's borders are so leaky that people from Mozambique can walk through the Kruger Park and into Mpumalanga undetected and unchecked (apart from a few incidents each year of lions killing such illegal immigrants).

As the millennium turns, the authorities say they are containing the problem, but population experts suggest that as many as 5 million people already in the country, perhaps nearly 12 per cent of the population, are by origin illegal immigrants. Many such people have been resident for years, if not generations, and never bothered with the paperwork. Many are thought to be migrant workers who simply stayed.

It is also known that some new immigrants do obtain identity documents and permanent residence on the black market or through corruption in the government offices – but we will not suggest you take this route.

• One positive step the authorities took in 1997 was to tighten up border controls by reducing the number of land border posts from 52 to 19 and the number of airports cleared to take international flights from 36 to 10. It was hoped that not only illegal immigration would be reduced by these steps but also smuggling of commercial goods and illegal drugs.

The fact remains, however, that even people from neighbouring countries who enter South Africa illegally, are found and deported, often simply wait a week and return by the same route they used before. There is no indication that such illegal activity is being hindered by the horrible conditions of the Department of Home Affairs transit camps or by the latest tightening up of border controls.

A growing trend of xenophobia

You will find repeated many times in this book the statement that one of the best assets of South Africa is the friendliness of its people. This remains true, despite the recent reputation the country has gained for crime and violence and despite all the racial tensions arising from apartheid which are still a reality in the minds of a substantial minority of people who are unwilling or unable to shift their allegiance to the new South Africa.

However, there is another side you should know about. The culture of friendliness is nowadays mixed with a growing xenophobia, especially in the informal sector (such as the competition between local street traders or hawkers and newcomers from different parts of Africa). South Africa, seen elsewhere in Africa as an economic power house, is undeniably an attraction for businessmen of an entrepreneurial nature, and it has proved easier in the 1990s for people from East and West Africa, as well as South Africa's immediate neighbours, to enter the country (legally or often illegally) and start a business. But very high levels of unemployment over long periods have made some South Africans suspicious of traders, entrepreneurs or workers from other countries, who are accused of taking jobs out of the hands of local people or bringing down wages because they are prepared to work for a pittance.

You probably will not encounter this uglier side of xenophobia, which has also seen police reportedly turning a blind eye to assaults against street traders from East Africa or police allegedly taking bribes from wealthy West African criminals who run drugs and prostitution rackets from cheap hotels in Berea or Hillbrow in Johannesburg.

Perhaps this isn't a real hatred of some foreigners, seen rightly or wrongly as economic competition for street-level survival. The xenophobia that sometimes spills into the streets is perhaps more a reflex of frustration from people who are unwillingly cast as the long-term unemployed. If an economic miracle can be wrought and the South African jobless given work and the economy gear up into consistent growth, the problem could largely solve itself.

Legal immigration and emigration
The figures for the legally controlled movement of people into and out of South Africa make for interesting reading.

- From 1960 to 1994 there were only five years when there were more people leaving the country than entering it. The years were all times of political crisis and general uncertainty: 1960 (the Sharpeville shootings), 1977 and 1978 (the two years following the Soweto riots), and 1986 and 1987 (two of the worst years of apartheid, with a state of emergency imposed).

Otherwise, for nearly 35 years South Africa was attracting more people to settle than chose to leave. And the numbers were high by today's standards. Looking at peak years, in 1975, for example, there were over 50,000 immigrants and just over 10,000 emigrants; in the year I entered the country, 1982, there were nearly 46,000 people coming in and only 7,000 leaving.

- In the four years 1994 to 1997, by contrast (the last year for which Home Affairs statistics are available), there were more people leaving than entering legally, with figures of about 4,500 to 6,000 immigrants a year against 8,500 to 10,000 emigrants. Indications are that this trend continued in 1998 and 1999.

Since 1940 there had never been more than two successive years of net loss to emigration. So is there a crisis – a brain drain, as the newspapers say?

Things are worse than the figures suggest

Before answering this, it should be said that the position is actually much worse than these official figures suggest.

- On the **immigration** side, it is naive to think that only 5,000 people are entering South Africa a year. Leaving aside the many thousands of migrant labourers (some of whom are probably illegal), commentators say there are tens of thousands of illegal immigrants coming in each year, and those deported often return, many times.

- On the **emigration** side, it is known from examining records in high commissions and embassies in South Africa that many leavers who stated they were exiting South Africa temporarily were actually emigrating. For example, in 1996, the official records showed that 1,767 South Africans emigrated to Australia, whereas the Australian High Commission recorded 3,200 South Africans entering Australia. In addition, many white South Africans travel on British or other foreign passports, making it impossible for the authorities to know when they leave for good.

We have seen that official figures are misleading and do not reflect the true scale of either emigration or immigration, but the trend is clear: South Africa is losing people to emigration in a way not seen in nearly 60 years, and the numbers of legal immigrants are low by comparison with earlier years.

So, is there a brain drain?

On any reasonable criteria, the answer must be yes. We base this on two factors: first, the reasons emigrants give for leaving and, second, the type of people who are going.

- In a March 1999 survey, analysts FSA-Contact found that **reasons given by emigrants for leaving** were as follows: 60 per cent cited crime, 47 per cent cited violence, 40 per cent education problems, 20 per cent poor health care, and 13 per cent falling living standards (respondents answered in more than one category, so the figures add up to more than 100 per cent).

- A survey in January 1999 by P-E Corporate Services showed much the same ranking of reasons for emigration, adding as other factors job insecurity and possible retrenchment.

In both surveys, the emigrants suggested that the 'push' factors making them leave South Africa outweighed the 'pull' factors of their destination countries. Few who left cited better job opportunities overseas as their reason.

- The FSA-Contact survey showed the **destinations of its emigrant sample** as follows: 38 per cent were heading for the USA, 26 per cent to the UK, 19 per cent to Australia, 9 per cent to Canada and 5 per cent to New Zealand. It is easy enough to see that these are all English-speaking countries, most of which are also members of the Commonwealth and by any standards First World.

Given that it is mainly managerial and executive-level or professional people who can afford to think of emigrating, and given that in South Africa at the millennium most people in these positions are still white males, it is not surprising that the majority of those taking the decision to leave are managerial-level, English-speaking, male and white. That is not to say there is no emigration among black, coloured and Indian South Africans, but it is as yet on a small scale.

What fields are the emigrants working in?

Two near the top of the list are information technology (IT) and accounting/financial services.

- **IT professionals** account for almost a quarter of total staff turnover in South Africa (the all-sector average is 10 per cent a year), and many IT people do emigrate, taking transportable skills with them. A proportion of them make for South African IT companies that have successfully established overseas, like Datatec, Didata, CCH and Top Info. It is calculated that up to 25 per cent of people legally emigrating from South Africa are IT professionals.

- Auditing firm Deloitte & Touche found in 1997 that 75 per cent of top newly qualified **chartered accountants** wanted to work abroad, despite being able to command salaries of up to R20,000 a month in South Africa.

What is the cost of the brain drain?

Estimates on such a matter will vary considerably when there is little agreement on the numbers of people involved, but the Unisa School of Business Leadership calculated in April 1999 that the brain drain cost South Africa R2.26 billion in 1997. This result was arrived at by taking the average earnings of graduates who left the country in that year. The mythical average graduate, the study said, would contribute R7.4 million to the economy in his or her working life.

Whatever the figure, the real cost is greater because not only have skills and experience been lost which are hard to replace, but those leaving are most likely to be risk-takers and accept challenges – such as the considerable risk of starting in a new country. Emigrants the world over are generally hard-working, and indeed South Africans settling overseas are often successful in their new business or profession.

The same Unisa survey found that in the period 1994–97 emigration cost the tax base R8.4 billion and as much as R285 billion in lost contributions to gross domestic product.

WHO CONTROLS IMMIGRATION?

We have painted a picture of a country enduring a brain drain perhaps modest in numbers but significant in its effect on the economy, and with no apparent end in sight to a number of successive years of net emigration loss. Surely this dire situation is an invitation to the South African government to liberalise its immigration rules – which, we must warn you, are not at all easy to negotiate – and promote a culture of welcoming qualified, willing workers, say in IT or auditing, who have the nation-building skills the country needs and is losing? One might indeed think so, but, regrettably, this is not the case.

Before we examine the nuts and bolts of immigration, we should briefly look at the legislation governing the process in South Africa.

The Aliens Control Act 1962

Perhaps the very name of the governing Act gives the game away: in 1962, and still today, migration policy is all about controlling alien, and hence threatening or dangerous, forces which could undermine the Republic. The Act was slightly amended in 1995 but still remains substantially in force as promulgated some forty years ago – just two years after the shock to the apartheid government of the Sharpeville resistance and massacres. The legislation governing immigration is still defensive, reactionary and exclusionary.

There is a possibility of a new migration policy, but the White Paper on International Migration, issued in early 1999, may take a year or more to progress into legislation. We will come back to this later. For now the 1962 Act controls government policy.

The Department of Home Affairs

The Department of Home Affairs is the organ of the state administering migration policy. It considers legal immigration requests on an individual, ad hoc basis.

• There is no **quota system**, unlike, say, in Australia or New Zealand, where immigrants are scored on a points basis, according to age, qualification, sector in which employed and so on, then matched to a wants list of needed occupations, which changes according to circumstances ('this year we need radiographers, not brain surgeons').

Dealing with Home Affairs, we must advise you, is not an easy or uplifting experience. The offices tend to be old, unwelcoming and difficult to negotiate ('this queue is for form A, not form B: go back and stand in the other queue'). The culture of the department – and there is no other way to say this – tends to be Afrikaner, conservative and obstructive.

The talk on Bureaucracy Street is that Home Affairs is the most conservative organ of government and the least able to change. One immigration lawyer was quoted by the *Financial Mail* in early 1999 as saying there had been an explosion of cases brought by would-be immigrants against Home Affairs in recent months, and 'Home Affairs' interpretation of some of the provisions [of the 1962 Act] is becoming more conservative and xenophobic'.

Such comments are not intended to deter you from coming to South Africa to settle. Not at all. But you should know that for some people the process of getting the proper paperwork in order and waiting for replies can be trying. No two immigrants have the same experience, and yours may be easy and quick; but be prepared for it not to be.

Offices of Home Affairs can be found in the leading cities of South Africa: check the back of the local telephone book under 'Government Departments'. If you can use a smaller office rather than one in a big city, you might find the queues smaller and the treatment more humane.

Anticipating what we will advise later, let's suggest at this point that the best way to find your way through the immigration minefield is: (a) to go to an immigration agent, who will help you walk through the minefield safely, or (b) to be in a job situation in which you are transferred to South Africa and your employer does the paperwork for you.

THE NUTS AND BOLTS OF IMMIGRATION

So, after all this preamble, how do you go about the immigration process? You may be applying from a South African Embassy or High Commission outside the country or to a Home Affairs office when inside South Africa.

- Everybody has to go through the route of applying for temporary residence, and thereafter permanent residence.

Application for temporary residence (B1-159A)
The basic form everybody must complete is B1-159A, **the application for temporary residence in South Africa**. This can cover an individual or a whole family, and it must accompany all other detailed permit applications, described in (a) to (e) below. This basic form contains:

- the personal details of each applicant
- citizenship and passport details
- own addresses and those of friends or relatives in South Africa
- intention of stay

- arrangements for repatriation (amount of available funds and details of return ticket)
- details of dependants
- security and health clearance (details of any convictions or infectious diseases contracted – the form mentions TB, but not HIV/Aids)
- a declaration.

Two photographs of the applicant are required, and on top of page 1 you must tick a small checklist which specifies the type of temporary permit you are applying for.

Applications for the temporary permit must include B1-159A and one of the five categories of detailed permit applications.

There are five categories, which we will look at in turn:

(a) workseeker's permit
(b) work permit – temporary employment
(c) work permit – self-employed/own business
(d) work permit – arts and entertainment industry
(e) study permit.

(a) Workseeker's permit (B1-159B)
This permit is for people wanting to enter South Africa to assess employment opportunities and attend job interviews. Applicants wishing to explore prospects in setting up a business in the country must complete this form and that for self-employment or own business (B1-159D). Applicants must return to their country of origin/residence to await the outcome of their application.

The form asks applicants to be specific in outlining:

- their chosen occupation
- level of position sought
- reasons for wanting to work in South Africa
- whether recruited or approached by an agency or local business/ overseas principal of a local subsidiary or responding to an advertisement
- specific companies intended to approach, and why
- qualifications and experience
- declaration.

Comment: It may all sound promising, but an executive immigration expert advises that this permit rarely secures a positive reaction from Home Affairs (where the application is sent for assessment), and is an unlikely route to a successful immigration application. So now consider:

(b) Work permit – temporary employment (B1-159C)
This is the normal employment application for people seeking work in South Africa as an employee, and you need your prospective employer's help in completing the form (see Figure 3). You are asked to supply:

- educational qualifications
- work experience, covering all jobs held, dates, salary and position held
- declaration.

The prospective employer is asked to supply:

- details of the company and its business
- numbers of employees, in categories such as key personnel, management, administrative and artisans; and how many South African citizens, approved immigrants and holders of temporary work permits are employed in each of these categories
- details of recruitment process followed – Department of Manpower contacted for possible applicants, employment agencies approached, media advertising used
- reasons why local candidates were not appointed
- details of special skills offered by the candidate, not available locally
- additional explicit motivation to support selection of the applicant
- details of offer made to the candidate
- declaration.

Comment: The pressure here is definitely on the would-be employer to convince Home Affairs that considerable efforts have been made to recruit locally. The exhaustive process of approaching the Department of Manpower and various employment agencies (an executive immigration agency says at least three should be used) plus advertising (with copies of the print advertisement, names of media where placed, the number of inserts and amount spent in recruitment advertising) has to be gone through and everything documented scrupulously.

G.P.-S. 017-0695

BI-159: C

REPUBLIC OF SOUTH AFRICA

DEPARTMENT OF HOME AFFAIRS

APPLICATION FOR A WORK PERMIT—CATEGORY: TEMPORARY EMPLOYMENT

IMPORTANT:

(i) This form must be submitted together with the basic application form BI-159: A.

(ii) All applicants are required to personally complete paragraphs 1, 2, 3 and 4 and their prospective employers paragraphs 5 to 9.

(iii) The following documentation must be attached in the space allocated on form BI-159: A:

(a) A certified copy of the applicant's highest educational and any additional qualifications plus testimonials or certificates of employment from previous employers.
(b) A letterhead from the prospective employer onto which press clippings of the advertisements relative to the specific position have been affixed.
(c) The documentation as specified in item 6 of form BI-159: A relative to the applicant's maintenance in and possible repatriation from South Africa.

AS SUBMITTED BY:

Surname/Family name	Given names	Date of birth

1. Please provide details of **your workseeker's permit,** if applicable:

1.1 Issued at:	1.2 On:
1.3 Reference No.:	1.4 Valid until:
1.5 Proposed occupation:	
1.6 **If you do not hold a workseeker's permit,** reason:	

2. QUALIFICATIONS:

2.1 School qualifications	2.2 Total number of years	2.3 From	2.4 To	2.5 Name and location of school
Primary school				
Secondary/High school				
Professional school				
2.6 Highest examination passed				
2.7 Major subjects				
2.8 Higher qualifications or special training:				
2.9 Name and location of college, university or other educational institution attended:				
2.10 Prescribed duration of course				

Fig. 3. Application for a work permit – category:
temporary employment (B1-159C).

63

2.11 Period attended	2.12 From	2.13 To	2.14 Major subjects		
2.15 Degree, diploma or certificate obtained					
2.16 Trade qualifications					
2.17 Prescribed duration of apprenticeship					
2.18 Period served			2.19 From		2.20 To
2.21 Trade in which qualified			2.22 To which trade union do you belong?		
2.23 Details of any additional "in service" or practical training					

3. EXPERIENCE:

EMPLOYMENT RECORD (IN CHRONOLOGICAL ORDER, COVERING FULL PERIOD OF EMPLOYMENT INCLUDING PERIODS OF UNEMPLOYMENT)

3.1 Period		3.2 Name and address of employer	3.3 Type of business	3.4 Position/ Occupation	3.5 Monthly salary
From:	To:				
From:	To:				
From:	To:				
From:	To:				
From:	To:				

3.6 DETAILS OF ANY ADDITIONAL EXPERIENCE AND/OR SPECIAL SKILLS GAINED TO ASSIST APPLICANT IN HIS/HER PROPOSED FIELD OF EMPLOYMENT

4. DECLARATION BY APPLICANT:

I acknowledge that I understand the contents and implications of this application. I solemnly declare that the above particulars provided by me are true and correct and that the following is a bona fide offer of employment obtained in accordance with legitimate procedures.

....

Signature of applicant   *Signature of witness*

Signed at.. this ....day of.. 19 ....

2

Fig. 3. Cont.

TO BE COMPLETED BY PROSPECTIVE EMPLOYER

5. OFFER OF EMPLOYMENT

IMPORTANT:

(a) Employers must note that the overriding consideration in dealing with applications for work permits is whether the employment or task to be performed cannot be undertaken by a South African citizen or an approved immigrant. Employers must therefore indicate below the steps taken by them to obtain the services of suitable candidates from the local labour market.

(b) The applicant is by law precluded from commencing employment, whether remunerated or otherwise, until he/she is in possession of a valid work permit for the specific purpose. Non-compliance can lead to heavy penalties being imposed on both the employer and employee.

(c) Separate sheets may be attached if the space provided is insufficient to include full information/replies.

6. BACKGROUND DETAILS OF PROSPECTIVE EMPLOYER AND POSITION OFFERED

6.1 Title of Company/Organization:	
6.2 Physical address:	6.3 Mailing address:
6.4 Telephone number: (code) (number)	6.5 Facsimile number: (code) (number)
6.6 Employer's business registration number:	6.7 Employer's tax reference number:
6.8 If a subsidiary, principal company and location:	
6.9 Nature of business conducted:	Number of employees:

Category	Key personnel	Management	Administrative	Artisans	Labourers	Other (specify)
6.10 SA citizens						
6.11 Approved immigrants						
6.12 Holders of temporary work permits						

6.13.1 The position offered has been vacant since:
6.13.2 or, If a newly created position, details:
6.14 Details of the recent dismissal of any employees in this specific category:
6.15.1 Is the applicant related to you or anyone else in the business: No ☐ Yes ☐   6.15.2 Details
6.16 The position was brought to the attention of the applicant by the following means:

7. RECRUITMENT AND INTERVIEWING OF SA CITIZENS/RESIDENTS TO FILL THE POSITION

7.1.1 The Department of Labour was approached: No ☐ Yes ☐   7.1.2 Branch:
7.2.1 Employment agencies were approached: No ☐ Yes ☐   7.2.2 Agencies:
7.3 Media advertisement inserted in: (name of publication)   from   to

Note: The relevant press cuttings must be affixed to an original, official letterhead (which includes details of the directors/owner members of the business) and submitted with the application. Please also attach relevant copies of replies received from the Department of Labour and employment agencies.

3

Fig. 3. Cont.

7.4 Full details of the outcome to the above and reasons why suitably qualified local candidates were not appointed:

....
....
....
....
....
....
....
....

7.5 Does the applicant possess any special skills, not available locally, that have been tested by you and make him/her the most suitable candidate for this position:

7.5.1 No ☐   Yes ☐

7.5.2 Details ....
....

7.6 Additional explicit motivation to support the selection of an alien incumbent...
....
....
....
....
....

8.   DETAILS OF OFFER MADE TO APPLICANT:

8.1 Title of occupation to be followed:	
8.2 Salary offered: R per month.	8.3 Additional benefits, if any:
8.4 Nature of offer: Permanent................. Temporary................. For a period of.................weeks/months.	
8.5 Summary of delegated duties..	
8.6 Preferred date of commencement of employment: / /	

9.   DECLARATION BY EMPLOYER

I, (full name)... ID Number ....in my

capacity as .... of the company/organization known as ....

hereby undertake full responsibility for the above-namedapplicant...and solemnly declare that I am authorized to make this offer of employment on behalfof the aforesaid company/organization, that this offer is made in good faith and will be honoured and that the above particulars provided by me are true and correct.

....
              Signature of employer   *Signature of witness*

Signed at .... this ....day of .... 19 ....

4

Fig. 3. Cont.

The process essentially is one of persuading Home Affairs that the would-be immigrant is uniquely qualified to undertake the job and there is no possibility of a local candidate coming forward. The employer has to put in a great deal of work to make this application stick, and Home Affairs is under no obligation to explain why it refuses an impeccable overseas candidate.

(c) Work permit – self-employed/own business (B1-159D)
Along with form B1-159A, this permit is to be completed by applicants for:

- existing businesses (audited financial statements are required)
- branches or subsidiaries to be established (audited statements plus information on overseas holding company)
- new businesses (certified statements on applicants'/partners' assets and liabilities)
- and feasibility studies and statement of business objectives.

The form asks for the following information:

- details of existing business
- the amount of foreign capital to invest and available for running expenses
- the number of local citizens, permanent residents and temporary residents plus employees to be recruited and transferred from abroad
- details of business and educational qualifications.

Comment: Immigrant experts advise that the practical criterion is amount of money to be invested and the quantity of job creation offered by the applicant. In practice, an amount of R500,000 is a good starting point, say the experts. Additionally, the business must be viable already or likely to prosper. Would-be immigrants usually find this route less difficult than others, but discovering the right employer at the right time may not be easy. At least the applications in this category tend to be processed quickly (it can be a few days rather than several weeks as in most of the other categories).

(d) Work permit – arts and entertainment industry (B1-159E)
This special category is for crew and cast of overseas film and TV production companies applying to work in South Africa.

(e) Study permit (B1-159F)
Study permits are offered to tertiary level students who want to take courses available only in South Africa (for example, South African history or anthropology or one of the southern African languages) and who are not by their presence excluding a deserving local candidate. The form B1-159F involves:

- giving a motivation giving detailed reasons why he/she wishes to pursue studies in South Africa
- signing an undertaking to leave the country on completion of the studies
- getting a medical report signed by his/her doctor
- for primary and secondary students, obtaining an undertaking by the educational institution to pay the cost of the student's repatriation, if necessary; and for a tertiary level student, making a bank deposit or giving a bank guarantee for repatriation purposes, if necessary.

Application for extension of existing permits and change of use

The application for **renewal of an existing permit (B1-159G)** must be completed in good time before expiry of the old permit, or you run the risk of being declared a prohibited person and deported. **The usual length of permit is one year**.

A motivation for the extension should be supplied by the applicant, together with relevant supporting documentation, from employer, educational institution, etc. as appropriate.

A **temporary work permit**, for example, will only be renewed if the employer asserts that the applicant's continued employment is required. Proof must be provided by the employer that vigorous efforts were made to obtain the services of a South African citizen to replace the applicant, and a motivation offered for retention of the candidate.

A **study permit** will be renewed only if a South African citizen is not being displaced, if the student complies with language requirements (this may mean learning Afrikaans or another language), if the student can pay his/her fees and the repatriation undertaking remains in effect.

Comment: Applications for temporary renewal have not in the past been problematic (some people have renewed their permits once a year for 30 years or more). But there is evidence that from about

1998 Home Affairs has taken a keener interest in long-time residents who are still on temporary permits. The advice is to try and convert to a permanent residence permit as soon as possible (see below).

Application for change of purpose and/or conditions of existing permit (B1-159H)

This largely covers a proposed change of employer by a temporary work permit holder. The applicant fills in the details of existing permit held and a motivation for the change of conditions, and the prospective employer must complete the same details as provided by the initial employer for form B1-159C (e.g. proof of approach to Department of Manpower, recruitment agency and media advertisements placed, plus a motivation).

Comment: As in the applications for temporary renewal, those for change of purpose are coming under more scrutiny than in former years. An immigration expert advises that since July 1996 it has proved difficult to get Home Affairs to change purpose of entry, certainly while the applicant is waiting within South Africa. Applicants are being told to return to their country of origin/residence and reapply from there. The general advice is to upgrade to permanent residence if possible, without delay.

Application for permanent residence (B1-947 [IM 9E(i)])

There is no formal minimum or maximum period for applying to become a permanent resident of South Africa. An immigration adviser suggests you wait at least three months if a temporary resident (to demonstrate financial independence) and at least a year if self-employed (to show a set of annual accounts), but these are not statutory periods.

> **Students cannot become permanent residents in their student capacity.**

The appropriate application form (see Figure 4) has changed little in many years. For instance, it still asks applicants if they have ever belonged to the Communist Party or 'sympathised with or supported any communistically orientated organisation or doctrine'. One can understand the National Party in the 1970s designating such a question, when the SA Communist Party was banned, but, ironically, the post-1994 democratically elected governments are bristling with SACP members.

Other questions asked include:

- declaration of convictions of a criminal offence ('even if such conviction is no longer on record against you or the person concerned')
- declarations of insolvency or civil suits against the applicant
- questions on debt, physical or mental disability and previous emigration history, whether in South Africa or to other countries.

In some ways this is an easy form to complete, but the killer is the **attachments**. Here is a short list of what must be appended with all **permanent residence applications**:

- photograph
- birth certificate (original document only)
- medical report (less than six months old)
- radiological report (ditto)
- immigration questionnaire (form B1-757)
- character reference (from a 'person of standing')
- educational certificates
- work references
- offer of employment (from employer)
- proof of financial resources (for retirees to South Africa and the self-employed)
- citizenship declaration form.

Comment: Having submitted this battery of forms and documents to Home Affairs, there is nothing much else for the applicant to do but wait. The waiting period may be weeks and more often months, and it follows that applications should be made early in the life of a temporary permit so there is no overlap problem.

If one has got this far, it is hoped the application will be successful, and there is no indication that Home Affairs is turning people down as yet for quota or other affirmative action reasons.

Citizenship

If you work your way through the immigration hoops successfully, you may decide take the further step of seeking citizenship. The procedure, in brief, involves your having a good police record for six years after gaining permanent residence, taking various oaths and

G.P.-S. 017-0113

BI-9×7 [IM 9E (i)]

REPUBLIC OF SOUTH AFRICA

APPLICATION FOR A PERMANENT RESIDENCE PERMIT

(Hierdie vorm is ook in Afrikaans beskikbaar)

Please read and comply with the instructions on page 4

Note.—(a) Read all items carefully and complete them in detail. A mere dash (—) is not acceptable.

(b) The completed form MUST be accompanied by the documents listed on page 4.

(c) In the case of married couples both the husband and the wife must sign and date this form.

FOR OFFICIAL USE ONLY

Interviewed ....

....

APPROVED: Signature ....

Date..................

Previous correspondence ....

1. **DETAILS OF APPLICANT** (block letters): SURNAME.................... FORENAME(S) ....

Sex	Marital status (never married/married/ widowed/divorced)	Date of birth	Country and place (town/city) of birth	Highest educational and vocational qualifications (or number of years of schooling completed successfully)	Present nationality	Religion	Denomination of your church	For official use Permit numbers

PRESENT RESIDENTIAL ADDRESS: No. .... Street .... Suburb and town/city....................

2. (a) Details of: (i) Wife; (ii) husband if the wife is the applicant; (iii) unmarried children under the age of 21 of both husband and wife including those born out of previous marriages or out of wedlock; (iv) children, if any, of unmarried applicants. Full details are required whether the persons concerned intend to proceed to South Africa or not or are already in South Africa. If the applicant is a child details of parents, brothers and sisters under 21 years must be furnished.

Surname	Forename(s)	Relationship to applicant, e.g. wife, husband, son, daughter	Date of birth	Country and place (town/ city) of birth	Highest educational and vocational qualifications (or number of years of schooling completed successfully)	Occu-pation	Present nationality	Religion	Denomi-nation of your church

(b) Wife's maiden name.................... ; and (c) any other former surnames....................

(d) Names of the persons mentioned under paragraph 2 (a) who do not wish to apply for permanent residence and the reasons therefor:

3. If a wife and children wish to join a husband who is already in South Africa, or if a husband who is in South Africa wishes his wife and children to join him, the address of husband or wife must be furnished below:

Present address ....

Fig. 4. Application for a permanent residence permit (B1-947[IM 9E(i)]).

71

For official use

4. DETAILS REGARDING APPLICANT AND (IF APPLICABLE) WIFE AND CHILDREN

The following questions relate to you (the applicant) as well as to any person mentioned under paragraph 2 (a), and must be answered "YES" or "NO":

(a) Have you or any of the persons concerned ever been—

    (i) convicted of a criminal offence even if such conviction is no longer on record against you or the person concerned: ....

    (ii) declared insolvent? ....

    (iii) the subject of a civil action? ....

(b) Will you or any of the persons concerned leave any debts behind on your departure or, if you are already in South Africa, did you leave any debts behind abroad?. ....

(c) Is there a civil or criminal enquiry pending against you or any of the persons concerned? ....

(d) Have you or any of the persons concerned previously applied to immigrate to or to settle permanently in South Africa? ....

(e) Have you or any of the persons concerned ever been refused permanent residence in or entry to or been repatriated or deported from South African or any other country? ....

(f) Have you or any of the persons concerned ever previously been to South Africa for longer than three months? ....

(g) Do you or any of the persons concerned suffer, or have any of you ever suffered from or been treated for any physical or mental disability? ....

(h) Have you or any of the persons concerned ever belonged to the Communist Party or sympathised with or supported any communistically orientated organisation or doctrine? ....

N.B.—If the answer to any of the questions 4 (a) to (h) above is "YES" give FULL details below. In connection with question (a) (ii) state whether or not you or the persons concerned have been rehabilitated. In respect of question (f) actual periods and addresses of residence must be furnished.

....

....

....

5. Have you or any of the persons concerned ever emigrated to another country? If so, please state which person(s), the countries of previous immigration, and the year in each case. ....

....

....

2

Fig. 4. Cont.

For official use

6. (a) What is your occupation? ....

   (b) What occupation do you intend following in South Africa? ....

7. Name and address of present employer ....

8. Address at which you can be contacted in South Africa:

   ....

   Note.—Any incorrect information or false documents furnished in support of this application may result in the applicant and his/her dependants being refused permission to enter into or to remain in South Africa.

9. I/We, the undersigned, declare that the photograph(s) submitted in support of this application are a true likeness of the person(s) whose **names** appear on the reverse side thereof and that the details reflected in this application and supporting documents are true and correct, that it is my/our intention to reside permanently in South Africa and that neither I/we nor any of the persons mentioned under paragraph 2 (a) have ever received any financial assistance from the South African Government, or any agency acting on its behalf, for the purpose of proceeding to and settling in South Africa. I/We further declare that I/we have received the information pamphlets and that I/we have studied them, particularly the two entitled "Assisted Immigration—a Handbook on your journey to and arrival in the Republic of South Africa" and "Employment in the Republic of South Africa". I undertake to ensure that my offer of employment will remain valid at all times.

Signature of applicant.. Date..........................

Signature of legal spouse.. Date..........................

**FOR OFFICIAL USE
(PHOTOGRAPHS)**

Fig. 4. Cont.

PLEASE READ THE FOLLOWING IN CONJUNCTION WITH THE ACCOMPANYING INSTRUCTIONS:

IMPORTANT.— (a) The documents listed below *must* be submitted by the persons indicated.

(b) "**Applicants**" on this page includes all persons whose names appear under paragraphs 1 and 2 (a) on page 1 and who intend to apply for a permanent residence permit.

(c) Documents which are not in English, Afrikaans or Dutch must be accompanied by **certified translations** into English or Afrikaans.

(d) The applicant and his/her spouse *must* sign this form. Where the applicant is a child both parents *must* sign this form.

1	Photograph, not less than 3,80 cm × 3,80 cm.	All applicants	A recent, passport-type, full-face photograph bearing the names of the applicants on the reverse side thereof. Machine-type or instant photographs are not acceptable.
2	Birth certificate, or extract from birth record.	All applicants.	Only original documents are acceptable.
2.1	Change of name document i.e. Statutory Declaration or Deed Poll.	All applicants, where applicable.	
3	Medical report, form BI 811 (IM 10).	All applicants.	Must not be older than six months at time of submission.
4	Radiological report, form BI 806 (IM 13).	All applicants 12 years of age and older	The report must not be more than six months old at time of submission. ("Mass X-ray" cards and separate radiological reports acceptable.
5	Questionnaire, form BI 757 (IM 418).	All applicants 18 years of age and older.	
6	Police certificate(s)	All applicants 18 years of age and older	In respect of all countries of residence in excess of 12 months.
7	Marriage certificate, or extract from marriage record	All married applicants.	
8	Final divorce decree(s) and all relevant court orders regarding custody of children and maintenance	All applicants who have been divorced	Required irrespective of whether or not the person concerned has since re-married.
9	Death certificate of late spouse	All widows and widowers.	
10	Character reference, form BI 843 (IM 361)	All applicants (excluding wives and/or children)	The character reference must be submitted by a person of standing.
11	Questionnaire, form BI 897 (IM 88) **if not already submitted**	All applicants who will be employed in South Africa	*N.B.*—(a) Full details of both training and experience are essential to confirm an applicant's ability to perform the intended occupation in South Africa. (b) Documents submitted in support of this section must indicate the actual dates of training and/or employment and also the capacity or occupation in which trained and/or employed. (c) Present employer's work reference may be submitted at a later date if so desired.
12	Highest educational, trade and/or professional certificates	All applicants who will be employed in South Africa	
13	Work references or certificates of service (covering at least the last five years)	All applicants who will be employed in South Africa	
14	Offer of employment	All applicants proceeding to pre-arranged employment	The job offer must state clearly the occupation to be followed and salary offered and must not be older than six months at time of submission.
15	Proof of financial resources.	All applicants who are retiring to South Africa, who will be self-employed or who will be entering into a business partnership.	
16	Consent of both parents or guardian.	All single applicants under the age of 21.	
17	Citizenship declaration, form BI 939 (IM 427)	All applicants 21 years of age and older and/or by both parents where under 21 years of age.	

4

Fig. 4. Cont.

filling in more forms. Six years after your last big form-filling exercise you can probably bear to face the process again.

Dual citizenship as between, say, the UK and South Africa, is reasonably straightforward to obtain.

WHAT DO THE PERMITS COST?

In April 1999 there was an increase in the fee levels to be paid to Home Affairs, with costs going up dramatically. It was not clear whether this was a revenue-gathering move or a deterrent to less affluent would-be immigrants.

- Extensions to temporary work permits went up from R500 to R1,020, for one year.
- Permanent residence permits increased from R7,750 to R10,020, with no time limit.
- Education permit extensions doubled from R500 to R1,020, for one year.

USING AN IMMIGRATION AGENCY

The foregoing account may have proved sober and perhaps discouraging reading. I can assure you, however, that the considerable effort and strain involved in the immigration process is worthwhile, because living in South Africa remains rewarding, with manifold opportunities in a dynamically evolving and generally positive society.

As said before, the process is a minefield, and the best advice we can offer is to take the help of an expert in this area. But a **word of warning**: there are many unregistered immigration agencies, which are best avoided because they have no legal or even business status *vis-à-vis* the Home Affairs Department.

An experienced agency, perhaps with staff previously employed by Home Affairs, knows the culture of the department and the plus points in an application which win approval. The experts also know how best and when to offer the various application forms and which criteria or attachments really count. This can save time and eventually money.

One such agency is **Execu Immigration**, which claims to be the biggest of its kind in South Africa, and which has Home Affairs accreditation. It has offices at Johannesburg International Airport

(Tel: 011 390 1567/8) and Durban (Tel: 031 222 809). The email for both South African offices is izak@execu.co.za and the website is www.execu.co.za.

The **Department of Home Affairs** itself has a toll-free number: 0 800 601190, but had no website accessible to the public at the time of writing.

THE FUTURE

As mentioned above, the 1962 Aliens Control Act remains the governing legislation for immigration and emigration, but change is coming, if recommendations of the **1999 White Paper on International Migration** are enacted in legislation, possibly in 2000 or the following year.

Some of the recommendations of the White Paper are as follows. Even if they are not enacted, the proposals do serve to show the way Home Affairs (which appointed the task force which drew up the White Paper) is moving and thinking.

- Renewable three months' free entry for all except prohibited persons.
- Greater latitude for entry of tourists, traders and businessmen, who will be eligible for once-renewable three-month entry permits.
- A new immigration service to be established, plus a new immigration court and security force.
- Shift from border control to community, workplace and educational institution inspection of foreign workers.
- Stricter controls on employers who employ foreign workers, with compulsory payment of set sums into a skills training fund expressly for South African workers.
- Permanent residence for all temporary legal workers after five years, provided there is a permanent job offer and no local candidate is available.
- Permanent residence may be sought before five years, on application to the National Economic, Development and Labour Council, which will set sector quotas.
- Foreign investors will have to undertake training of South African workers in their employ.
- Foreigners who are self-employed will need to bring in sufficient funds to live on and produce job opportunities.

- Foreigners will no longer have to apply for entry permits from their home countries.
- Corporate visas may be negotiated, with the companies responsible for administration and eventual repatriation of foreign workers – this covers chiefly the mines and agriculture.
- Spouses of people with South African citizenship will automatically qualify for permanent residence.

Comment: The policy goal is clearly to try to stem illegal immigration and put South African workers at the head of the employment queue, even in cases where legal workers from abroad are needed to fill specific positions.

There is a shift to making entry into the country more flexible but increasing controls over conditions of stay. One commentator said in respect of legal temporary immigrants that they have to 'work' their way into permanent residence over a new five-year period, which is like 'being condemned to five years of insecurity'.

While still dominated by a preoccupation with control of unwelcome foreigners, by which the authorities still imply illegal, unskilled African workers, the new policy shows signs of being informed by market forces and a macroeconomic, growth point of view.

There does appear to be space still in this radically new policy for skilled, foreign immigrants, such as the readers of this book – although how the details would work in your case remains uncertain at the time of writing. However, if you take expert and professional immigration assistance, as suggested earlier, there is cause to be optimistic that the new South Africa will continue to welcome you.

How you go about settling in forms the subject matter of the next chapter.

4

Settling In

So you have arrived at Johannesburg International (or Cape Town or Durban), with some sort of permission to stay in South Africa. What do you do to settle in? Let's look at your alternatives in finding accommodation, the services you can obtain as a resident and some facets of everyday life, before we go into specialist chapters on employment, retirement, social life, getting around and so on.

FINDING SOMEWHERE TO LIVE

Immediate accommodation

Where do you stay for your first night in the country, if your employer or family or friends have not made plans for you? (By the by, you'll soon discover that 'we'll make a plan' is the national phrase for intending to do something, although you should know it can also be a polite way of putting you off.)

- Starting at the airport, you can get over your jet lag at various **airport hotels**.

- Going a bit further afield but still near the three main airports, the **Formule 1** hotel group will probably have a conveniently located building which will cost a few rand in the taxi to reach. The selling feature of Formule 1, in South Africa as elsewhere, is cheapish accommodation paid for by the room, whether one, two or three people share.

- If you're not too keen on staying in hotels for more than a night or two, there is a growing range of **bed and breakfast** (b&b) establishments in the major towns, and not only on the tourist routes. Lists of authorised b&bs are published annually, and most CNA bookshops or larger hotels will have such lists on hand.

- If you really have little money, **youth hostels** and **backpack lodges**

78

can be found in the larger cities, but these are crowded in the summer months.

- Instead go downmarket by changing the **suburb** you are prepared to live in (try Germiston instead of Bryanston, Woodstock instead of Claremont).

- If **self-catering** is to your taste, the Don Suites Hotel Group is one specialist offering good facilities in upmarket suburbs, with lettings by the day, week, month or longer.

The rental route

But a hotel or b&b may not be your idea of a settled place to live, especially if you are a family man or woman and have some capital in hand. What about something more permanent?

Renting in contemporary South Africa is actually not an easy option because the supply of rental accommodation is drying up. Rent control has applied to rental property built before 1949, but the apartments are usually in bad repair and in areas where landlords cannot sell because of downgrading (as in Johannesburg's Berea and Hillbrow). The Act governing rent control was repealed in 1999, so that landlords would be free, after notice periods of up to three years, to charge market-related prices.

Another avenue for rentals is from people paying off a house and who have to move around the country with their job (as in many of the banks and insurance groups and mining houses). It may be desirable for them to offer a short-term rental rather than sell. The snag here is that with a recent history of high interest rates (peaking at 25.5 per cent in October 1998), the mortgage payer will often have to pitch the rent on the steep side to continue with high monthly payments. Rates had fallen progressively to 16.5 per cent by July 1999, with further cuts possible – still very high in European terms and still about 8 per cent above the cost of inflation, leaving considerable room for more reductions.

Word of mouth, estate agents and the classifieds are your traditional ways of **finding rentals**, and increasingly the information is supplied on the Internet as well as in the Saturday newspapers. These days many companies do offer staff housing subsidies in the case of purchases or help with rental accommodation, and these are considered as 'perks' by the taxman.

If you can find good rental accommodation, such as a 'cottage' at the back of an older house (this would usually be an upgraded 'servants' quarters'), you may be lucky and have use of the garden, pool and garage as well as fairly cheap payments (less than R2,000 a month in most cities).

As a tenant you don't have to pay for **maintenance**, which is the responsibility of the leaseholder or landlord; you also have some protection in the law against the landlord raising rentals when his mortgage bond goes up (though watch out for the time when your agreement is renewed and the landlord may try to get more out of you to set against his increased costs).

There is little sign that the government is targeting rental accommodation as a viable part of the housing economy.

Is home-buying a better option?

The advice the experts give is to buy if you are likely to stay in one place for at least 7 and preferably 10 or 15 years. Frequent moves lose you money because of the inbuilt factor of paying off interest charges to the mortgage company for some years before the principal cost comes down, and expensive lawyer's fees or transfer duty, which can tot up to 10 per cent of the value of your property.

Before you start you will normally have to find a deposit of 10 per cent of the house value and pay this to the bank or mortgage company. You are not obliged to stay with your regular bank in the house-buying process and are at liberty to shop around, though your bank may offer discount in some form to keep your business. But the 10 per cent deposit rule does seem standard, even in low-cost housing schemes.

Strategies to beat the system

As for the period of the mortgage, the smart move would be to take a **bond** (as the mortgage is commonly called) for as short a period as you can afford. The mortgage company will want you to lock into a 20-year bond, which brings them maximum advantage, but if you can manage it, try and pay off in five years.

- On a R200,000 bond the five-year option will cost you R5,188 a month, while the 20-year bond will be R3,241 a month. The interest on the 20-year bond would be R577,000 and on the five-year bond only R111,286 (at August 1999 values).

If you cannot go this route, in South Africa's still-high interest-rate environment, it makes good sense to increase the amount you pay. Adding just 10 per cent to the standard monthly bond repayment could halve your pay-off term.

Paying earlier each month, for example, five days before the end of the month, when the bond repayment falls due on the first of the next month, can reduce the home loan term and the amount of interest you pay.

Other strategies to think about are multiple payments during the month (because interest charges are calculated on the outstanding daily balance), and payment of a lump sum into the mortgage account.

More considerations in buying a home

A rule of thumb adopted by the banks and other mortgage lenders is that the bond repayments should not exceed 30 per cent of your income. And don't forget you will have to buy a homeowner's comprehensive insurance in order to get the mortgage in the first place, pay household contents insurance on top of this and also some form of municipal rates or levy for services.

Some careful homework is needed before you decide what you can afford, and some strength of character to resist the blandishments of an enthusiastic estate agent trying to get you to exceed your budget.

All the same, location is a key factor in choice of property. Going for the cheapest property in the most expensive area is a strategy that could pay off. Keeping your ear to the ground about new roads coming through an area or the proximity of a squatter camp (which do sometimes arise almost overnight) is also advisable: ratepayers' associations can be more helpful here than local councils.

- If you earn, say, R10,000 before deductions a month, and are paying off R2,000 on your car, you are unlikely to be able to manage more than R2,500 on a bond and R750 on rates/levy, but that would fetch you a R200,000 home, paid for over 20 years.

- To pay it off in five years the car might have to go and moonlight work and a second income might be needed, but this high-risk strategy would mean you can live rent-free while you are still employed, and you'll get ahead of the mortgage game once and for all. No more landlords, no more interest rate disasters – how wonderful!

For help in working out payments on your home loan, a useful website number is www.persfin.co.za, the site of *Personal Finance* newspaper supplement, part of Independent Newspapers.

A competitor for the banks

A new alternative to sourcing housing finance with the banks emerged in late 1998 with a company called **SA Home Loans**. This company deals only in mortgage finance and does not support the same costly overheads as the banks.

SA Home Loans lends out money and puts the debts together as 'mortgage-backed securities', which are sold to retirement funds and life assurers, which need interest income. The criterion for joining the scheme is to have a minimum loan of R100,000 and have 30 per cent of your own money invested (paid up) in your property. The benefit will be a loan that is two or more percentage points lower than the big four banks, which generally all offer the same interest rates.

The toll free number for SA Home Loans is: 086 0100 178.

What kind of property scheme do you want?

South Africa in the 1990s has become the land of high security fences, with homeowners obsessed with crime and security. For many people a traditional suburban house and garden has become an unsafe option, and this fear has given impetus to the proliferation of townhouses, cluster homes and other developments with security as their main attraction.

This is not merely a 'frightened white' phenomenon, and you will find this '**fortress South Africa**' syndrome throughout all groups and around the country. While the reality and the perception of crime take on ever more frightening aspects, it is unlikely the trend will reverse.

One home-buying option much in vogue is **sectional title**. Here a block of flats or a townhouse, say, is run by a corporate body made up of representatives of the homeowners and the managing agent, but the individuals (unit holders) buy their own apartments through their own mortgage companies. As an owner you are eligible to be a trustee of the corporate body. The corporate body sets the levies, looks after security, parking, the gardens, swimming pool, tennis court or whatever other facilities are common to the group. It also maintains the general exterior appearance of the property (an individual cannot build an extension, say, without the corporate body's approval). The advantage to the individual purchaser is that the cost of big things, like replacing the roof or building an extra security fence, is shared, and there is usually a supervisor who works with the agent in finding tradesmen to complete repairs to individuals' homes. In effect, the property in general is managed but the individual does as he pleases within his four walls.

Cluster homes operate along similar principles but with a distinct boundary to the property. The individual has freehold and there is no corporate body. Many cluster developments do form a homeowners' association to look after general operational and administrative issues, for which a levy is payable.

Developers of new units, like townhouses or clusters, often build one or two properties, which they then use as show houses for the public. The idea here is to buy 'off plan', meaning that your unit has still to be built. A deposit is put down to secure the right to that unit, and there is flexibility to change the interior finishes. The developer will sell to you on sectional title lines.

Another route is to **build your own house**. It is not a proposition to be taken lightly and will involve a considerable cash outflow over an extended period, but with luck you will get the house of your dreams. Get expert help before embarking on this specialised option.

MUNICIPAL SERVICES IN GENERAL

The general distinction for payment of municipal services, mentioned above, is between **rates** and **levies**. Rates are paid direct to the municipality in which a residence or business is located, while levies are paid to an agent in a townhouse or sectional title development, among others, and the agent deals with the municipality concerned.

A messy business: the new municipalities

It is a fact of recent South African history that the **rates boycott** was a powerful and effective way for the ordinary black person (who was not yet a citizen of his own country) to register a protest against the apartheid government. By refusing to pay for water and electricity, the township resident could show solidarity with banned liberation movements like the ANC and PAC. As often as the services were shut off by the white authorities, they were reconnected by the activists.

The rates boycott of the old South Africa did, however, leave a legacy of non-payment of rates which besets local administrations in the new. Meanwhile, the municipalities have themselves been overhauled, with formerly white and formerly black jurisdictions combined, new boundaries created and a wholesale replacement of mainly white staff by mainly black, as many previous municipal employees 'took the package' of early retirement. Both the culture of non-payment and the settling down of new administrators have made running an effective municipality difficult. In late 1998 a survey indicated that of 843 municipalities in South Africa, one-third were regarded as viable, one-third as marginal and one-third as unviable.

Under the 1994 Constitution local governments are obliged to provide basic services in areas under their jurisdiction, and the goal is for 90 per cent of revenue to be raised locally. Some authorities took the line of raising rates by abnormal, once-off amounts in the mid-1990s, and an unequal rating structure in adjacent munici-palities remains a focus of bitter debate. Racial polarities have come into the equation, as formerly black and formerly white authorities have been brought together.

In fact, there has been a post-apartheid renewal of the 'non-payment' phenomenon, as big business and individuals in areas like Sandton refused to pay escalating rates, which the new authorities said were needed to uplift the adjacent black township of Alexandra. Boycotts and 'tax revolts' in traditionally white areas continue to smoulder, and Eskom, the electricity supplier, has taken a tougher line in disconnecting persistent defaulters.

The system of local government in place at the time of writing is described as 'transitional', although the financial straits of whatever local authorities replace the present 'substructures' will probably remain acute. However, against this unsettled background the provision of services in most urban areas remains fairly settled and regular.

MUNICIPAL SERVICES YOU CAN EXPECT

Electricity

The provision of electricity made up about 40 per cent of local government income in 1996–97. Eskom is the state electricity supplier, and is among the cheapest national grids in the world, owing to an abundance of cheap, open-cast coal. Electricity is one of South Africa's best assets, and regional growth, if not a continental presence, beckons in the new millennium.

- In January 1998 South Africa produced industrial electricity at just over 2 UK pence per kilowatt hour; New Zealand was just below this rate, but the UK was at almost 5p, the USA was just over 3p and Japan was at 5.5p.

Coal-fired power stations provide nearly all the country's electricity (and a lot of its pollution – just breathe the air of Witbank, a city in Mpumalanga flanked by power stations and a major steel works). Eskom is a key part of the government's reconstruction and development programme, with a target of electrifying 1.75 million homes in the period from 1994 to 2000. Municipalities were tasked with making 750,000 connections. Analysts said it was likely that Eskom's goal at least would be reached. **Electrification** is seen as vital in extending education, promoting entrepreneurship and reducing crime (by creating or improving street lighting). It also releases people from the chores of collecting firewood in townships and rural areas.

The chances are that in an urban environment you will have access to safe, cheap and reliable electricity (about 80 per cent of urban households had electricity in 1998). In rural areas the service is much spottier, with only some 30 per cent of households connected at the same date. What these percentages hide is that as many as 17 million people, at the end of 1996, had no access to electricity, according to the Institute for Strategic Studies.

- One word of warning about your electricity supply: especially in summer on the highveld **violent electrical storms** may disrupt power supplies and lightning can damage phones, computer equipment and other home or business electrical devices. A lightning protector and relevant insurance policy are worth considering.

The **current** across the country is 220/230 volts at 50 cycles a second, and round three-pin plugs are in general use. For some reason the current in Pretoria is 250 volts.

Electricity in the form of **street lighting** is a municipal affair, and visitors may be surprised that some of the wealthiest parts of the country, such as Sandton and parts of Bryanston, in Johannesburg, still lack proper street lighting. In this they have something in common with most of the townships, where street lighting has hitherto been non-existent.

Water
The supply of water services comprised about 12 per cent of local government income in 1996–97. The provision of cheap and potable

water (you can safely drink the water out of almost any tap in the country) has been a real success story of the post-1994 governments.

While up to 1994 government policy focused on building expensive dams, like the Lesotho Highlands Water Project, and moving water through pipelines to the centres of population and industry, like Gauteng, the Mandela government took active steps to bring water supplies to the 12 to 15 million rural people who lacked clean water and the 21 million who had no hygienic sanitation. Delivery became the watchword of the Department of Water Affairs and Forestry, led by the dynamic minister, Professor Kader Asmal (who took the education portfolio after the 1999 election). Water was to be paid for by users in accordance with the amounts used, with provision for use by people too poor to pay, a right propounded in the constitution and defended in the new Water Acts passed by the government.

South Africa has an average rainfall of 464 mm, against the world average of 800 mm, and is effectively a semi-desert region with areas of higher rainfall, like the KwaZulu-Natal coast and parts of the Cape coast. It is to the credit of Professor Asmal and his department that the message of water as a valuable and scarce resource has been readily accepted. Not long after the 1999 election the minister announced that over 250,000 jobs had been created in the water sector in the previous five years and 4 million people had gained new access to water.

Sanitation

What you really need to know is whether the sanitation works and is reliable. The answer must be that it depends on where you live and which municipality looks after your interests. The basic standard, however, is high, and most rubbish is removed on a regular basis.

One thing, regrettably, that most parts of South Africa have in common is **littering** and a culture of not clearing up your mess at the rugby game, at the school sports day, in the street. There are few prosecutions, although by-laws are in place to charge offenders, and perhaps because there are more urgent needs South Africa is likely to have to suffer dirty public streets and facilities for the time being.

Public **toilets** are scarcer than they should be, although newer malls and public buildings have better provision than their predecessors. Toilet facilities for the handicapped, along with ramps, are also few and far between, again with the exception of the most recent offices, buildings and malls.

The streets and parks

Streetside **car parking** can be a problem in busy city centres and suburban shopping areas, and do watch out for kerbside yellow lines where parking is forbidden and violations are punished. Parking meters seem to be being phased out in favour of multi-storey car parks where the takings are better. So you may be able to park freely at meters in some city streets.

Don't expect to find many **cycle lanes** in South Africa. It's not an idea that has taken off. In fact, cycling in general is still growing towards the point of being accepted and carrying any consumer clout.

A feature of many South African city streets is the proliferation of **posters** on trees, street lights and telephone poles. The posters cover event advertising, the daily and weekend press, auctions and liquidations and some commercial advertising, not to mention political campaigns at election times. What some people regard as a vibrant, pretty well-regulated and informative part of community life, others regard with anger. One such oppositional group in Johannesburg's northern suburbs is Crapp – Citizens' Revolt Against Poster Pollution. Such groups have had successes in drawing attention to regulation of poster use, but when councils find the renting of space to be profitable, the cause of the would-be banners faces big barriers. Johannesburg's Adopt a Light scheme in 1999 said that putting up 5,000 posters in frames could bring in R80 million a year for the council, enough to install 140 kilometres of new lights. As one local newspaper put it, the council's poster scheme and Crapp were 'poles apart'.

Public parks have been low on the agenda for municipalities, and standards of safety, cleanliness and service have shown a marked deterioration in the 1990s. Some well-established parks were threatened by developers, including Johannesburg's Zoo Lake gardens, but in this case a public outcry kept the marauders at bay.

Increased environmental protection, not only for parks but for private residences too, was enacted by the Mandela government, but commercial interests have continued to bulldoze (sometimes literally) the public interest. Once again, the silent South African consumer has been slow to stand up for his or her rights, even though these have been strengthened by the constitution and a growing body of law.

Library services

Libraries are also minor items on the council agenda but even ill-resourced libraries provide vital reading rooms for students and basic reference books, as well as the books and other services (like audio cassettes and CDs) for recreational lending.

The story everywhere in municipal terms is of reduced budgets for new books, no money for building repairs and no replacements for departing staff. At the same time private commercial libraries seem to be growing in numbers and resources. All the big mining houses, law firms, chambers of commerce and stockbrokers, to take but four examples, have enviable and up-to-date holdings.

For the expatriate and homesick Briton, the **British Council** services a lending library and a training centre and has information on studying in the UK. The Johannesburg office at 76 Juta Street, Braamfontein (Tel: 011 403 3316 or 339 3715) will be able to connect you to British Council offices in other centres and possibly be a good networking opportunity too.

Emergency services

Rescue and emergency services, such as fire, ambulance, the 'jaws of life' for retrieving injured people from motor accidents, mountain rescue services and lifeboats at the coast, are going through bad times as the millennium ticks over.

- On a recent weekend in Sandown, a part of Sandton, in the second-busiest **fire station** in Africa, there was not a single fire engine on duty, as all the machines were in for repair. The minimum number was supposed to be three functioning fire engines and one water pumper.

- The Greater Johannesburg Metro Council said there were not only equipment problems, brought about by budget cuts and reorganisation of the geographical areas covered by the municipalities, but severe staff shortages, again caused by **reduced budgets**.

- The lack of staff and usable equipment following the reorganisation of local government post-1994 may have contributed to the sharp increase in the number of **industrial fires** in this period. Payouts by insurance companies for fire were some R400 million in 1989 and up to R2 billion in 1997.

- It is hard to link property owners with deliberate **arson** to collect insurance money, at least in a court of law, but insurers have increasingly complained that arson is on the increase, and that the fire services are becoming less effective by the day.

- **Ambulance services** run by the state hospitals face a similar crisis of resources and manpower. The private ambulance services, like De Vries and St John Ambulance, carry on as they did before, but more and more it is the private hospitals that have the best equipment in terms of new motor vehicles and access to helicopters.

PERSONAL SERVICES

Let's spend a moment on who will actually be living in your home or on your property. South Africa is still the land of **maids and madams**, no matter whether you happen to be white, black or brown. If you have some disposable income and a family, it is likely you will employ a maid.

It should be no surprise that the best-loved comic strip in the country is 'Madam & Eve'. Not only is it part of the way of life of the 'madam' to have somebody helping with the cleaning, ironing, and sometimes the cooking and child-rearing, but the 'maids' too need this work to keep their own families going. So rather than jump in and condemn the practice of domestic service, it should be acknowledged that both Madam and Eve gained much from it, and still do. It has started to come good for the maids – or domestic employees – too, because they are now covered by the Basic Conditions of Employment Act and should have a written contract (see Chapter 5).

It was an odd and rather touching part of the apartheid period that even the most lily-white of neighbourhoods were always full of black domestics and gardeners. While the streets and house fronts appeared to be a white enclave, around the back, in the cottages and rooms, were whole families of domestic workers and dependants. The two lived in a complex symbiosis, taking benefit from each other, even when the pass laws and Group Areas Act were in force.

Taking the plunge into being a domestic employer
How do families find maids and gardeners? Usually it is by word of mouth. Once the word is out, somebody will arrive, depend upon it. And with that person could come dependants – which may or may not be what you want.

It is advisable to approach the whole process as if you were an employer, because according to the new rules that is what you are. Not only wages but work conditions, time off, medical help, holidays, a pension, provision of a uniform and even a burial plan could come into the negotiations.

If all this is beyond you, the thing to do is to ring a labour lawyer for a consultation and take your domestic employee along, with a view to agreeing a simple contract that suits both parties. Your local public library or nearest university department of law or the Bar Society could also be of help.

Other services

Let us begin this section with a South African passion – the **garden pool**. Even modest houses often have a pool, as do most blocks of flats and townhouses, and poolside relaxation is as South African as the braai – indeed, both things often go together.

It follows that having a **good pool service** is important, and on the same par as a good 'gynie' (gynaecologist) to many 'kugels' (see page 161). After all, did not the country invent both the Barracuda and Kreepy Krauly automatic pool cleaners? The usual advice applies: ask people you know whether a big or small pool company did good work for them, and follow up. There is a national trade association which gives accreditation to the more professional groups. Regular servicing of both pool and equipment is advised.

One heavy item on the monthly household expenditure column is begrudged by all but is commonly regarded as a necessity these days. This is the **security company**.

Property-owning South Africa has progressed in a generation from bars on the windows to small and later high walls, guard dogs and latterly electric fences. This is 'fortress South Africa', a term which well describes the typical embattled, defensive suburban house or townhouse complex across the country's cities. Paranoia has reached the stage where whole suburbs in the major cities have closed off certain access roads and pay for armed guards in little huts controlling traffic booms on the one access road left open, and all within the law.

And everywhere there are security companies. For an initial installation fee, your security company will rig up secret panic buttons around the property and advise you on access and control procedures. For your monthly fee, they will be on 24-hour call at a central office and also often patrol in fast cars, waiting for customers to call in or to check on unattended sounding alarms. Security is an established national industry and a part of life in the new South Africa. Security companies far outnumber the police, and many are led by ex-policemen who made the switch to advance their careers.

The 1999 *Yellow Pages* for Johannesburg contains 20 pages of security company advertisements. Sometimes there are interesting variations, such as the householders who use geese instead of guard dogs. I came across one farmer in the Northern Province who swore that his ostriches were far better and quicker than any dog in deterring would-be intruders.

We look at crime in detail in a later chapter, but let us ask for now how you choose from the ranks of security companies.

The general point to make is that a large security company that is well run would offer a superior service to a small, well-run one. Reaction time is critical, and if you need a car in your neighbourhood, you need one now. The chances of getting this increase if your company has more cars on the road. The big names have achieved their position by delivering service, and they usually belong to the trade associations (the Security Officers' Board and the Security Association of South Africa). They offer a wide range of services, including armed and unarmed guards, and often have a national network. Some of the leading names include BBR Security, Sentry Security, Fidelity Guards and Chubb, but if you want to hire your personal guard or use a one-car company that is your choice.

Other domestic services, like TV and the telephone, are covered in a later chapter, and health and schooling are important enough to get their own chapter, but we should put in a word here about **handymen**, like plumbers and electricians.

The *Yellow Pages* have good lists of such services, but how do you choose among them? Asking your neighbour or townhouse supervisor is a good first step. I have found that handymen who are jacked up enough to issue flyers and employ people to hand these out at 'robots' usually also offer good service. Another route you might take is to find an umbrella group that offers a spread of services through different independent suppliers. One recent flyer had a single number for the following services: conferences, entertainment, gardening, guttering, home appliances, insurance, irrigation, painting, plumbing, pools, removals, security and tour operators.

There is usually a standard call-out charge and parts and labour on top.

FINANCIAL SERVICES

The banks

What of your banking requirements? How well does South Africa rank in terms of personal service and electronic delivery? The answer is: surprisingly well. It is **a well-banked country** in international comparisons, and by far Africa's banking leader.

The 'big four' banks dominate the local industry, though not quite so overwhelmingly as before. In 1998:

- ABSA had 26 per cent market share (29 per cent in 1994)
- Standard had 20 per cent (21 per cent in 1994)
- FNB – which in 1998 became FirstRand, with the merger of First National Bank with Rand Merchant Bank, Momentum and Southern Life – had 16 per cent (against 19 per cent)
- Nedcor had 15 per cent against 14 per cent in 1994.

The difference was essentially the growth of 'other banks' from 6 per cent to 9 per cent and in foreign banks from 1 per cent to 5 per cent; two other large banks, BOE (from 6 per cent to 7 per cent) and Investec (static at 3 per cent), did not change much in the five-year comparison.

Total assets in the industry were estimated at R662 billion in March 1999. In the same year there were 31 locally controlled banks, nine foreign-controlled banks, 12 foreign-controlled branches and 59 representative offices of foreign banks operating in South Africa.

Banking services

- The banking system at retail level, which means you and me, is characterised by numerous branches nationwide, with First World electronic, Internet and telephone banking services.

- **Customer service** has generally improved as competition has hotted up from newly registered foreign banks, and as consumers have exerted some pressure to benefit from the latest technical expertise.

- It is now routine, for example, to buy unit trusts, service your mortgage bond and pay your utility bills at an ATM with a simple entry of your PIN number. And it doesn't even have to be the ATM for your bank, because the big four are all linked electronically through Saswitch (though you will pay a higher service charge).

- You can easily find out your cash balance over the phone, buy an insurance policy and go Internet shopping with your credit card (as discussed in the section on shopping in Chapter 8).

- You can also buy foreign exchange at most banks (you will need to show your air ticket and passport).

- Most retail banks open from 9am to 3.30pm on weekdays and from 8.30am to 11am on Saturdays.

Credit facilities

It is relatively easy for bank clients to get a **credit card** – perhaps too easy, say some critics – and smart cards are breaking into consumer finance in a big way. For example, many labourers are paid at the bank through their credit cards rather than getting cash at work, partly for security reasons but also because people in general can cope with the technological demands of personal finance.

Financial advice

It is also relatively easy to find a **personal finance adviser**, either at your bank or privately. The magic acronyms here are CA, a chartered accountant as approved by the SA Institute of Chartered Accountants, or FILPA, a fellow of the Institute of Life and Pensions Advisers. The latter group is recommended for retirement advice (see Chapter 6). If you can find an adviser with either of these formal accreditations, you may pay more than for your friend's nephew who is a BCom at Wits, but you also know you have recourse to a recognised institution with internationally recognised qualifications, a code of conduct and the power to expel defaulters.

Insurance

It's somewhat similar with **insurance**, where brokers – your interface with the industry – come in two categories. These might be called the risky amateur and the qualified professional.

For years the SA Insurance Brokers' Association has tried to persuade the government to insist on broker qualifications, and it may be that the campaign is bearing fruit, with legislation in the pipeline to make registration of brokers compulsory, as a measure to protect the public.

Final words of caution

- It should be added that while banking, personal finance and insurance systems are up to date and easy to access, the financial sector as a whole is enduring tough times at the start of the new millennium. Try to get an overdraft for a new, small business; try to find reduced insurance premiums for your car or office; try to cut your bank charges; try to get a home loan if you live in a township – and you will find the service ethic more restrictive than cooperative.

- The difficulties and cost of doing business, even before tax, are both growing, and the trend is for costs to escalate further and service to operate in narrower bands. It is partly a matter of a depreciating rand; partly the costs of technology; partly increased competition both from overseas rivals now welcomed in the country and from empowerment rivals within the country; and partly the loss of key personnel at top management levels. So be prepared for uneven service in a fast-changing financial world.

5

Working For a Living

THE SOUTH AFRICAN WORKFORCE

To give an idea of the workforce in South Africa we have to go back to October 1995 figures, which show 14.4 million people in the 'economically active population' (EAP) aged 15 and over. Of these 8.4 million people (59 per cent) were in the formal sector, 1.7 million (12 per cent) in the informal sector and 4.2 million (29 per cent) unemployed. More recent figures, say analysts, would reflect a decrease in the number of jobs in the **formal sector** (which includes normal salaried or wage-paid work in both public and private sectors), and increases in **informal work** (which includes all types of unregistered and non-taxpaying activities), and the number of people **unemployed**.

- Breaking down the 14.4 million total a bit further, 69 per cent of the EAP were black, followed by whites (17 per cent), coloured people (11 per cent) and Asians (3 per cent).

- You would be most likely to find a job in Gauteng, with 25 per cent of the EAP, followed by KwaZulu-Natal at 19 per cent, and the Western and Eastern Cape, both at 12 per cent. You would be least likely to find a job in the Northern Cape, with 2 per cent of the EAP – although if you were a sheep farmer this might be the place to start!

WORK TRENDS

The traditional jobs in South Africa have been in mining, agriculture, manufacturing, retail and various service industries, not to mention a large number of domestic workers. Most of these industries have experienced rapid change in recent years, which has usually meant fewer jobs being available than before.

By some definitions, since the mid-1990s South Africa has become a job-shedding rather than a job-creating economy. Most emigrants have been skilled, economically active and often professional people whose abilities are not being replaced. Among the reasons contributing to reduction in job opportunities are effects of global competition, downsizing and mergers, technological progress and government attempts to change the nature of the workforce, including affirmative action policies.

- To give one example of government action to save costs and restructure the economy, in 1996 President Mandela introduced a programme to cut numbers of civil servants by 300,000. In practice it was found that a few, mainly skilled personnel 'took the package', leaving less able people in office, and adding to bureaucratic problems.

Despite rapid change and declining numbers, the traditional work sectors do remain the backbone of the country's economy. However, competition for available advertised jobs, it is fair to say, has become more intense.

So, what are the **new industries** in which South Africa is building its economic future, and which offer the most scope for entrepreneurs?

- In October 1998 the National Jobs Summit, which brought together government, business and labour, decided to focus on **tourism**, and set up a fund to raise R1 billion to promote tourism as an industry. The fund target had been virtually reached by mid-1999. It was expected that R65 billion income annually would come from tourism by 2004, yielding over 1.8 million new jobs.

- Other expanding job sectors include **information technology**, **e-commerce** on the Internet, **telecommunications**, **entertainment** including gambling and leisure, **franchising**, **training** and **outsourcing**. More on these below.

LAW AND THE WORKER

The Mandela government of 1994–99 was particularly active in introducing labour legislation to define and protect workers' rights. Some of the important recent laws which now govern the workplace are described below.

Basic Conditions of Employment Act 1997

This Act came into force in December 1998 to enact the right to fair labour practices established in the country's new constitution. The Act covers virtually all workers, including for the first time domestic and agricultural workers, and sets minimum standards for working conditions, including:

- a 45-hour working week
- overtime at one and a half times normal wage, and double for Sundays and public holidays
- four months unpaid maternity leave
- prohibition of employment of children under 15
- on starting a job an employee must be given a detailed, written summary of the job, hours and days of work, wage rate, date of payment and so on
- three weeks leave for each year of work completed
- notice in the first four weeks of employment to be one week; in the first year two weeks; and thereafter 30 days.

The Act was criticised for failing to take the opportunity to set minimum wages, but this step was deferred, with considerable disagreement between unions and business on the principle.

A pro forma letter of appointment to ensure compliance with the Act is shown in Figure 5.

Labour Relations Act 1995

This Act covers the whole range of collective bargaining issues, allocating specific rights and privileges to unions and employer bodies.

- Unions are given for the first time the constitutional right to strike, and union members can take time off for union meetings.

- Collective bargaining is now the task of new bargaining councils at sector level.

- All discrimination on grounds of race, gender, ethnic or social origin, age, sexual orientation and so on is unlawful, including for job applicants.

- The Commission for Conciliation, Mediation and Arbitration (CCMA) and a new Labour Court were set up to handle disputes. Both have proved successful in coping with a mass of cases.

Pro-forma letter of appointment to ensure compliance with Section 29 of the Basic Conditions of Employment Act (No 75 of 1997)

Company name and address in full

....

....

A N Employee

....

....

Date:

Dear ....

Letter of Appointment

We take this opportunity of welcoming you to the Company, and confirm your appointment to the position of .... (occupation of the employee), with your particulars of employment as contained herein below:

1. Date of Engagement

Your employment with the company will commence on ......(day) ....'........................ (month) .... (year);

2. Brief Job Description

As a .... (occupation of the employee), you will be required to

....

....

....

....

.... (a brief description of the work for which the employee is employed);

3. Place(s) of Work

Your place of work will be:

....

....

(if applicable). You will, in addition to the above location, be required to render your services at the following branches of the company should the company deem this to be necessary to meet its objectives:

.... (branch)

.... (branch)

4.Hours of Work

Your ordinary hours of work shall be from ... h ... to ...h..., ...(day) to .... (day).

5. Overtime

It is a condition of your employment with the company that you agree to work such overtime as may reasonably be required of you by the company, from time to time. Such overtime shall be preceded by reasonable notice thereof and shall not exceed the maximum statutory amount of overtime permitted in law. Such overtime work shall be remunerated at a rate of one and one-half times your normal hourly rate of pay.

6. Rate of Pay (or) Salary

Your rate of pay/salary shall be R......................................
per week/month, and shall be payable weekly/monthly in arrears.

Additional benefits accruing to you are (optional):

....

....

....

....

* Any payment in kind is required to be included.

7. Deductions

The following deductions shall be made from your wage/salary weekly/monthly:

7.1 UIF Contributions

7.2 PAYE

7.3 Provident/Pension Fund (if applicable)

7.4 Medical aid (if applicable)

8. Annual Leave

You will be entitled to 21 consecutive days leave on full remuneration in respect of each annual leave cycle. Such annual leave must be taken at a time mutually convenient to both the company and yourself.

9. Sick Leave

9.1 During the first six months of employment, you will be entitled to one day's paid sick leave for every 26 days worked. Notwithstanding the aforesaid, you will be entitled to an amount of paid sick leave equal to the number of days you would normally work during a period of six weeks; you are therefore entitled to .... days sick leave per each 36 month sick leave cycle.

9.2 You must notify the company by 10am on the morning of any absence due to illness/injury.

9.3 A medical certificate must be produced to your superior after more than two consecutive days absence from work in order to qualify for paid sick leave. The certificate must be issued and signed by a medical practitioner or any other person who is certified to diagnose and treat patients and who is registered with a professional council established by an Act of Parliament.

10. Bargaining Council/Wage Determination (if applicable)

The company falls under the jurisdiction of the .... (Bargaining Council or Wage Determination).

11. Accrued Period of Past Employment (to be included if past employment is to be recognised, eg: in the context of the purchase of a "going concern").

It is recorded that your past employment with .... (company name) will be recognised and credited to you with respect to your employment relationship with .... (company name).

12. Termination of Employment

Your employment with the company is terminable by the company or yourself on notice of not less than:

12.1 One week in the first weeks or less of employment;

12.2 Two weeks, if your employment with the company has lasted more than four weeks, but less than one year;

12.3 Four weeks, if your employment with the company has endured for a period in excess of one year.

Notice of termination of the employment contract must be given in writing (unless tendered by an illiterate employee).

13. Policies and documents having jurisdiction over the employment contract

The employment with the company is subject to the provisions of (for example):

13.1 The company grievance and disciplinary policy

13.2 The pension/provident fund rules

Yours faithfully

A Manager

(Company name)

I, ... (employee's name) hereby accept the terms and conditions of employment as set out above.

Signed: ....

Date: ....

Drafted by: Tony Healy & Associates

Fig. 5. Pro forma letter of appointment under Basic Conditions of Employment Act.

Employment Equity Act 1998
This Act revoked all discriminatory laws not otherwise covered by the above Act and set out positive measures to assist certain groups, namely the disabled, women and black males.

- All businesses employing over 50 workers or with an annual turnover of R4 million must complete a job audit, in consultation with the workforce, reflecting the numerical goals to achieve representation of the population in the workplace.

- Annual reports must be submitted to the Department of Labour showing numbers of black, white and other workers, especially the prioritised groups.

- Failure to submit reports or to take steps to implement promotion of previously discriminated people would result in large fines and possible closure of businesses.

The Act came into force in August 1999 and the first reports were to be submitted by December 1999.

Skills Training and Development Act 1998
This Act plans to redress the acute skills shortage in the economy by instituting a training levy of 0.5 per cent of the payroll of all firms from 1 April 2000 and 1 per cent from 1 April 2001. Four-fifths of the fund would be distributed at sectoral level and one-fifth through a national skills fund. 'Learnerships' would replace the faltering apprenticeship system for artisan training.

The South African Chamber of Business (Sacob) called it an unjustified new tax on business and said it would not support it. Other critics said the Act offered no tax incentives for training and no tax breaks, while adding to the burden of the tax system in collecting another payroll tax.

UNEMPLOYMENT

Before looking at ways of finding a job and of starting your own business in South Africa, we should pick up on the alarmingly high figure for unemployment mentioned above. The problem is so large that it almost qualifies to be one of the national 'scourges' along with HIV/Aids and crime, mentioned in Chapter 9.

In April 1999 the *Financial Mail*, a leading business weekly, said the South African economy had shed 500,000 jobs since 1994, and joblessness was rising by nearly 3 per cent a year. The new entrants to the job market each year could be as many as 600,000 people by the early years of the new century. To put the figure in perspective, job creation had not run at more than 100,000 in any one year of the Mandela administration of 1994–99.

After violence, unemployment is the second most mentioned cause of concern in recent attitude surveys among South Africans. To be more precise, white people surveyed usually said violence was the worst problem, and unemployment was down the list, along with schooling and health; among black people, unemployment was seen overwhelmingly as the major social problem.

Statistics show that the highest levels of unemployment are among black, unskilled labour. Employment experts say such workers have low prospects, low pay, little mobility and high job insecurity. In some townships the unemployment rate is said to be over 70 per cent.

The position may have been worse in 1999 than that suggested in the 1995 figures mentioned at the start of this chapter.

- Statistics South Africa (SSA) has a **strict definition** of unemployment, which covers people over 15 not employed, available for work and who have tried to find work in a four-week period.

- SSA also has an **expanded definition**, which duplicates the strict definition but also includes people who have a desire to work, even if taking no steps to find it within a monthly period.

- **For 1997, unemployment by the strict definition was 22.9 per cent (16.9 per cent in 1995). By the expanded definition the figure was 37.6 per cent (29.2 per cent).**

Remember that South Africa has no social security net to catch the unemployed. Apart from the Unemployment Insurance Fund (see below), there is no provision for being unemployed except what you organise yourself, as in employment protection policies with insurers.

If you are retrenched you should receive a package of some type, depending on your contract of employment and some or all of your pension funds, again depending on your contract. But, as the employees of gold mine ERPM found out in late 1999, a company going into liquidation is not obliged to pay retrenchment monies, only holiday pay to a maximum of R2,500 per retrenched employee.

FINDING PAID WORK

There are three main ways job seekers can look for work:

- the newspapers and trade magazines
- the Department of Labour
- personnel agencies.

The newspapers and trade magazines

- The best-known jobs pages **nationally** are in the *Sunday Times* (weekly) and *The Star* (Workplace on Wednesday, plus weekday classifieds).

- **Regional papers** will be appropriate if you are seeking work in, say, Pietermaritzburg (*Natal Witness*) or Kimberley (*Diamond Fields Advertiser*).

- If you are **looking for work from outside the country**, try contacting the *Sunday Times* at PO Box 1742, Saxonwold 2132; Tel: 011 280 3000; Fax: 011 280 5150, sending a cheque for at least £3 to cover airmail postage per issue. The website is www.bigbreak.co.za. Figure 6 shows typical recruitment advertisements from this source.

- *The Star* is at PO Box 2014, Johannesburg 2000; Tel: 011 633 2420; Fax: 011 836 8398; or website is www.star@co.za. A cheque for £2 should cover airmail charges per issue. The email is at class@star.co.za.

- South Africa has a plethora of **trade magazines**, some commercially sold and others in-house. It could be useful to locate the particular local magazine in your field, both for trends and for job advertisements. The best way to do this would be to consult a press guide, like *Willings*, or in South Africa the regularly updated listing by SA Rates and Data (*SARAD*), the bible of the advertising industry: SARAD, PO Box 2647, Randburg 2125; Tel: 011 787 2070; Fax: 011 787 2064.

Department of Labour

This may be a long shot for actually getting work, but it could be useful to register with the appropriate regional branch of the department, over and above bureaucratic reasons for doing so.

The latest figures (for September 1998) show 63,000 registered job seekers, which is a drop in the ocean of unemployed, but on the

Fig. 6. Typical job advertisements in a Sunday paper.

Fig. 6. Cont.

principle that every stone must be turned, here are the telephone numbers of Department of Labour offices in main centres:

Pretoria	012 309 5000
Johannesburg	011 497 3000
Cape Town	021 460 5911
Durban	031 336 1500
Bloemfontein	051 430 3001

Personnel agencies

South Africa has the well-known agency names, like Kelly, Drake, PAG and Emmanuel, for both temporary and permanent positions. Find contact details in the *Yellow Pages* for each main centre under 'personnel consultants'.

Management consultants also feature in the *Yellow Pages*, again with a mix of international and local names. Although they are not in the jobs business as such, it could be worth your while trying some lateral thinking by seeking such advice on trends and growth areas.

Other means of getting work

South Africa is still small enough to have an 'old boy' approach to finding people for jobs. Call it networking or affirmative action, but who you know may just get you an introduction and an interview.

I know, it happened to me. I applied for one job at a book publisher, had the interview over lunch with the MD and was offered a completely different and unexpected job. The MD thought I'd be useful to the business, but he only came to that conclusion on a face-to-face meeting, and then created a new position for me.

If you thought 'old boys' networks' were for men only, here are three South African groups which cater for **women only**:

- National Association of Women Business Owners; Tel: 011 402 8268
- Executive Women's Club; Tel: 011 887 0809
- Professional Women and Leaders' Development Organisation.

This isn't the place to go into good interview techniques or compiling a compelling CV (other *How To* books do this very well), but getting a foot in the door is a vital first step. It pays to enlarge your range of contacts by attending trade conferences or exhibitions, reading the trade press, going to country clubs or sports clubs (South Africa is very big on its health clubs and every sport, particularly outdoors and active) and finding your way into a social circle of like-minded people.

A helpful book, with checklists and logical steps to follow, in researching markets and opportunities, is Guy Macleod's *Starting Your Own Business in South Africa* (see below). If you want a motto for creative job-seeking, remember the words of a slogan for a leading South African Sunday newspaper, 'Great minds never think alike.'

STARTING YOUR OWN BUSINESS

Guy Macleod's book mentioned above (published by Oxford University Press in Cape Town and in its ninth edition in 1999) is a complete introduction to the subject and is recommended.

South Africa is not yet a particularly friendly environment for small business, and interest groups are often seen campaigning for removal of inflexible laws and what they call an excess of red tape. Value-added tax has been a particular source of frustration (see below on taxes), along with a reluctance by banks to lend to entrepreneurs and a shortage of available risk capital from other sources. Yet entrepreneurs point out that they are achieving what the state has failed to do for many years: creating jobs and being profitable.

Government plans to help small business
The government, it should be said, has made efforts to help small business, or as it is now known, the **SMME sector** (small, medium and micro enterprises).

- **Business Partners**, formerly the Small Business Development Corporation, targets small and medium enterprises rather than the micro sector. It is 20 per cent owned by the state and is a commercial enterprise. It helps business people qualify for loans if they have fewer than 500 staff, total assets of under R30 million and need finance between R150,000 and R30 million.

   In 1997–98 Business Partners made loans in such sectors as manufacturing, retailing, professional and personal services, the motor trade, restaurants, hotels and guest houses. There are regional offices in five provinces, with the head office at PO Box 7780, Johannesburg 2000; Tel: 011 480 8700; Fax: 011 642 2791.

- **Ntsika Enterprise Promotion Agency** is a unit of the Department of Trade and Industry targeting the SMME sector, with divisions in management and entrepreneur development; technology; business development services; targeted assistance; marketing and business linkages; and policy, research and information. Ntsika is headquartered at PO Box 56714, Arcadia 0007; Tel: 012 341 1120; Fax: 012 341 1929.

- **Khula Enterprise Finance Ltd** is another unit of the Department of Trade and Industry and is mandated to make loan finance and equity finance available to SMMEs through authorised intermediaries. There is a list of these intermediary groups, which on-lend to businesses, in Macleod's book, pages 224–25. The Khula toll-free help line is: 0800 11 38 57.

Let's now look at four areas offering good growth opportunities for small business in present-day South Africa.

1. Franchising

It is said that in the USA in the late 1990s, 42 per cent of retail sales were made through franchises; in South Africa the equivalent figure was 9 per cent. However, the industry is growing quickly in South Africa from small beginnings, and is often regarded as one of the less risky entrepreneurial opportunities, provided that seed capital, an ability to pay an ongoing royalty fee, and some business experience are at hand. A good franchisor trains and supports the franchisee, especially during the initial stages of the business.

The typical South African franchise has been in fast food (like Kentucky Fried Chicken, Spur, Juicy Lucy), but there are other areas, like instant printing, office services, vending, video hire shops, accounting and website design, which are expanding. One Soweto businessman has his own spin on franchising, with mobile hawkers' trolleys and stock made available at his stores.

Among the financial institutions, ABSA Bank has set up a dedicated franchising department, and insurer Liberty Life its own New Venture Academy for potential franchisors.

The national body is the **Franchise Association of South Africa**, PO Box 31708, Braamfontein 2017; Tel: 011 403 3468; Fax: 011 403 1279. Franchise information is available on the Internet at postnet.co.za.

2. Internet business

Not only is computer use still burgeoning in South Africa but the specific area of e-commerce is exploding. It was already a R1 billion market in 1998 and is expected to grow to R47 billion by 2002, according to consultants BMI Tech-Knowledge.

- Niche areas of expansion include leisure and travel, computer hardware, clothing, books, software, food and drink and entertainment.
- There were said to be a million or so Internet users in the country by the end of 1998, and the market was growing at 10 per cent *a month*.

It is hard to think of a better entrepreneurial opportunity than this!

3. Tourism, leisure, entertainment

We noted above how the government has targeted tourism as a growth engine for the South African economy into the first decade of the new century. This industry, along with leisure and entertainment, which economists have forecast will also grow rapidly, given the right security and regulatory environments, will undoubtedly offer opportunities for alert entrepreneurs. Growth areas will include game parks, guest houses, eco-tourism, palaeo-tourism (visiting sites of early humankind), river rafting, wilderness adventures and the like.

There is no national body covering this range of initiatives, so it is really every man and woman for themselves. There is just a beginning so far in educational courses in this area, e.g. Midrand Campus offers game-ranging qualifications, and more development can be expected.

4. Outsourcing or subcontracting

There is a growing market for production and service skills in narrow niche markets where companies, both big and small, have opted to place certain operations in specialist hands.

This could mean producing blow-moulded plastics, editing a book, office cleaning, translating services, routine data processing or payroll handling, offering training courses in Internet business and website design, making jewellery or supplying components to the motor industry, to name a very few of the opportunities that are there if you look for them.

The outsourcing trend is growing, by all accounts, and is an area where skills are rewarded and age not penalised. Typically for the self-employed person, such work is usually referred by word of mouth and networking rather than more formal (and competitive) means.

Other useful contacts for small business

- If you have access to the Internet, a relevant site is the **Business Referral and Information Network (BRAIN)**, a Department of Trade and Industry initiative for SMMEs. The home page is www.brain.org.za.

- Another well-regarded agency is the **Small Business Advisory Bureau**, Potchefstroom University, PO Box 1880, Potchefstroom 2520; Tel: 0148 299 1002.

- **Entrepreneurial Business School** offers a correspondence course in entrepreneurial business administration (EBA), along the lines of the MBA, and is one of the first such qualifications in South Africa. Tel: 021 948 8319.

- **Small Business Exchange** is an Internet site at: www.americanexpress.com/smallbusiness.

- **The South African Small Business Employers' Association (SASBEO)** was founded in June 1999 to assist small business, representing its interests in arbitration disputes, new labour legislation and regulations. Tel: 011 646 7589.

- *South Africa Business Guidebook: The Essential Guide to Doing Business in SA* (annually updated and published by WriteStuff Publishing CC; Tel: 011 728 6902; Fax: 011 728 2479; email aslwrite@global.co.za; website www.guidessa.co.za) is intended for foreign investors but is also a convenient listing of business associations for each sector, provincial administrations and advice for business and small business.

TYPES OF BUSINESS ORGANISATION

- **Public companies** in South Africa are those quoted on the Johannesburg Stock Exchange. They raise public share capital and, with limited liability, have 'Limited' added to the company name.

- **Private companies** are owned by the members, to a maximum of 50 people, and are designated by Proprietary (more usually Pty) Ltd.

In 1998 there were some 400,000 companies registered by the **Registrar of Companies** in Pretoria, both public and private. The address is: Registrar of Companies and Close Corporations, PO Box 429, Pretoria 0001; Tel: 012 319 9111.

What may be surprising to newcomers to the country is that in the same year there were also 500,000 close corporations.

- The **close corporation** (CC) is a simplified, registered form of company organisation, with limited liability and no directors. There is no requirement for annual audits but normal annual accounts are to be presented. CCs must be registered at the Registrar of Close Corporations (address above), by completing forms CK1 and CK7, plus payment of R150. The forms are obtainable from most newsagents.

- Other forms of valid business association are **sole proprietors** and **partnerships**.

Of course, there are also many informal business people who are registered for neither business nor tax purposes but who, on the other hand, fall outside the ambit of labour legislation and cannot enjoy the protection of the law.

All businesses of whatever size in the formal sector should be registered and the business name given recognition and some degree of legal protection.

THE TAXMAN COMETH

In South Africa all individuals, all partners in a partnership, and all companies and CCs which derive a taxable income are liable for tax.

Income tax

The income tax is progressive, meaning that it increases for individuals from a base of R33,000 (for tax year ending 29 February 2000), taxed at 19 per cent, up to R120,000 and above, taxed at 45 per cent. See Figure 7 for the income bands.

Companies and CCs pay a flat rate of 30 per cent but may also be liable for a tax of 12.5 per cent on dividends, called the STC (**secondary tax on companies**). Special rules apply for tax in mining, farming and insurance.

Taxable income is annual income, excluding capital receipts, less allowed deductions. These deductions include pension payments,

Taxable income	Tax rates
R	
0 – 33,000	19% of each R1
33,001 – 50,000	R6,270 +30% of amount above R33,000
50,001 – 60,000	R11,370 +35% " " R50,000
60,001 – 70,000	R14,870 +40% " " R60,000
70,001 –120,000	R18,870 +44% " " R70,000
120,001 and above	R40,870 +45% " " R120,000

Fig. 7. Tax table for the year ending 29 February 2000.

medical expenses, donations to a university or other tertiary institutions, and retirement annuities, and others in the case of home-based self-employed people (like office rental, proportion of electricity used for office, etc.).

From this taxable amount, the taxpayer then deducts the **primary rebate**, granted to all taxpayers (R3,710 for 2000 tax year), plus age rebate, for those aged 65 years or older (R2,775 for 2000 tax year).

Employed people receive a basic **employee's tax certificate**, the **IRP5**, which lists gross remuneration, made up of salary, lump sum payments, allowances for travel and entertainment, use of car, bond subsidies, low or interest-free loans and others. It also shows on the deduction side amounts taken off by the employer for pension fund contributions, medical aid, SITE and PAYE taxes paid. This IRP5 form is the employee summary of that year's pay and deductions. See below for more details.

Provisional tax

Provisional tax is payable by companies, CCs and some individuals (self-employed among them) who receive income from sources other than remuneration that exceeds R1,000. The appropriate form is **IRP6(i)**, and it must be submitted by a provisional taxpayer even when no provisional tax is payable.

This is not another tax but payment of income tax in two provisional instalments in any one tax period. The idea is to get cash flowing into the tax coffers, but it also can serve as a salutary control on taxpayers who might be tempted not to save for an annual reckoning until too late. The tax authorities say: 'Provisional tax is not a separate tax, but merely a provision for the actual tax liability which will be determined on assessment.'

There is a third and 'voluntary' provisional instalment for individuals earning over R50,000 a year and companies/CCs earning over R20,000 a year. There is no penalty for non-payment of this third instalment.

Value-added tax (VAT)
This is the main indirect tax on consumption and is presently charged at 14 per cent on most goods.

- Each business or individual pays VAT to the tax office on successive stages of the production cycle of a product, with bi-monthly calculations and payment submitted to the Receiver of Revenue.

- Businesses or individuals with turnover of under R150,000 a year need not register for VAT.

- VAT is payable on goods rather than services.

Small business organisations expressed outrage in April 1999 when it was learned that they were expected to pay VAT on invoice, not on receipt of payment, i.e. pay before payment was received. The position is under review.

PAYE and SITE
- **Pay As You Earn (PAYE)** is the form of income tax paid by employers to the Receiver for those people not registered by the employer as provisional taxpayers. PAYE is not payable for people earning under R18,500 a year or for staff aged over 65 and earning under R31,950, but is payable for income exceeding R60,000.

- **Standard Income Tax on Employees (SITE)** applies to the first R60,000 of remuneration. People earning under this amount are not required to submit tax returns to the Receiver because their tax will have been deducted by the employer.

RSC Levies
Regional Services Council (RSC) levies are payable by businesses in some areas (the basis of RSC payments is being restructured), based on remuneration to staff and income paid by the businesses.

Self-employed people are liable to RSC levies.

Fringe benefits

Fringe benefits, like car allowances or payment of petrol, travel and entertainment expenses, payment in share options, bursaries, mortgage loans and the like, are matters of frequent revision in the government's Budget announcements (usually delivered in mid-February). People affected should consult their company human resources department or accountant for the latest position.

The same advice holds for the structuring of tax benefits and construction of a tax package, which can bring considerable tax advantages to the high net worth individual.

Although not strictly fringe benefits, in 1999, for the first time, the Receiver targeted employers' contributions to medical aid funds and provident funds.

Unemployment insurance

Unemployment Insurance Fund (UIF) deductions must be made by employers in respect of staff earning an annual income of under R63,648 (currently). These are monthly payments paid to the UIF office. UIF payments are made to people who have contributed and have become unemployed up to a total of 45 per cent of previous income for up to six months. Debate is continuing about bringing in higher-paid earners and graduating the payments so that lower-paid earners receive progressively more.

The UIF is South Africa's form of unemployment pay and, unfortunately, the fund has been the subject of financial mismanagement. Further, fewer than 10 per cent of the unemployed are said to benefit from the UIF. However, the UIF does cover maternity, illness and death benefits under certain circumstances.

There were over 320,000 UIF registrations at September 1998, the latest month for which data was available. The figure was up nearly 17 per cent on the year before.

FILLING IN YOUR TAX FORM

The **income tax form (IT12 BU)** for 1999 was a hefty 14 pages of A4 paper, closely typed, with 24 pages of explanation. But do not panic!

- You can get help from any **registered accountant**, for a smallish fee (maybe up to R250 if your documents are all at hand), and the **offices of the Receiver** are much more client-friendly than they used to be. In fact, if you get your papers in order and all your deduction claims listed, the Receiver will do your tax return there and then.

- If you prefer to do the sums yourself, there is an **annually updated guidebook** called *Paying Less Tax Made Simple*, by Ralf Metz (Metz Press, about R80). There are also **software packages** to take you through the tax form step by step. One is Brilliant Tax Return from Brilliant Business Systems, about R150, annually updated, with approval by the Receiver. Another program is WinTax 2000.

THE RECEIVER GETTING TOUGH

You should be aware that the Receiver of Revenue, as part of the South African Revenue Service (SARS), is making a concerted effort to widen the tax base and bring non-taxpayers into the net. A SARS representative said in April 1999 that they were hot on the heels of 'freelance prostitutes, taxi barons, informal traders, professional gamblers and even police informers'.

The target was to bring up to 1.5 million more taxpayers into line, using better information technology systems, in a bout of administrative efficiency. The Receiver was also looking for individuals who register as companies, such that they pay company tax at 30 per cent instead of individual tax at 45 per cent!

The perhaps appropriately named Nits (New Income Tax System) was being installed in 1999 at a cost of R300 million to link financial and other institutions with SARS. The linked systems will in time present an accurate and unassailable picture of an individual's financial dealings, from their salary to traffic fines, medical aid, UIF, share dealings, vehicle licence and bank, the Registrar of Companies and insurance company. The good news is that while malpractice will be highlighted, the online linkages will cut tax assessment time down from four months to one.

You have been warned! Co-operate rather than try to get away with it. As the Receiver's office will tell you and even show you, tax avoidance is fine and good, but tax evasion is illegal and will be punished!

6

Getting On in Life

What's life like in South Africa for older people, whether local or immigrant, or the increasing number of English-speaking retirees from overseas?

The short answer is that if you have worked for your retirement, put efficient financial policies in place, have funds to spare, are able to choose where you live and your health remains good, it is a wonderful place to spend your later years. The weather is generally excellent, the majority of South Africans are friendly and wish you well, it is an English-speaking culture in part, and the cost of living is relatively cheap – especially if you have a good pension payable in pounds or dollars.

STATE PENSIONS

The harsh reality

Few people, however, either local or immigrant, have all these ducks in a row or can afford a million-rand home in Constantia or Ballito Bay with a lifestyle to match. Experts estimate that under 10 per cent of South Africans have sufficient funds to retire on.

- The reality for most South Africans is a **basic state pension** per person of no more than R520 a month (the rate from July 1999), and that is the top level if you can show a means test official that you have minimum personal resources. Most people with any savings at all will receive less than this sum.

Living on R520 a month, to include accommodation, food, medical and all other expenses, is possible, because many people do it, but can it be a happy or fulfilling life? Without rent control on older flats, for example, many urban residents could not manage on their pension and other savings. As it is, many older people depend on their children, with varying degrees of success, or have to put their name on a long waiting list for a retirement home.

Will pensions go up?

The outlook for increased state pensions, which are payable only to South African citizens, is not promising. The bad old days of unequal pensions for whites and blacks have now gone, but the net has become wider and far more people qualify to receive some pension, whether state or disability. The government has recently put extra resources into welfare, but the net payout per person remains small.

Added to the small maximum sum available to people is a bureaucracy struggling to make a transition from 14 separate national and 'homeland' regimes under apartheid to the new, unified system. Tales of pensioners not receiving their cheques because of inefficiency, fraud or theft are common. Reported scams have shown people illegally claiming for dead or imaginary relatives.

At an institutional level, pension funds have not always been efficient or incorruptible. The government started in 1996 to claim a kind of hidden tax on pension and provident funds (it began at 17 per cent and went up in 1998 to 25 per cent), and these funds are too good a revenue target to escape further attention from the minister of finance. This will probably mean more pressure on both state and private pensions.

Other state pensions

From 1 July 1999, the following monthly rates apply for other forms of state pension:

- war veterans receive R538 a month (up from R518)
- disability grants go up to R520 from R500, for people 18 and over whose disability is found to qualify for the grant by a welfare examiner
- grant in aid to R94 from R90 for dependants with debilitating mental or physical conditions
- care dependency grants increase from R500 to R520, payable to parents or foster parents whose combined income is below R8,000 and who care for a severely disabled child of under 18
- foster child grant to R374 from R360, for fosterers looking after children prior to adoption
- child support grant, a new form of grant, set at R100 a month for each child.

Pensions are usually reviewed in the annual Budget in February.

A gloomy scenario

Longer term, the experts predict that the older part of the population could suffer the effects of the **HIV/Aids epidemic** in South Africa and the whole southern African region, which is forecast to reach a peak in the years 2005 to 2010. Aids is expected to devastate the 20 to 45 age group, which is normally the heart of the productive workforce.

- On this reading, there will be fewer workers, less national wealth, more sick people and, by implication, smaller welfare benefits, especially for older people, but with enlarged employee contributions to insurance and medical aid funds.

- While older people's age span is likely to rise towards 80 (about four years less for men in South Africa than for women, the same gender gap as in many other parts of the world), Metropolitan Life estimates that life expectancy in the 20–45 group will fall from 50 to 38 for men and from 54 to 37 for women in these years.

- All this will pressurise the state pension sector, and it is unlikely it will keep up with ever-growing demands to pay many previously unpensioned people a living pension rate.

The individual will be thrown more and more on their own resources, and if it has always been prudent to plan for one's future it becomes even more important now, and to begin that planning as early in life as possible.

PRIVATE RETIREMENT FUNDS

The sums you will need

Retirement planners and consultants generally advocate having funds at hand on retirement which are at least 15 times the size of the last annual pay. This sort of sum is clearly impossible to expect from state pensions, so private retirement planning is necessary. It is a truism, which few people heed, that the earlier such planning is undertaken the more advantage from compounding and cheap entry into schemes can be expected.

Even funds such as mentioned here may not be enough if:

(a) inflation keeps rising at its 1998–99 range of 5 to 10 per cent and eats into fixed payments (hence the advice to pay more of your productive earnings into **inflation-index linked pensions**); and

(b) your health remains generally good and you live well into your 80s or 90s, but your funds do not cover you adequately for the later years, when medical expenses are likely to be heaviest.

The choice of retirement funds
The recognised and generally applied private retirement fund types in South Africa are:

- defined benefit pension funds
- defined contribution pension funds
- defined contribution provident funds
- retirement annuity funds
- pure endowments.

This account can do no more than skim through the options in a general way, and you are advised to consult a qualified financial planner or retirement expert (and not just a friend from the club or pub) to explain the finer points of specific policies on offer.

Defined benefit pension funds
These are the traditional pension funds, where you as employee and your employer both put in each month, and you receive a defined pension based on your years of service. Often the salary for the last two years is taken as the average, plus a small percentage added on for each year of service.

On retirement you can take a maximum of one-third of your pension as cash, the **lump sum**, and the balance of your pension is reduced by one-third.

The amounts you receive are fixed and known, which is to your advantage, but the snag is that most such pensions are not inflation index-linked. Another disadvantage is that if the pension fund itself performs well it is not obliged to pass on increased benefits to you – this is up to the trustees rather than an automatic benefit. Worse still, if you change jobs you may not be able to take more than your own contributions with you.

Defined benefits worked well in older times when 'jobs for life' were more common, for the privileged few at least, but this pattern is changing. The average South African will change jobs at last seven times in a career, it is said, not to mention bouts of unemployment.

Employers, too, are finding the fixed nature of the benefits onerous and are trying to move their own retirement planning to funds of the fixed or defined contribution type.

Defined contribution pension funds
The key points of this type of fund are:

- Both you and your employer make set contributions.
- These contributions on both sides are fixed on entry to the fund, as a percentage of pensionable salary.
- The employer guarantees to make a contribution but not to pay a fixed amount for your pension.
- When you retire you may take a third in cash, calculated according to how much you have built up in the fund (the **full** or **accrued benefit**).
- The balance after withdrawing the lump sum of one-third must then be used to purchase a pension or compulsory annuity.

Good investment performance of the fund could well mean a higher pension for you; or the converse may be true. When you change jobs, with this type of fund you may be able to take the full benefit with you after a certain number of years of service.

You do have more say in investment of the funds, as between, say, an **equities portfolio**, related to the stock market, or a **smoothed performance portfolio**, where the average growth of the market is used.

Your choice is wider because, following recent legislation, the membership of pension fund trustees has been opened up, so that union and employee representatives now have a right to share in administering the fund with company management.

However, as can be seen, defined contribution pension funds are more at the risk of market forces, for good or for ill. They are also rarely inflation index-linked.

Defined contribution provident funds
These funds are also defined but differ from the last fund type in the tax treatment of your contributions and benefits, and the need to take the balance of your benefits, after the lump sum of one-third, as a monthly pension.

Under defined contribution pensions you delay paying tax until retirement, because you can deduct contributions from tax. With defined contribution provident funds, however, your contributions are not tax-deductible. At retirement your lump sum is calculated as for the pension fund, but you can now claim your contributions, with a current minimum of R24,000.

Advisers suggest your provident fund should be on a **non-contributory basis**, which means the employer pays all the contributions (he can claim against tax for this but you cannot). Salary packages structured to provide for the employer to pay are sometimes called **salary sacrifices**.

Contributions on both sides are fixed when you join the provident fund, as a percentage of pensionable salary. As with the defined contribution pension fund, the amount you receive is related to the performance of the fund on the market.

Critically, when you retire, all the benefits, including your contributions and your employer's, plus income and capital growth, called the **full benefit**, are paid to you as a lump sum. You then make the investment decisions, as no pension is payable by the fund.

When changing jobs, the full benefit is normally taken with you, after a certain period of service. This can be a disadvantage if you withdraw and spend the windfall.

So the provident fund pays you a single lump sum on retirement, and you choose your next move, such as buying retirement annuities or investing on the market or in a new business. The advantage and the risk are both yours.

Retirement annuities (RAs)

These types of investment mature from age 55, must be taken before 70, and have good tax benefits, especially if you have a long period of membership.

RAs are a good way to save because they are locked in until you reach 55 (whether male or female). Historically they have beaten inflation, and can be supplemented by life or disability cover for dependants (payable if you do not attain the maturity age).

When the RA falls due you can take a third of the value as a lump sum in cash, which is tax-free up to R120,000 but taxed at the average rate above that. With the two-thirds balance you must buy an annuity (pension). The formula is R4,500 $\times$ n, where n is the number of years you have been paying in.

The main choices of annuity are **life annuity**, which ends at your death, but gives the highest pension; **guaranteed term**, for, say, 10 years, and ceasing on your death, or **joint and survivor**, to cover you and your spouse and ending on the death of the surviving spouse. Another, newer alternative is the **living annuity**.

Note that you cannot use an RA as collateral or draw cash against it; it is non-assignable.

Linked product companies

This new form of investment opportunity should be mentioned briefly. Linked product companies offer a spread of investments, at retirement or before, for the more entrepreneurially minded personal finance planner.

Such groups, usually the bigger insurance companies, are not so much advisers as administrators of a portfolio, but their advantage is to offer a wide umbrella of products not normally linked. Examples include RAs (for savings), **living annuities** (another form of RA), **preservation funds** (mainly to keep retirement funds intact as you change jobs – see below) and **wrap funds** (including shares and unit trusts).

As you see, the choices of retirement funds or alternatives are manifold, and further research into the subject is recommended. See the list of further reading at the end of this book for the leading titles to study; and, of course, a good investment adviser is indispensable.

OTHER ASPECTS OF RETIREMENT

Retirement villages

South Africa is well up with overseas trends in the rapid expansion of retirement villages. Their appeal includes independence, security, a communal lifestyle and recreational facilities, along with the possibility of scaling down to a room with board or frail care if necessary. However, not as many new projects were built in the late 1990s as earlier in the decade, so it is a good idea to get on waiting lists long before you want to move (many villages take people from 55).

- There is most choice at the luxury end, including a number of dedicated golf and fishing villages in the Western Cape, Gauteng and Mpumalanga in particular.

- If you have adequate means you could look out for a modest cottage in a pleasant complex.

- If your means are limited you should target a suite or room in a retirement home, which would be secure and comfortable but with more restrictions.

- There are a number of state-supported old age homes as well as private organisations for special interest groups (e.g. Jewish or Methodist homes, ex-servicemen's homes).

One way to access a list of retirement villages in these various categories is through the **SA Council for the Aged** and the **SA Association of Retired Persons** (see useful addresses for contact details).

Health care for the elderly

Unforeseen medical expenses can do more to undermine careful retirement plans than almost any other contingency. As you get older one thing or another has to go wrong with your health or that of your spouse, so it is prudent to be prepared for the inevitable.

The first piece of advice is self-evident: look after yourself physically – stay fit or take exercise to get fit, within limits. Eating right and having more frequent medical checks are platitudes but nonetheless sensible precautions and part of a healthy lifestyle.

Some experts say that meeting your medical needs should be top of your list when deciding whether to move to a new and perhaps smaller house or flat on retirement and thereafter.

- **If you are a member of a medical aid scheme at retirement the employer must continue your benefits until your death.** Illness or old age do not constitute grounds for an employer stopping your membership of the medical aid; and your spouse or dependants will continue to be supported after your death.

But, and this is the big but, the level of employer contributions to medical aids is generally going down and that of employees is generally rising. Costs of medical inflation are rising higher than core inflation, and as the balance of providing the service swings towards the employee/retiree, so the range of services offered is being limited by cash constraints.

The experts advise that rather than the traditional, one-size-fits-all medical aids, employed people, and the self-employed in particular, should look at new generation medical schemes. These are generally tax-efficient, use insurance and provident funds to back schemes and can be more individually tailored. Managed health care and access to a range of private hospitals around the country are part of this new-look medical aid policy.

Employees should take the bull by the horns and get advice from registered financial brokers about the private schemes on offer and negotiate with their employer. In any event it is wise for everybody to put more away in savings, especially through retirement annuities, for the inevitable increase in all medical costs as medical inflation continues and as HIV/Aids spreads even more widely in southern Africa.

Tax deductions for medical and dental care

- **Below age 65** you can claim some medical costs against taxable income, to the greater of R1,000 or 5 per cent of your taxable income. Included are your contributions to any medical aid, medical expenses paid to a doctor or hospital that are not covered by your scheme, and costs arising from a medical disability.

- **Above age 65** all medical expenses are claimable against your taxable income, without limits.

Work for senior citizens

One of the alternatives to retirement, available to some people – especially the self-employed, owners of businesses or those who are or could be consultants – is to keep on working. If you follow the advice of an accountant or other qualified adviser, it is possible to be tax-efficient by working on into retirement years.

One well-established employment agency which specialises in the over-50s is the **Senior Citizen Employment Agency**, with branches in the main urban centres (head office in Johannesburg; Tel: 011 835 8660; Fax: 011 835 5780).

The agency offers both temporary and permanent positions, and staff benefits such as flexitime, insurance payments, paid holidays and payments into the Unemployment Insurance Fund. The target client is the older person who wants a second or even a third job rather than the retiree as such.

Not all companies or small businesses value the contribution older people can make, but this agency has shown there is a market for the skills and experience of the older age group.

TAX AND RETIREMENT

We mentioned above the benefits of pensions and provident funds and retirement annuities. Let's look now at how to make a tax-efficient retirement in South Africa, as the law stands at the turn of the millennium.

The basis of your retirement tax planning should be a two-year cycle, as explained below:

- To reduce the tax you pay in retirement you must bring down your average rate. This means (a) reduce your income or (b) increase your deductions from taxable income in **the year before and year of your retirement**. The comments that follow apply equally to men or women.

- **Retire early in the tax year,** which runs from 1 March to the following 28 or 29 February. If you retire in March you will not have generated any income, although you still need to have reduced your income in the previous tax year.

- **Limit the interest income** you receive from investments and maximise income from non-interest sources. So invest in shares and endowments, and avoid fixed deposits, rental income and government bonds in this two-year period.

- **Maximise deductions from tax**, for example, by buying a retirement annuity in the year before you retire and putting the maximum tax-deductible amount into it.

- **Get more tax-free income** by repurchasing unit trusts or from an access bond facility.

- Look at buying **second-hand endowments** near maturity.

- If you resign, are fired or retrenched you can transfer your withdrawal benefit or lump sum from a pension or provident fund to a **pension or provident preservation fund** and leave it there until you want to retire. This presupposes you have other funds to live on that enable you to take a couple of years until your tax settles down to a low rate. A preservation fund is a special retirement fund that preserves benefits until retirement is taken. You gain by deferring tax and you receive your money at preferential rates, including the first R120,000 of any lump sum tax free. You can make only one withdrawal from a preservation fund and are taxed after the first R1,800 of such a withdrawal. The rate of tax is the average (probably about 19 per cent) rather than the higher rate of say 25 per cent or 30 per cent at the time of retirement.

- If you have several **retirement annuities** due to mature at the same time, stagger their maturity dates and hence reduce tax.

- A **trust** is a good way to minimise estate duty by putting growth assets into it. Each spouse can donate R25,000 a year to the trust tax free, which can also reduce the respective estates handily.

Do you pay SA tax as a UK retiree drawing a British pension?
The key principle here is that South African tax law levies taxes on a source basis.

The Income Tax Act of 1962, plus annual amendments following the Budget each year, provide that a pension is only taxable in South Africa if in at least two out of the preceding ten years before the pension becomes due there are earnings within South Africa. If there are no such earnings, or services, as the Income Tax Act calls them, then no tax is payable on a foreign pension in South Africa.

Note, however, that this refers to overseas-paid pensions (and social security payments too). If you have income from abroad in the form of an annuity, interest, rentals or royalties, these do constitute taxable income in South Africa.

Help for British residents living abroad
The Inland Revenue has a number of useful leaflets for British residents living abroad, all in 'plain English texts'. Among them are:

- *IR20: Residents and non-residents – Liability to tax in the UK.*
- *IR58: Going to work abroad? A guide to the tax position of UK residents living abroad.*
- *IR138: Living or retiring abroad? A guide to UK tax on your income and pension.*
- *IR139: Income from abroad? A guide to UK tax on overseas income.*

These are available in the UK at Tax Enquiry Centres or Tax Offices, listed in the phone book under Inland Revenue, or in libraries and Citizens' Advice Bureaux.

The Inland Revenue advises that people intending to leave the UK for full-time work overseas should complete form P85 to help determine their residence status and hence tax status.

LOOKING AT ESTATE DUTY

The level of duty of 25 per cent on the minimum estate of a personal estate of R1 million or more was fixed as far back as 1988. Experts say the minimum estate should be more like R4 million, taking inflation into account.

An estate of R1 million may still sound high, but it does include life assurance. Add in the value of your house and other personal assets, and you may be surprised that you are worth over the million, and hence will attract estate duty if you don't make provision.

So what is your next move? In three words: **consult an expert**. It may be best to invest sums abroad annually (see below), or to set up a trust.

SETTING UP A TRUST

There are two kinds of trust in South African estate planning: *inter vivos* and testamentary.

- To shield wealth from duty and pass it to heirs, the ***inter vivos*** trust is a popular method. The words mean a trust made in the lifetime of the founder, who transfers his assets to a trustee to administer on behalf of a third party, the beneficiary. The idea is that future growth takes place in the trust, not in the estate, hence avoiding the creeping rise in value towards the R1 million mark. The process is known as 'pegging' or 'freezing' the value.

- **Testamentary** trusts are established in a will. There is no cost attached, as opposed to a cost of between R3,500 and R10,000 plus VAT to set up an *inter vivos* trust. The testamentary trusts only take effect on the death of the testator.

In favour of both kinds of trust is that assets are protected and controlled, with ongoing management; a trust is confidential, even after death, whereas a will is a public document; there is an element of pegging the value in *inter vivos* trusts; and the rights of minors or a surviving spouse can be safeguarded (and incidentally protecting the assets against children who might waste them).

Against the *inter vivos* trust is the initial cost involved and the fact that it will not be necessary if the estate is worth under R1 million. On the other hand, the cost would usually be less than the amount the heirs save in estate duty in due course.

Property bought in the name of a trust attracts transfer duty at a flat rate of 10 per cent, and transferring shares to a trust will attract 0.25 per cent in marketable securities tax.

If one partner leaves all assets unconditionally to the spouse, estate duty will not apply.

You can set up as many trusts as you wish, including individual ones for each child, or in tax havens overseas, which means offshore assets will not be included in your estate at death, while the heirs continue to benefit.

Expert opinion is that the above situation may change, as the government continues to look for ways to tax the individual. Be aware of the annual Budget, in February, and ask your financial adviser to keep you informed of any new situation as it arises.

MAKING A WILL

Here are three good reasons why you should make a will in South Africa (or anywhere else):

- A will states your last wishes clearly and unequivocally, even if you have few assets.

- Confusion will be caused in winding up the estate if there is no will. The matter would go to the Master of the High Court, who appoints an executor. Far better to choose an executor you know and trust, and avoid the long process of winding up (which may take a year or more).

- When minor children are involved, the court insists on assets being sold and placed in a trust for the children. This will be a low-risk, low-return type. Again, it's far better to opt for a trust that will offer real value to your heirs.

Making a will is straightforward and inexpensive in most cases, relative to the costs and inconvenience to others of dying intestate.

INVESTING OVERSEAS

For many years the South African or South African-resident investor was denied the legal opportunity to invest overseas, and exchange controls are still applicable to some extent at the start of the new millennium. However, in 1997, 1998 and 1999 the Reserve

Bank announced progressive new foreign investment allowances, which at the time of writing stand at R500,000 per taxpayer.

This means anybody over the age of 18 and in good standing with the SA Revenue Service can presently invest R500,000 abroad. The trend towards final abolition of exchange control has been signalled, and one day the individual will be able to own assets overseas as well as invest in them.

Given that the local financial market remains volatile, it is recommended that at least one-third of a personal portfolio is invested globally. This also ensures advantages in terms of estate planning. Again it is vital to talk to a registered expert.

KEEPING UP WITH FRIENDS

Finally, a word about friendship associations. Mainly existing to offer reduced airfares between South Africa and the UK, these clubs also enable cut-price travel within the two countries, have lists of recommended accommodation and arrange for travel insurance.

Contact details for **Friends of the Lion** in South Africa and **Friends of the Springbok** in London are given in the list of useful addresses at the end of the book.

There are many regimental, school, sporting, gardening and other groups with cross-links between the two countries which could add to your networking opportunities. This is an area where there is no official help offered and you need to be resourceful in making the most of your contacts.

Let us now turn to two areas of social policy that will concern most immigrants – education and health.

7

Education and Health

OVERWHELMING CHALLENGES IN SOCIAL POLICY

The last chapter took us out of chronological sequence, moving from working life to retirement. In this chapter we'll step back into the hurly-burly of everyday living and look at ways to survive and thrive under the considerable challenges posed by education and health in contemporary South Africa.

Social and political transformation

The education and health portfolios have been high profile in both the Mandela and Mbeki administrations. The government has attempted to fashion radical new approaches to its social programme, highlighting education and health, with huge extra demands on the public purse. At the same time the pressure of popular expectation has grown for a basic and professional service for all, and not merely for an older white or a newer black élite.

As we have found in many other areas of South African life, the issues arising in such key areas of social policy as education and health originate in the rapid transformation from an apartheid to a democratic dispensation.

Bureaucratic transformation

We refer elsewhere to the massive challenges of HIV/Aids, crime, unemployment and the brain drain. In the present case, combining multiple levels of racially divided education and health administrations into inclusive national and provincial structures will take years yet to settle into an effective and cost-effective system – and many critics doubt it will ever happen.

We would be wise to remember it is still early days in the new South Africa, as it enters its second decade. On the other hand, the voting public, trade unions and other organs of civil society demand immediate action and improvement as they face unprecedented real pressures on the ground, in education and health as in the other crisis areas.

ANC policy emphases
In addition to the crucial challenges of reforming old bureaucracies, the two portfolios we are instancing here have carried much of the ANC's brand of socialism, and particularly redistribution. In health this has meant an emphasis on primary health care at the expense of high-technology medicine, along with free care for nursing mothers and children up to six years of age and abortion on demand. In education it has been the much-trumpeted, if stuttering, introduction of 'outcomes-based education' or Curriculum 2005.

The issue is delivery
Both departments face critical issues of survival despite levels of state spending which are high by international standards. In both services the bulk of available money goes into salaries rather than medical equipment or classrooms and textbooks, and often the salaries are for unproductive office staff rather than those in the front line.

The pressing need for all social spending departments in modern-day South Africa is to put the money and resources available to better use, cut the bureaucracies, reduce corruption and improve service, while empowering private–public partnerships so that the majority can benefit. In a single word that has become the current mantra, the issue is delivery.

THE STATE SCHOOLS SECTOR

A radical new approach
About 80 per cent of the nearly R50 billion state budget for education in 1999-2000 was earmarked for the schools sector rather than tertiary education, as the government attempted to take effective action at the ground level where the needs were greatest.

The main pillars of state policy were the **Schools Act** of 1996 and **Curriculum 2005**, which we will look at in turn.

The Schools Act 1996
The Schools Act provides for compulsory education from the year in which a child turns 7 to age 15, or the ninth grade, whichever comes sooner.

- Education must be made freely available to all, though not necessarily free (independent or private schools are allowed to operate). No pupil may be refused entry on grounds of inability to pay school fees.

- All schools must be open to all races, as racial discrimination and segregation in education are formally abolished, confirming the country's constitution.

- Corporal punishment in schools is declared illegal.

- School fees are set by the school in consultation with parents in the school governing body.

- Pupils, parents and educators are the new partners with the state in creating and maintaining good learning. Parents are given an unprecedented responsibility and role on school governing bodies.

Curriculum 2005

Curriculum 2005 or outcomes-based education is the government's main policy innovation in the education sector. Following considerable public discussion, the policy began to take effect from 1997.

The idea was to develop, by 2005, a vocational and national needs-based education system which would both create an educated workforce for the country and fit children for a competitive local and international jobs market. National needs or outcomes (whether 'critical' or 'specific', as the jargon went) were identified and the curriculum in schools would be altered to meet them. In the process traditional examination methods would be scrapped.

This implied that subjects like English, mathematics and sciences in their present form would go, and the school certificate (better known as matric) would be abolished. The eight new 'learning areas' would be: arts and culture; communications, literacy and language learning; economic and management sciences; human and social sciences; life orientation; natural sciences; numeracy and mathematics, and technology.

In place of one end-of-school examination, which also served as a university entrance qualification, schools would engage in continuous assessment of pupils, while a form of external assessment would be carried out after grades 3 and 6, with a comprehensive external assessment after grades 9 and 12.

What has happened in practice?

The Schools Act has attracted surprisingly little attention, given its far-reaching plans to transform the education sector. Perhaps it has been overshadowed by even more critical and immediate needs, like unemployment, crime and hospital queues.

In the event there have been isolated cases of opposition, such as the racial violence at the high school in Vryheid, an Afrikaans-speaking town, in 1998 and 1999, when the new governing body elected a black headmaster and the largely white parents and pupils objected.

There was also considerable delay in many rural areas in setting up the new governing bodies, with many parents unprepared for their new responsibilities. Some private schools, on the other hand, said the change was easy for them because they had been using democratic governing methods for many years.

Introduction of outcomes-based education was slow, with grade 1 beginning in 1998, grade 2 in 1999 and a planned extension to grade 7 in 2000. At this rate the whole system would take far longer than 2005 to be introduced. At the time of writing, there was no sign that matric examinations would be abolished, with employers, universities, teachers, parents and even students insisting they preferred the existing nationally recognised process, with all its faults.

Crisis in the schools system

Opposition parties were not slow to point out that according to the government's own statistics there was a huge crisis in the system, which the new initiatives could not mask or address.

- Looking at infrastructure, for example, in 1998 of the country's 30,000 or so schools (with a school population of about 12 million children) only 75 per cent had a water supply, 43 per cent had electric power and only 33 per cent had flush toilets. About 49 per cent had appropriate textbooks, only 27 per cent had learning equipment and 31 per cent had teaching materials; the number in the public schools sector with facilities like PCs and CD-Roms was minuscule.

- Unicef noted in 1998 that nearly 10 million men and 11 million women in South Africa had no education. Close on 15 million South Africans could not read.

- The rate of matric success had fallen markedly in the new South Africa, from a pass rate of about 70 per cent in 1988 to nearer 50 per cent in the late 1990s. Matric exemption for university entrance had dropped from 24 per cent in 1988 to under 14 per cent in 1998.

- The pass rate varied considerably between the provinces, with the Western Cape, KwaZulu-Natal and Gauteng at the top and the traditionally poorer provinces of Northern Cape and Northern Province at the bottom.

- One telling statistic published in the *Sowetan* at the start of the 1998 school year was that 942 schools in the Northern Province had no headteacher.

- Among other areas of criticism were ill-prepared and poorly motivated teaching staff, excessive pupil–teacher ratios, textbooks not ordered and sexual abuse of students. The Democratic Party summarised the situation in 1999 as 'shambolic'.

Minister Asmal takes the helm

One person in government willing to take these criticisms to heart was Professor Kader Asmal, the incoming minister of education in the Mbeki administration of April 1999. After a few weeks of consultations Asmal confirmed that 'it would not be an exaggeration to say there is a crisis at every level of the system', with large parts of it dysfunctional and 'carrying deadly baggage from the past'.

In July 1999 the minister launched a new nine-point programme, which is worth itemising here as a sign of government intentions and priorities in the first years of the millennium. The priorities were listed as:

- making the provincial education system work in harmony with the national department
- eliminating illiteracy among adults and youth
- ensuring that schools become centres of community and cultural life
- creating better physical conditions at schools
- developing the teaching profession
- ensuring the success of outcomes-based education
- creating a vibrant further education and training system
- developing a higher education system which understands the challenges facing the country
- dealing with HIV/Aids through education and training.

The plan was well received, and the minister (who had been an effective water minister in the Mandela cabinet) was widely accepted as the right man for a hugely challenging job. Some commentators noted that there were the budgetary resources available and the political will to make the nine-point plan stick. Now it was a matter of delivery.

The likelihood was that, however many plans the government made, the crucial difference would be made by a very few educators who had the gift and commitment to teach, in the most basic and under-resourced of conditions. Year after year school inspectors going to a remote township school that somehow managed high matric passes would discover the same lack of classrooms or toilets or telephones as elsewhere, but a passion to learn had been fuelled by an exceptional teacher.

THE NUTS AND BOLTS OF GOING TO SCHOOL

At ground level, far below questions of national policy and programmes, what awaits a new pupil arriving at a South African school?

Note to begin with that in the South African context a public school is exactly that, and a private school is private, in contrast to the British system where a public school is actually a private school! Here we are looking initially at the public, state education sector in South Africa.

Ages, terms, hours and years

The first thing to note is that the **starting age for school** as from January 2000 is put at the year in which a child turns 7. The raising of the age from 6 years was likely to save the government about R1.4 billion a year, since up to 70 per cent of starters at the former age were found to be repeating their first year. The new policy would also release teachers and classrooms for productive use, it was suggested.

The policy would put an extra burden on the pre-primary sector, most of which was privately rather than state-supported. Schools variously offered play-only facilities, partial learning and full learning options for the 3–6 age group, and half- and full-day care.

- **School terms** run from January to December, with matric examinations presently in October and November. Four terms are usual in all provinces, with variations in individual dates as set by the provinces.

- **School holidays** include five weeks in December and January (midsummer), and shorter breaks at Easter and the southern hemisphere spring and winter.

- **School hours** are generally 8am to 1.30 or 2pm in the public sector, with extramural activities, if offered, after 2pm. 'Mom's taxi' is a factor of everyday life in South Africa, as elsewhere. On the other hand, the competitive and expensive occasion of matric balls and gowns is all South African, as every 17-year-old knows.

- **School years** in South Africa formerly covered standards 1 to 12, where standard 12 was matric year, usually at 17 or 18 (or even older if more years had to be repeated). Under Curriculum 2005 terminology, 'standards' become 'grades', also from 1 to 12, and 'pupils' become 'learners'.

There is no formal division between **primary and secondary education.** Nonetheless, a majority of state schools (70 per cent of the total) are primary only, 19.6 per cent are secondary only, 9.4 per cent are combined and 1 per cent are 'special' (remedial, gifted and so on). There is no national examination between primary and secondary levels (between 11 and 13 years of age).

Visas and permits
See the chapter on immigration for the rules regarding **education visas for immigrants**. This largely concerns tertiary education, and study permits are issued subject to repatriation guarantees.

Fees
Comparative costs of schooling are instructive, and the *Sunday Times* of 18 October 1998 provided the following four examples. They indicate well the enormous range of schooling options and the huge disparity in fees which remains. The first two are white boys and the second pair black girls:

- Roy Jones, a Grade 9 pupil at Jeppe Boys' High, Johannesburg (a well-off state school), at R6,000 a year

- Craig Jennings, a Grade 11 pupil at St Stithians, Randburg (a top-level private school), at R21,000 a year

- Jane Radebe, a pupil at Excelsior College, Johannesburg (an inner-city private school), at R2,640 a year

- Zandile Nkosi, a Grade 7 pupil at Thembelihle Primary, East Rand (a poor state school), at R40 a year – and half of the school's 536 pupils cannot afford to pay even this small fee.

AREAS OF EDUCATIONAL EXCELLENCE

Kumon – mathematics tuition at home

While South Africa performs very poorly in global comparisons for mathematics education, some students are rising above the general level of mediocrity.

Kumon is a Japanese programme of maths education known to over 2.5 million students worldwide. It was introduced on a meaningful scale to South Africa in 1997, and over 10,000 students were following its precepts within two years.

The programme involves 10 to 20 minutes of daily maths practice at home, with active parental supervision. Set tasks have to be completed before the next graded exercise is undertaken. Costs are around R100 a month, and success rates are gratifyingly high. A telephone contact number is: 011 788 4303.

Sunshine Books – making early literacy fun

Sunshine Books, published by Wendy Pye Publications in New Zealand and distributed in South Africa, offer a fun programme of literacy learning. The books encourage group reading and story-telling, with classroom discussions about the stories.

Sunshine has the additional virtue of being affordable, costing some R50 a child per year for three years and of being outcomes-based, in line with current educational philosophies.

The Sunshine catalogue of over 200 fiction and non-fiction titles, alphabet books and oversized books has been introduced into grades 2 and 3 in a number of schools, with considerable success, in association with the READ educational support group.

An award-winning newspaper supplement for young readers

The *readRight* supplement to the weekly *Sunday Times* was the winner of the 1999 world Young Reader Prize, awarded annually to a newspaper for innovative activities in developing young reader-ship.

As well as appearing in the newspaper, the four-page, colour broadsheet was supplied in mid-1999 to over 900 schools, thanks to sponsorship from insurance, paper and educational publishing concerns. The supplement is designed to reinforce scarce textbook materials in term time.

An online learning channel for educational television

The Learning Channel Campus is a pioneering educational teaching company, which began in 1998, and was a world leader in distance education within a year. It produces high-quality educational material on video and CD-Rom, in newspapers and on TV, with the aim of helping students 'learn to learn'.

Access to the website (www.learn.co.za) is free. Complete syllabuses of grades 10–12 in all subjects should be available by early 2000, according to the channel, and students can test themselves, receiving instant results and full answers on the website.

Crawford Schools – private and progressive education

Over the last decade or so, Crawford Schools at pre-school, primary, secondary and tertiary levels have developed a reputation for academic, extracurricular and sporting success.

The formula of low pupil–teacher ratios, a non-racial and non-denominational entrance policy, an approach of 'think, understand and apply', careful selection of students and above all teaching excellence, has helped produce a creative learning environment, say parents.

Each student in grades 4 to 12 signs a code of conduct that becomes the basis of the school's discipline policy. The website is student-driven (at www.crawford.co.za), and there are seven campuses so far in Gauteng and KwaZulu-Natal.

Graeme Crawford's approach of applying a proven formula to the business of opening private schools and making a profit in the process has aroused considerable opposition among educators, but in the combative South African education environment success in matric and other forums remains a compelling argument for those able to afford private schooling.

THE PRIVATE SCHOOLS SECTOR

There has been much focus on private schooling in the new South Africa, but it is important to put the numbers in perspective. Recent research by the Independent Schools Council showed that in the late 1990s there were approximately a thousand private schools (the number varied according to definitions of 'private'), and the student body made up under 3 per cent of the total South African school population.

Included in this figure of a thousand schools were the top-quality, established private schools and a number of inner-city fee-based schools which were often of the fly-by-night persuasion and offered little more than basic literacy and numeracy at nominal fees.

Pressure grows on the private system

The education department went to some pains in 1998 to appeal to parents not to desert state schools in favour of private education, arguing that standards in the state schools had not fallen. Many parents, both black and white, begged to differ, which led to increased pressure on the private sector, especially in the Western Cape, many parents' preferred destination for student relocation.

- Woodmead Preparatory School, north of Johannesburg, a well-known private school with impeccable 'struggle' credentials, was one loser, reporting in late 1998 that 26 out of 350 students had left for reasons of emigration, with a further 20 relocating within Africa.

Another type of school migration noted increasingly at the end of the 1990s was flight from schools in the old townships, like Soweto (largely black) and Lenasia (largely Indian), to the suburbs of Johannesburg (still largely white). Inner-city schools and formerly white-only state and private schools suffered increased pressure on their resources as the township schools emptied.

Parents were willing to follow quality education, at the cost of mounting taxi fares (some children were paying over R250 a month to travel to school by 1999) and rising school fees.

The government continued to offer limited financial support to the private system as the 1990s closed, but there were indications that even this assistance would have to end as pressures on the public system continued to mount. It did not help that educational inflation was growing at a rate calculated at 6 per cent above the general inflation rate by 1997.

It was in such an environment of growing need for educational provision that both inner-city schools and concepts like Crawford Schools (see above) could expand to meet the desperate longing of parents and children for a competent education.

How parents can pay for private education

- To give an idea of the costs involved, Standard Bank in June 1999 calculated that for a child born in 1999 parents would need at least R450,000 to cover both state schooling and tertiary education; if the parents opted for private schooling that cost would exceed R1 million, or R537 a month from birth.

- Sage Education Trust estimated in 1998 that parents of a newborn child should save at least R200 a month just to cover the child's tertiary education. To illustrate the loss from five years of missed compounding and the rate of educational inflation, the figure would more than double to R480 a month if the saving plan was started when the child was five.

The consensus of informed advice was that default payment methods like student loans, overdrafts and funding out of current income would become increasingly impractical for personal educational provision in the new millennium. Competition for private school and university bursaries would only increase.

In these circumstances parents were exposed to ever more vocal calls by service providers, many of which were newly listed on the Johannesburg Stock Exchange, to open savings plans for their child's private education at birth or even before. The proposition makes considerable sense, provided recognised independent financial advisers are consulted.

Other parts of the private education system

- **Special schools** are a minor part of the education system in numbers but are extremely important for those children who have particular needs. Despite crippling cost pressures on the schools concerned, there is usually a place for a special child to take up, provided the parent looks hard for it, whether the need is for a gifted, remedial or handicapped student, a Waldorf or a Montessori school, or a Jewish or Islamic school.

- As another alternative one might possibly investigate **home schooling**, which remains legal in the new South Africa. The Association of Home Schooling estimated in 1997 that there were about 1,500 home schooling families in the country (making about 2,500 students). Up to a third of this number were organised and the rest 'underground', the association estimated.

TERTIARY EDUCATION

Tertiary education is usually thought of in terms of the public

Nkosi Johnson, a brave education pioneer

The Star reported in August 1999 the uplifting story of 10-year-old Nkosi Johnson, a sufferer from HIV. Two years before, Nkosi had tried to gain access to a state primary school in Melville, Johannesburg, and a storm erupted because his adoptive mother, Gail Johnson, had chosen to reveal the boy's HIV status.

The education department in the province and nationally had no policy in place at the time, but Nkosi's application obliged it to formulate new measures. After widespread consultation a promulgation in a *Government Gazette* in August 1999 prescribed that all public schools, education and training establishments could not turn away students or teachers with HIV/Aids because of their medical condition alone.

Testing of students for HIV/Aids before admittance to a school was also prohibited, and teachers should not be put through an HIV/Aids test as a requirement for appointment.

In addition, if and when students became incapacitated through the disease, they should be provided with work for home study.

In line with the education ministry's new nine-point policy, education would be highlighted in the fight against Aids/HIV. Nkosi Johnson was an unwitting participant in this lengthy process.

institutions, comprising 21 state or traditional universities and 15 technikons, many of which were formerly segregated but all of which are now theoretically open to all.

However, there is another element, which caters for an increasing number of tertiary students – the private sector, featuring institutions like Varsity College, Damelin, Midrand Campus, Boston City Campus and Allenby Campus. Legislation was enacted in 1997 to recognise the private sector institutions as universities.

A comparison of state and private provision in tertiary education

- The traditional universities are given recognition overseas as centres of research, based on the grading of researchers on the academic staff list. Private universities tend to have a shorter history of research but often use industry specialists as lecturers, which adds to the hands-on value of the lectures.

- Traditional universities offer a wide range of courses and career options, while private universities are still mainly in the BA, BCom area, with some BSc degrees through outsourcing.

- Traditional universities have developed their own syllabuses, while the private universities usually follow Unisa or overseas (usually US or UK) syllabuses.

- Traditional universities are much bigger, with lecture rooms of up to 250 students, while private universities have smaller class sizes and smaller bureaucracies.

- Both types insist on matric exemption for entrance, but recognition for the degrees awarded remains contentious in the case of private universities, which might lead to problems for postgraduate study abroad.

A shift to the technikons

The growth area in state tertiary education is in the technikons. These are a middle range of mainly vocational institutions between the universities on the one hand and teachers' training and technical colleges on the other.

Once almost wholly white institutions, technikons in the new South Africa are predominantly black and are spreading rapidly. Total enrolments grew by 46 per cent from 1993 to 1997 (from 147,000 to 215,000 students). Expansion is expected to continue to 262,000 by 2001, according to estimates published in August 1999.

The African component rose from 41 per cent in 1993 to 57 per cent in 1997 and could increase to 60 per cent by 2001. Meanwhile white numbers had dropped from 229,000 in 1993 to 187,000 in 1997 and an estimated 186,000 in 2001.

There was a feeling noted among white students and parents that technikon standards were falling, which had led more whites to enrol in private universities or overseas.

Expansion at the universities

Enrolments were also escalating at the public universities, with growth of 8.6 per cent between 1993 and 1997 and an expected further rise of 12 per cent by 2001 (numbers were 349,000 in 1993, 379,000 in 1997 and 423,000 expected in 2001).

Overall growth in both universities and technikons was put at 20 per cent between 1993 and 1997, with an estimated additional growth of 18 per cent by 2001. Further and tertiary education could together comprise 1.5 million students by 2005, experts calculated.

Growth trends included a decrease in historically black institutions, an increase in historically Afrikaans institutions and steady numbers at traditionally English-speaking universities.

The largest university by far in the country remains Unisa (the University of South Africa), a renowned distance education campus, with over 124,000 students registered in 1997. Also over the 20,000 mark were Vista (28,600), Pretoria (26,000) and Rand Afrikaans (21,600); next in line was Wits, the University of the Witwatersrand, with a student body of 18,000.

Funding for state universities and technikons

The former white universities and technikons still received the lion's share of the R6 billion subsidy from the state for tertiary education in the 1999–2000 budget, mid-1999 figures revealed.

The former white institutions received R3 billion out of the R4.4 billion allocated to universities, and former white technikons shared R1.1 billion out of a R1.7 billion budget. The country's 10 historically black universities shared R1.4 billion, and the black technikons received R604 million between them.

Student debt was approaching R600 million overall. The debt arose mainly from non-payment of fees, either through inability to afford them or a political motivation including the culture of non-payment. The government has repeated many times its policy platform of 'no free education', despite loud calls to write off student and other debts and to increase its 'redress' for apartheid disadvantages.

A new funding framework for higher education is due to be phased in from 2000, with partnership between the state and civil society a strong theme. Parents and business will most probably be asked to pay more for tertiary education in all its forms.

A tax benefit to remember

The South African tax system is notably stingy in giving benefits to taxpayers for donations. The exception is that donations to a university or other tertiary institution are tax-deductible.

You need a receipt from the institution to say the donation has been approved in terms of the Income Tax Act. The deduction is limited to R500 or 2 per cent of your taxable income, whichever is the greater.

CARING FOR THE COUNTRY'S HEALTH

High spending, low impact

Health spending is the second largest social expense of the South African government, although a long way behind education. In the 1998–99 budget the allocation for health was R25 billion, up 24 per cent from the previous year's R20 billion. Nonetheless it comprised 12 per cent of the total domestic budget, with government planning to increase the amount to R28 billion by 2000–01, keeping the proportion at the 12 per cent level.

In 1995 South Africa's health expenditure (including both public and private) was higher as a fraction of the budget than that in Sweden, New Zealand and China, though less in proportionate terms than in the USA and Germany.

However, at US $77 per head, the actual expenditure in South Africa that year was dwarfed by others (the USA spent $2,765 per person and Sweden $2,343, against China's $11). The population per physician was a very high 1,527 in South Africa, against 385 in the USA, 393 in Sweden and even China's 633.

As becomes clear to anyone in any way involved in the South African health system, it is not the amount of money thrown at a problem that counts. How the money gets to the needs on the ground is crucial, and too much of the budget is still supporting inefficient posts and bureaucracies. New funding cuts at trauma units rightly make more impact in the press than protecting an administrator's pension fund.

HOSPITALS AT BOTH ENDS OF THE SPECTRUM

A suffering public hospital system

Make no mistake, the public health system in South Africa is under considerable pressure and often spills over into crisis. Once newspapers can show, as they did in July 1999, that two babies had died because of staff funding cuts at Coronation Hospital in Johannesburg, government and provincial authorities had to accept that immediate measures on the ground mattered as much as long-term planning. Following the public outcry a number of key posts at Coronation were unfrozen and money found from somewhere to keep critical nursing and other medical positions occupied.

At Chris Hani Baragwanath Hospital, located between Johannesburg and Soweto, the largest hospital in the southern hemisphere and one of the biggest in the world, journalists have reported constant long lines of patients clamouring for treatment, day-long queues at the pharmacy counter, a continuous shortage of beds, dirty floors, a huge drugs and sheets stealing operation behind the scenes, doctors being hijacked or attacked, and ever-increasing numbers of victims of gunshot wounds and mothers presenting with HIV/Aids. Yet the hospital, along with many others, somehow manages to keep going, despite the cash shortage, the emigration of doctors and defections to the private sector.

Many people ask exactly how four public hospitals (Johannesburg, Chris Hani Baragwanath, Coronation and Helen Joseph) can ever be expected to serve up to 10 million people in Gauteng, plus referrals from all over Africa, and still provide the service South Africans are entitled to in terms of the constitution. Can the circle be squared?

The nuts and bolts of the hospital system

- In 1997 there were 426 **public hospitals**, said the Department of Health, supplying 110,000 beds; add in 108 health centres and academic hospitals and there were 542 facilities. The number of public beds had decreased by 27,000 in the previous four years.

  - An audit in 1998 showed that under one-fifth of all health care facilities were 'ideal' and about a half were 'acceptable'. One-tenth were so bad they should be 'condemned', the audit stated. At least R500 million was to be awarded to hospital upgrading by 2000.

  - Public hospitals were reclassified from 1997 as district, regional, central and specialist.

- In 1996 there were 304 **private hospitals**, said the department; another survey with a different definition showed 323. The number of beds was put at 21,000, and growing rapidly.

- The **health sector as a whole** was a R60 billion a year industry in 1999, according to a survey that totalled public, private and out-of-pocket personal health expenditure.

- Although the pace of hospital and rural clinic building had markedly increased during the Mandela administration, guided by the much-criticised health minister, Dr Zuma (with 567 clinics built from April 1994 to December 1997), there remained **huge differences between public and private resources**.

  A 1997 survey, for example, revealed that 50 per cent of rural clinics had no telephone, 22 per cent had no taps and 20 per cent lacked electricity. The contrast between an overrun and under-resourced Third World state hospital sector and a well-functioning and well-equipped First World private sector could not be more marked.

Making high-tech medicine relevant in the new millennium

South Africa earned a global reputation for high-tech medicine after 1967 with the first heart transplant, carried out by Dr. Christiaan Barnard at Groote Schuur Hospital in Cape Town.

Since those heady pioneering days the country's academic hospitals have been battered by budget cuts, emigration of key staff, non-replacement of state-of-the-art medical technology and the new emphasis on primary health care. But if South Africa's high-tech lead in medical innovation seemed to have been thrown away, in mid-1999 there was announced a government initiative which offered hope of restoring something of the lost glory.

An international and local empowerment consortium was awarded a tender by the department of health for piloting a study of **telemedicine**. By using advanced equipment, a patient in a rural clinic could in effect deal with a virtual doctor over the Internet in a combination of high-end technology for low-end, affordable public health.

The scheme was hailed as a potentially revolutionary contribution to President Mbeki's African Renaissance, although much development work remained to be done before success could be claimed.

A PHILOSOPHY OF PRIMARY HEALTH CARE

On its accession to office in 1994 the Mandela government made clear its priorities for health:

- unification of apartheid structures into an integrated national system
- reduction of inequalities in delivery and improvement of access to primary health care services
- the primacy of child, maternal and women's health

- mobilisation of interested parties to support a national health insurance scheme.

How far had these worthy aims been met by the millennium? Pretty well, by any score. In addition to rural clinics, the department had introduced abortion on demand, successful vaccination campaigns, a national child feeding plan, free hospital treatment for all children up to the age of 6 and for pregnant mothers, and the drafting in of Cuban doctors to fill shortages in rural areas (over 350 doctors arrived from 1995 to early 1998).

The health insurance plan moved closer to legislation as 2000 approached, later than anticipated but still on course.

Yet the feisty minister, Dr Zuma, (who moved on to the foreign affairs portfolio in April 1999), had made many enemies in her drive to improve health care for the poorest. For example, medical interns resisted her law which made obligatory one-year 'community service' in rural areas, with some calling it medical conscription. Whether the scheme will be introduced in practice remains unclear at the time of writing.

Another and larger confrontation was with the pharmaceutical industry. The minister acquired powers to regulate drug prices, allow wider importing of generic medicines and open up the pharmaceutical business to all comers, with supermarkets able to compete with pharmacies. Not only were domestic manufacturers' noses put out of joint but big business in the USA and Europe threatened trade sanctions if their intellectual property rights were not better protected.

The minister also managed to offend the tobacco industry by banning smoking in all public places and forbidding tobacco sponsorship in sport, but once more actual enforcement proved harder than enactment.

Yet a start had been made in the drive towards a free and equal public health care system for all citizens, and the health ministry had become the highest profile of all the social service departments of government. By the end of the 1990s most people in employment could gain access to medical help, whether a GP or hospital, public or private, new state rural clinic or urban private clinic, or the growing trend to personal health care by alternative methods.

HOW HEALTHY IS SOUTH AFRICA?

As so often in this book, we must note bizarre paradoxes in describing the new South Africa. With one of the healthiest climates in the world, by common agreement, why does the country have, for example, the worst **tuberculosis** (TB) epidemic in 150 countries surveyed, according to the World Health Organisation?

- There were 159,000 notified cases of TB in 1996, with over 10,000 deaths. The infection rate was a high 362 per 100,000 of the population. About a quarter of the TB cases reported that year could be attributed to HIV infection.

There is little doubt TB numbers are on the rise, from both increased reporting by patients and an absolute growth in cases. The infection rate was double that of other developing countries and over 50 times greater than in the USA or Europe. The main groups at risk were known to be the coloured and African populations of the Western Cape.

Some analysts said the problem was at base educational. TB victims were not made aware that their treatment had to be carried out for a full six months and that incomplete treatments were a cause of a new and deadly infection, multi drug resistant (MDR) TB. This spreads through the air as vapour from coughs and sneezes, especially in densely populated areas like townships.

- If TB was the worst of South Africa's notifiable diseases, **malaria** and **measles** followed (with rates of 24 and 20 per 100,000 of the population respectively in 1996). Measles and polio were probably on the way out, with national vaccination campaigns in full swing; measles could be eradicated by 2002, health authorities said.

- **HIV/Aids** was not notifiable at the time of writing, which meant the extent of the most deadly scourge of all was still not officially known. Added to the TB death count, one survey suggested over 3.5 million people would suffer from HIV/Aids by 2005, and already in 1999 1,500 people a day were said to be becoming infected (see Chapter 9).

- But this was not all. South Africa had the highest incidence of various kinds of **cancer** in the world. African men were most at risk from oesophogeal cancer, white and coloured men from prostate cancer and Indian men from stomach cancer. Among black and coloured women, cancer of the cervix was most frequent, and among Indian and white women, breast cancer.

- Among more elective complaints South Africans also suffered from **lung cancer** and **alcoholism** in large numbers.

Yet this is a country with a strong tradition of endurance sports, a thriving health and fitness industry, a fondness for outdoor life and exercise, and some of the best fruit and vegetables and cleanest air still available anywhere. It is a strange paradox indeed, this simultaneous straddling of wide extremes, but how typically South African!

ALTERNATIVE SYSTEMS OF HEALTH CARE

All that has been said so far has been related to western medicine, yet the South African health care system is far from exclusively a matter of postcolonial medical ways. Far from disappearing, the **traditional herbal medicine** of *sangomas* and *nyangas* (types of traditional healers) is flourishing as never before, alongside and below conventional pharmaceutical and surgical methods.

A start has been made in integrating traditional African healing systems at basic rural levels with western medicine, with patients free to choose their regime. Traditional systems tend to be far cheaper and more familiar to many country people. However, if you also go through the streets of big cities, near the taxi and bus stops, you will find *muti* (medicine) peddlers and small shops with stacks of strange roots and dried plants for sale.

The problem for *sangomas*, brought about by their growing popularity, is maintaining a good supply of herbal medicines, with unprecedented competition for collection of naturally occurring plants. A start has recently been made to organise the growing, harvesting and controlled preparation of the most frequently used species.

This attempt at creating a more professionalised traditional African health regime was welcomed by the health authorities, who generally have proved themselves prepared to work alongside other widely accepted health methods.

- **Other alternative healing regimes** such as homeopathy, reflexology, osteopathy, naturopathy, ayurveda and Chinese medicine are available in South Africa. Practitioners can be found through referral by friends, and through health shops and publications they carry, such as *Link Up* and *Odyssey* magazines.

- Some of these regimes may be included in medical schemes, but you would normally expect to pay for treatment on an out-of-pocket basis.

- **Vegetarianism** is a thriving alternative to the country's love affair with *braaivleis*, especially in the traditional Indian communities. An increasing number of other South Africans are choosing vegetarianism as their principled way of life – in addition to the many who are too poor to afford meat in the first place.

PUTTING MEDICAL SCHEMES IN CONTEXT

Given the state of health care in millennial South Africa, there is only one top prize for personal health care for you and your family, and that is to belong to a medical scheme or medical aid, which usually means you are in full-time employment.

An Old Mutual survey in 1997 found that 60 per cent of companies offered a company medical scheme, while 40 per cent opted for external commercial schemes. The survey also established that while 90 per cent of employees were eligible for membership, as many as 40 per cent did not belong to an employer-sponsored medical aid.

Employers are currently spending far more on the health needs of the workforce than, say, twenty years ago. Hollandia Reinsurance Group found in 1997 that employers spent between 10 per cent and 15 per cent of payroll that year on health care, whereas in 1977 the figure was 1 per cent.

What are medical schemes?

- A **medical scheme** is an insurance to cover your health. You pay in regularly so that you can draw on your funds as you need them. As well as being an insurance, a medical scheme is also a type of trust fund over which you have some control on how much you spend.

- A **company medical scheme** is an employee benefit giving you access to private medical care. Your contributions against salary are supplemented by the employer, with the details forming part of your contract of employment.

- **Open market public health care schemes** are those in which you contribute the whole amount, through financial institutions such as Liberty Life, Momentum or Fedsure.

- **The Representative Association of Medical Schemes (Rams)** is the national body to which most medical schemes belong. It lays down fees, referred to as the **scale of benefits**.

- If a doctor is '**contracted in**', this means you will pay Rams' scale of benefits rates. Your doctor or dentist will usually submit your account to your medical scheme for payment.

- If your practitioner is '**contracted out**', you will pay more than the scale of benefits, often at private fee levels set by the doctor or the professional body to which doctors belong. Here you would normally settle the account yourself.

New generation medical schemes
New generation medical schemes have been around since the early 1990s and are contrasted with **traditional medical schemes**.

The new generation model emphasises risk rating and management, and gives incentives to doctors to cut their costs. Traditional schemes, on the other hand, charge on a fee-for-service basis and actually encourage practitioners to spend more on drugs to recoup more from the scheme. It was this inefficiency in the system that provided the impetus for the newer schemes to enter the arena, a move which has tacitly received government support.

Health for all
The Board of Healthcare Funders is a government body set up in July 1999 as a new umbrella association for the whole health care industry. The constituency is large, covering some 7 million individuals, and many more dependants, and spending of some R25 billion a year. The basis of the board's work is to act as an agent of transformation from health care for an affluent élite to universal care from the primary level upwards.

The **National Health Plan** is due to become law in 2000, if the lengthy consultation process is completed and legislation drawn up by then. It aims to formalise the first comprehensive and integrated health system in South Africa, with 'health for all' within a decade as the target.

Among other components of the plan, it would become obligatory for all employees in the formal sector to contribute to their own health spending. Medical schemes would not be allowed to exclude anybody, including HIV/Aids patients, on grounds of health risk. It would be compulsory for medical schemes to continue with benefits to members who were pensioners and widows, as well as retrenched people. The government would also insist on licensing of the burgeoning private hospitals sector.

CONCLUSION

The nation's health has been a central plank in the new South African government's reconstruction plans, and progress has been rapid in establishing primary health care as the cornerstone of the country's medical system. The transformation process has been painful, with public hospitals bursting at the seams and few signs that epidemics like HIV/Aids and TB are being controlled or even contained, and ongoing battles with established interests, including doctors and pharmaceutical and tobacco companies. Medical schemes are set to become available to more employees than ever before.

At the same time private hospitals are springing up around the country, offering excellent service at affordable prices by world standards. To the public eye the gulf between First and Third World medicine appears to be growing vaster, with ability to pay rather than medical need the apparent criterion, contrary to the precepts of ANC policy. It is a paradoxical situation repeated in many other aspects of South African life at the turn of the millennium.

8

Enjoying Your Social Life

This chapter will look at some of the things that South Africa shares with other societies in making everyday life bearable and pleasurable. The next chapter, on crime and HIV/Aids, will examine the grim details of two realities that are a scourge of South Africa at present and into the future. You should be aware of both sides because both are aspects of life in the 'new' South Africa which everybody shares.

We will cover leisure activities and sport in a later chapter. For now the focus will be on everyday living – how people keep in touch; what they see on TV, hear on the radio or read in the papers or magazines; the great South African shopping experience; and South Africa's love affair with eating, drinking and smoking.

KEEPING IN TOUCH

Mobile phones

We mention in the chapter on moving around how in South Africa – which is essentially a large country with a population concentrated in a relatively few areas separated by big tracts of farm land – it is not always easy using public transport. Having a vehicle of your own is almost indispensable if you want the luxury, or perhaps the necessity, of mobility.

In a similar way, at the turn of the millennium, not having a **cellular phone** (the term mobile phone is relatively unknown in South Africa) means you rely on older and largely state-owned means of communication, like the Post Office and Telkom, which suffer the usual inefficiencies of big, entrenched bureaucracies.

South Africa has taken to cellular communications with abandon, and is thought to be among the top ten countries in the world in speed of adoption and use of this relatively new technology. The two licensed national networks, MTN and Vodacom, were themselves taken by surprise by the swift 'roll out' of the system in the mid-

1990s, reaching their first million subscribers in about one year rather than the estimated three. The subscriber base was close to two million as the millennium began, and it seems that every second person in the big cities has their signature cellphone. No longer just the 'Gauteng earring', cellphones are everywhere. Black or white user, madam or maid, business person or teenager – South Africans have a passion for talking to each other that surprises even themselves.

- The geographical spread of the networks is excellent, covering almost the whole country apart from remote or inaccessible country areas. Where Telkom has not yet penetrated with land lines, it is not unusual to see villagers with their cellphones, going straight and readily to space age technology before the old technology reaches them.

- The service is relatively cheap (modest use would cost up to about R300 a month, once the phone has been bought), and certainly comparable with land lines. Prepaid cards have multiplied the accessibility of cellphones and given another impetus to their spread. Using special offers, you could get talking for under R500 in CNA stores in mid-1999.

- It is easy to sign on and buy the phones, through dedicated phone shops, in bigger supermarkets, by following up advertisements in the press and through the many cellphone companies, each of which has a sales organisation in the country.

- The big international names operating in South Africa include Nokia, Ericsson, Siemens and Motorola, while local offerings include Nashua, Teljoy and Radiospoor. Renting is also an available option.

- What isn't so good, or safe, is the way many South African car drivers routinely drive and use their cellphones at the same time. Hands-free phone kits are available but have not really caught on, and the law against driving with a cellphone seems seldom to be applied. So, be warned: the driver wobbling all over the road ahead of you may be drunk but also may be lost in a telephone conversation!

The government has agreed that a third cellular operator should join MTN and Vodacom, and the name of the winning bidder was to be announced late in 1999. All the bidding consortiums have a strong empowerment component, and the winner will be under pressure to deliver an even cheaper service to the townships and impoverished rural areas than has been achieved so far.

Postal services

The **Post Office** has gone a long way to transforming itself from an apartheid institution into a modern service industry. In 1991 the old Department of Posts and Telecommunications became the **South African Post Office Ltd** and **Telkom Ltd**, both government-owned public companies.

In mid-1999 the Post Office appointed the New Zealand Post Office and an arm of the British Post Office as its business partners in an attempt to improve its administration and service, and make the operation profitable.

- While many of the smaller **local post offices** were closed in the 1990s, there are still over 1,500 offices offering the basic postal services. Posting a letter is relatively cheap by global standards (a local letter or postcard cost under R2 and a light airmail letter under R6 at the time of writing), although the prices had escalated in the 1990s.

- When moving to a new area, check if you are supposed to get **postal deliveries**. Some suburbs as well as many areas in the country do not have a delivery service and you are expected to open a post office box (cost is around R130 a year but has risen sharply in recent years).

The modernisation and automation of the service, and its opening up to a new generation of empowerment employees, not to mention high-profile cases of theft or corruption, have damaged the organisation's reputation in recent years. However, the basic service could be said to be excellent by African standards and reasonable by First World standards.

- **Private postal services**, like Postnet, offer a good alternative to the government system, where Postnet shops (a franchise operation) are available. Many customers have found it convenient to have one-stop facilities for buying stationery, sending a fax, receiving mail in a private box and being assured a guaranteed postal delivery.

Telecommunications

Telkom is the state telephone system, and was partly privatised in 1997 when 30 per cent of its equity was sold to a combination consortium of SBC Communications and Telecom Malaysia. The price of nearly R6 billion was the biggest single injection of capital into South Africa then recorded.

The consortium agreed to install 2.8 million new lines (the country had under 4 million lines at the time), including 120,000 pay phones, and replace 1.25 million analogue lines by March 2002.

The roll out process is well under way as this book is written. However, while this is admirable, as a consumer you still have to wait, perhaps one week to three, depending on whether you have cables in your area, for your instrument to be connected. This waiting time is less than half what it was in the 1980s, but it is still unacceptably high, especially in an era of instant access by cellphones.

- Telkom costs are reasonable by global standards, though there is no free concession on local calls, as in many American cities. You can have an instrument installed for under R300 and pay rental of under R50 a month (invoices are issued monthly). Calls are charged on a time and distance basis in various bands, but there is a discount for local calls and off-peak (Callmore Time) periods.

While the new Telkom is part of national life and experience and accepted as such, things are different on the Internet side, where it faces fierce opposition for its quasi-monopoly position.

BROADCASTING

Radio

Let's start with the medium that is most widespread but is often ignored by manufacturers and advertisers: good old-fashioned radio. Regional radio has existed for many years, alongside the SABC national radio services, but there was a proliferation of local and regional services in the 1990s once the SABC monopoly was broken up and a freer market in broadcasting began.

The situation in radio at the millennium is that nearly a hundred radio stations have been licensed to operate, most of them community-based and broadcasting to a specific community. Each of the 11 African official languages has a station, as have some

European language communities (e.g. Greek, Portuguese). Some stations target specific age groups (like youth station Yfm or 'oldies' channel Radio Today) or interests (Classic FM or 5FM, a pop music channel, both of these being SABC stations).

There are talk channels (e.g. Radio 702 in the Gauteng area and Cape Talk in the Western Cape, both being private commercial stations), campus and hospital services and religious broadcasts of various persuasions.

The SABC itself currently runs 19 stations, and claims an audience of 15 million, from the gospel station Radio Sunshine at the small end to a top audience (of nearly 4 million listeners) for Ukhozi FM.

Portable radios are cheap, readily available and a familiar part of most households, whether shack or townhouse. Advertisers support nearly all of the stations, and rates are relatively cheap, as compared to print and TV. The radio has come into its own as a wide-reaching, inexpensive advertising medium in the two democratic elections so far, both for the government and for opposition political parties.

- The latest innovation in radio, which sounds old-fashioned but is actually new and the work of a Cape-based inventor, is the **clockwork wind-up radio**. The factory is staffed almost exclusively by handicapped people, a case of 'sheltered' employment serving a genuine market niche. Made specifically for the poorest person, who cannot afford any radio or even a supply of batteries, the wind-up radio has been attracting attention elsewhere in Africa and as a First World gimmick, but it has penetrated relatively little yet into South Africa's heartland.

Television
Television has been in South Africa only since 1976, when one channel broadcast, in an amateurish way in black and white for limited hours on weekdays, mixing up English and Afrikaans programmes (but not any African languages).

The **SABC**, now called a public rather than a state broadcaster, today runs three channels (SABC 1, 2 and 3), with time apportioned to all 11 languages. The SABC is the TV licence issuer, although more of its income is derived from advertising than licences, paying which has been easily evaded in the past.

The other national channels are **e-tv**, a privately owned commercial operation, which began in 1998, and pay-TV operator **M-Net**.

- M-Net is interesting in that it was founded by leading South African newspaper groups as a pre-emptive effort to build up advertising revenue which was falling off at the then state broadcaster, the SABC. Their investment has paid off because M-Net has grown to over a million viewers in southern Africa, as well as a smaller but significant presence in East and North Africa and in a number of European broadcast and telecommunications ventures.

- M-Net is not allowed to broadcast news (a provision that was lifted for e-tv, after much debate), and is primarily an entertainment and sports channel (sports are shown on its associated channels Super Sport one and two).

- Another channel which has made the transition into the 'new' South Africa is **Bop TV**, once state-owned but now privatised. It broadcasts mainly in the old Bophutatswana area, in the west of present Gauteng.

- Special mention should be made of South Africa's own weekday '**soap**' called *Egoli* (meaning city of gold, Johannesburg), with a multiracial cast, multi-language script and multinational appeal. *Egoli* earns probably more from sales to the rest of Africa and Europe than at home, and has won international awards.

Other developments
- **Educational TV** is improving, with the SABC channels doing highly popular matric revision classes, particularly the mathematics and life sciences programmes with William Smith. However, far more needs to be done in getting television into poorer and rural schools, although many would say building classrooms and buying textbooks are more urgent priorities than obtaining TVs and cheap PCs.

- A successful locally developed TV series in the **edutainment** field is *Soul City*, in which health issues like HIV/Aids, TB, drinking, drug-taking and smoking are explored in a lively entertainment format and shown in prime-time. Celebrity appearances and endorsements, along with support in the form of workbooks, posters and events, make the programme an interactive experience for the teenage target audience.

- There has been a steady spread of **satellite channels**. DStv is the M-Net satellite service, carrying over 40 channels using digital technology. A satellite decoder, smart card and satellite dish cost around R3,000 to R4,000 in mid-1999, with running costs at about R150–R200 a month. Radio is also broadcast on the service, as well as the SABC channels.

So what is the verdict on South Africa's TV service?
It must be said it is much improved from the state-run and propaganda-spreading service of the 1980s. And so it should be, with a huge management and cultural shake-up in the 1990s, refocusing on a public rather than a state broadcasting role, and charging a licence fee of around R200 a year at the turn of the millennium.

There is a better service in the African languages, coming from a zero base, and Afrikaans has been much reduced, some say too far, to the status of one of the 11 official languages rather than one of the 'big two', with English. All the same, there is still far too much imported American and British 'pap' programming, too little in local social documentary and wildlife, where there is so much to be said and done. It is good on local music but weak on local drama, better in news but still stilted and arbitrary, and it makes too little of its potential in combating HIV/Aids and other social ills. But see for yourself and make up your own mind!

Cinema
Is there a South African film industry? Well, not on a Hollywood or Bollywood scale, certainly. There are good production facilities and a few famous locally made movies – like *The Gods Must Be Crazy*, the TV series *Shaka Zulu* and the comedy films made by Leon Schuster (the title of one of his most recent films, *Lipstick, Dipstick,* will give a flavour of what South Africa finds funny among local films). But an industry now to match the flourishing Killarney film studios of Johannesburg from the 1940s to 1960s, no.

However, the world's movie-makers have discovered South Africa as a location. There is a long and mainly dry summer in the Cape, when it's winter in the Northern Hemisphere; there are beautiful and varied locations; there is excellent infrastructure, with technical film-making expertise and advanced digital editing equipment; and above all the costs are low as compared to more established film industries, and trade unions are compliant.

Many low-budget films for the cinema and TV have been made in the 1990s, especially in the Cape, and more are planned. Perhaps more regular in terms of continuity of production, TV advertising work by foreign companies has come to South Africa in a big way.

Movie-going
Yet if South Africa doesn't yet have a developed local movie-making industry, South Africans are an avid movie-going people. The two big cinema chains are **Ster-Kinekor** and **Nu Metro**, which between them must account for 90 per cent of the movie houses. And how many there are!

Look in the Johannesburg paper, say the *Tonight!* section of *The Star*, and you'll have the choice of some 200 movies in greater Johannesburg and Soweto. Sandton City has 16 screens, Eastgate has 12 and plenty of others have 10. The story is similar in all the major cities around the country.

What is being shown is mainstream Hollywood product, but you do find art and subtitled movies at the 11-screen Cinema Nouveau in Rosebank, Johannesburg, for example. It is owned by Ster-Kinekor. A multi-screen art movie house is not a concept you find outside London or Paris, say.

The latest development is for Hindi movies made in Bollywood (Bombay or Mumbai) to break out of being shown only in predominantly Indian areas like Lenasia and Chatsworth. After the success of *Kutch, Kutch...* in certain English-speaking areas in 1998, in mid-1999 the big Indian hit *Hum dil de Chuke Sanam* was tried out in three Nu-Metro centres in Gauteng.

Advertising
Back to advertising for a moment, a mention should be made of South Africa's entry into the big international league, dating really from the 1999 Cannes International Advertising Festival. In the press, poster and TV categories South Africa was judged on a par with the UK, Brazil and the USA, the current global leaders in advertising creativity.

So, if there is an industry which carries the South African flag in terms of global competitiveness, perhaps it is presently advertising. Watch for the names of TBWA Hunt Lascaris, The Jupiter Drawing Room, Net#work, PCB Bosman Johnson, and Lowe Bull Calvert Pace, which were among the Cannes Lions winners.

THE MEDIA
We have been examining what South Africa listens to and watches,

including the advertisements which provide the oil for the broadcasting machine to function. Now let us answer briefly the question of what South Africa reads.

While South Africa lacks a rich reading culture such as that in Northern Europe or Israel – there are far too many illiterate or badly taught people in the country for that, not to mention inability to purchase reading materials – it does have a wide range of print options and a long-established newspaper and book publishing industry.

Newspapers

There are four leading **newspaper groups**: Independent Newspapers of South Africa (formerly the Argus Group), owned by Tony O'Reilly's Independent Group based in Ireland; Nasionale Media; Times Media; and Perskor. Times Media and Perskor are owned by 'black' interests.

There was a significant transfer of newspaper ownership from largely 'white' and foreign control to 'black' and local in the 1990s, although both former President Mandela and President Mbeki insisted the transfer so far had been insufficient. There were many more black, female and Indian editors or senior management appointments to local newspapers in the 1990s than before, but here again the pace of transformation was often criticised as too slow and lacking real depth.

The big four groups control something like 90 per cent of the daily press, a third of rural newspapers and half of the registered magazines, not to mention involvement in the electronic media (as in M-Net, see above).

- The main **daily newspapers** are *Sowetan* (circulation of 206,000 at December 1998); *The Star* (162,000), *The Citizen* (123,000); and *Burger* and *Beeld* (both Afrikaans, and both around 110,000). The only daily publication with something like a national circulation is *Business Report* (560,000), by virtue of being carried in *The Star, Pretoria News, The Mercury* and *Cape Times*.

- Among the **weekly newspapers**, the leaders are *Sunday Times* (450,000); *Rapport* (Afrikaans, 362,000); *City Press* (236,000); *Sunday Tribune* (110,000); and the biggest-selling African-language paper, *Ilanga* (116,000).

- The British *Daily Express* has a weekly South African version that is popular among immigrants from the UK and royal watchers, with a circulation of around 30,000.

Magazines

- Leading **weekly magazines** include the *Financial Mail* (34,000) and *Mail & Guardian* (36,000), both with an influence far beyond their circulation. The electronic version of the *M&G* available on the Internet (www.mg.co.za) receives by far the most 'hits' of any website in its category, and is updated daily.

- **Consumer magazines** also make an appearance with the weeklies. The best-known are probably *Huisgenoot* (430,000) and its English equivalent *You* (258,000). These are to be found, like most of the consumer magazines, at supermarket checkout counters as well as in CNAs and other booksellers.

- **Fortnightlies** doing well include the consumer magazines *Fair Lady* (104,000), *Rooi Rose* (Afrikaans, 125,000) and *Sarie* (Afrikaans, 180,000).

- There is a huge selection of **monthly magazines**, including imports and local products. In the women's market, for example, local versions of *Cosmopolitan*, *Femina*, *Marie Claire* and *Elle* fight it out with an older age group publication *Woman's Value*. Car, sports, health, gardening, wildlife, home decoration and family magazines all compete in the monthly category for increasingly rare advertising rands.

- Specifically **'black' local publications** like *Bona* (214,000), *Drum* (106,000) and *Pace* (75,000) have kept their readership by editorial innovation and good advertising support, while imported titles like *Ebony* have secured a smaller niche readership. However, African-language magazines barely exist as yet.

- **Big-selling monthlies** also include the TV guides and *Reader's Digest* (newly revamped in 1999), but the biggest of all, dwarfing all other monthlies, is the *Edgar's Club Magazine*, which was posted to over a million cardholders in one month in the mid-1990s.

Books

The book publishing sector is dominated by the **schoolbooks** publishers, which also serve (often in other divisions and with different names) as the general publishers.

While prescribed schoolbooks can have print orders of upwards of 500,000 per province, it is said that a sale of 5,000 copies for a local South African author makes a **bestseller**. So a Wilbur Smith (South Africa's biggest-selling author) selling over 20,000 of each new novel in the local market is a super-seller, and an exception.

A number of **literary awards**, like the M-Net, Sanlam and Boeke, help to publicise local publishing in the official languages, and not merely English and Afrikaans. Book sales and Christmas promotions also stimulate the general book market, but getting a novel or poetry published locally is hard work indeed.

Bookselling is dominated by the **CNA** chain, including brands like Exclusive Books, but a number of independent booksellers do carry on, adding diversity to the book market.

One South African bookbuying habit worth noting is the **book club**. Found all over the country and often being the stimulus for publishers to increase print runs, book clubs are usually small (up to a dozen members), informal, usually female and active (one buyer may purchase 10 new books, with members' funds and often at a discount). Club members meet in each others' houses to discuss the books they have decided to buy, and along the way talk about the children and what's new in the shops.

SHOPPING

Which leads, in a roundabout way, to the matter of shopping, one of South Africa's best-loved activities. The country has a full range of shopping options, from streetside hawkers to hypermarkets, from mail order catalogues to e-commerce and cyber shopping, to satisfy all tastes and pockets.

There's a case to be made that some South African shoppers are world class, with a deep knowledge of European fashion, say, and the spare cash to indulge their passion. Is not a *kugel* – an indefinable term, but including in its qualities a northern suburbs Johannesburg, usually Jewish, young woman with infinite taste and some wealth – above all a consummate shopper? She (and her male equivalent, the *bagel*) are lucky to have the excellent shops, bars and restaurants to shop in and be seen in. But let's start at a more basic level.

The informal sector
- It is only a decade or so since municipal regulations were

liberalised to allow **streetside hawkers** to sell their wares on city pavements. Hawking is one way immigrants from other African countries or people coming to the town from the countryside can make a start, and you will often see people with little plastic plates containing three apples or guavas or potatoes sitting on a street corner hoping to earn R5 in a day. On the other hand, some hawkers are well enough organised to buy fresh fruit and vegetables at the city produce markets, have removable display boxes or cabinets and do a good trade at important city intersections. The demand for their services is there, and even if some city residents complain of the build-up of refuse after the hawkers pack up and leave for the night, hawking as a feature of city life is here to stay.

- A relatively new South African shopping lifestyle is the proliferation of **marketing at 'robots'** (or 'robos'), South Africa's name for traffic lights. Once upon a time you'd only buy your newspaper as the light changed but now you can also purchase rubbish bags, wire models, fruit in season, footballs, penknives and other nick-nacks. You may only occasionally find value, but what convenience!

- Not many products can be bought these days from **travelling street vendors**, but you don't have to be in South Africa long to come across the one exception. In season it's a familiar city experience to hear the plaintive cry of 'mielies!', and you know somebody is selling maize cobs. Women sellers seem to carry their stock on their heads as they ply the streets, while for some reason the men often have bicycles. But either way it's nice to have one glimpse of an almost vanished time when most shopping was done in the street by colourful itinerant pedlars.

- A growth area in some places is the **'tuck shop'**, a small, family-run shop selling a few necessities, like bread, milk, sweets and cigarettes. A step up from the hawker, the tuck shop is still an informal arrangement, usually without a trading licence but allowed to function by the authorities. The largely Indian city of Chatsworth, near Durban, for example, has dozens of these tuck shops.

- While still in the area of informal-sector shopping, South Africa has its share of **jumble sales** and **car boot sales**, often advertised on the street posters that cling to every available post or pole in most of the cities. These occasions tend to be small and parochial, and there is not yet a culture of universal second-hand buying such as is found in the UK.

- What South Africa is really fond of is its **flea markets**. From virtually none in the mid-1980s to scores at the end of the 1990s, flea markets of various sizes and pretensions have cropped up all over the country. The larger ones, like Flea Market World at Bruma Lake, in eastern Johannesburg, or The Stables in Durban, are well organised, professionally run, with high entry limits for traders and customer guarantees, and spill over into weekday trading.

What all these informal-sector initiatives have in common, from hawkers to flea markets, is a personal touch, an interaction based on service and satisfaction for the customer, quite over and above the bargain-hunting.

The formal sector

- In the formal sector of shopping, the **neighbourhood stores** have been the inevitable losers to supermarkets, which have huge stocks, lower prices and better parking, although some local stores in convenient locations continue to make a living. Specialist shops and delicatessens can be found, with a little searching, in most cities.

- **Supermarkets** are most South Africans' idea of 'shops' in the new millennium. The big chains, like Pick 'n Pay, Shoprite-Checkers, Dions, Makro, Game and Clicks, serve not only South Africa but also have outreach into neighbouring countries.

- **Cash and carry stores**, like Makro and Game, are often used by smaller stores as their source of discounted goods, and individual buyers can obtain discount membership cards. Having such cards makes purchasing of big-ticket items, like furniture and beds, an affordable option, and home delivery might be part of the deal.

- **Woolworths** in South Africa is quite an upmarket brand, with its food and clothes stores in the better-off suburbs. It is often compared to Marks & Spencer in the UK in terms of the quality of its goods and informed service.

Supermarkets come in a variety of sizes, from national franchise operations, such as Spar, and smaller regional supermarkets to giant hypermarkets where you can buy not only groceries but clothes, sporting equipment, furniture and garden materials.

South Africa's supermarkets are respected in the wider commercial world as pioneers or early adopters in shopping technology, merchandising and making the whole experience customer-friendly. It's already possible, for example, to pay telephone accounts in larger Pick 'n Pays. Scanning devices are promised soon which itemise a whole trolley of goods in a supermarket within two minutes – an improvement on the long minutes it presently takes to reach checkout counters and the slow, one-by-one swipe method to cash up goods.

In general, busy Saturday morning shopping, with the kids, on a hot day and in crowded malls may not be as easy-going a supermarket experience as you might wish for.

- Our advice is: if you can, go early in the morning or late evening, or on a Sunday morning. Most supermarkets will be open on weekdays and Saturdays from 8.30am or 9am until at least 5.30pm, but sometimes to 7.30pm or even 9pm, and on Sunday mornings to 1pm. Shopping hours vary from store to store, so you should check before you embark on a shopping expedition.

- Long opening hours may also apply for many shops other than supermarkets, and some shops, such as the convenience stores attached to larger garages on the motorways, are open 24 hours, like the garages themselves.

Customer service

It has to be conceded that **service to the customer** in the formal shopping sector in South Africa lags far behind standards taken as normal in Europe or the USA, and the consumer has been generally too timid or unaware to complain.

Consumerism has been slow to take off in South Africa, but it grew through the 1990s, with TV slots, campaigning columns in some newspapers, a statutory watchdog, a small claims court and other signs of a gathering awareness that being ripped off or offered shoddy service is no longer acceptable.

Exploring the malls

Shopping malls, like Sandton City near Johannesburg, Cavendish Square in Cape Town, and the Pavilion in Westville near Durban, are First World shopping experiences. Foreign shoppers are often surprised by the quality of brands and range of luxury goods on offer, at prices that translate into bargains in dollar or sterling equivalents.

South Africa's yuppies and buppies (the black version of yuppie) keep many clothes boutiques, coffee shops, wine bars and latterly cigar bars going nicely in the more upmarket malls.

Many teenagers and even younger schoolchildren have also made the malls their weekend 'hang-outs', showing off their fashionwear and meeting their friends and opposite sex. This precocious behaviour concerns many parents, but on the other hand, they admit there is some security in the malls and the kids do have to go somewhere at the weekend.

Armchair shopping

Shopping from home is a growing trend. Mail order shopping has never really caught on in South Africa, and there is no equivalent of a Sears-Roebuck catalogue in the USA or Littlewoods in the UK, although direct mail concerns like HomeChoice or Glomail would dearly like to be as big as their Anglo-American cousins once were.

However, direct marketing on the TV is escalating, and mid-mornings on the TV seem to be a procession of long 'infomercials' for health and security products. Shops like Verimark or Glomail, which sell the goods direct-marketed on TV, are to be found in some shopping malls.

Thrupps in Johannesburg is one of the few old-style stores which still offers a **delivery service**, in this case of quality foods. However, many fast food outlets, like the pizza houses, also do deliveries in the cities.

Shopping on the Internet

E-commerce is taking off in South Africa, although many shoppers admit to a residual caution or fear of giving credit card information over the Internet.

Cyber shoppers who have taken the plunge have discovered, for example, the speed and efficiency of Amazon.com for buying books, beating the service offered by local booksellers.

The South African market is certainly growing, leaping from R500 million in 1997 to R1.2 billion in 1998. Projections are for e-commerce spending of R2.7 billion in 1999 and R5 billion in 2000, and thereafter, the experts say, it will seem so normal that it will be as commonplace as using an ATM has become.

While the Internet has bargains available – already in 1999 South

Africa had good car-buying, home-buying, and auction sites – the overseas sites which offer far more choice and seeming low prices may trap the unwary. The poor rand exchange rate and delivery charges from the USA or Europe, plus possible customs charges, may shift the 'bargain' into the luxury class.

- On the matter of e-commerce phobia, local technology experts advise looking for a digital certificate which authenticates the owner of the website. An unbroken icon of a **padlock** or a **key** in the tool bar, for example, will indicate a site is secure.

One local directory, shops.ecnet.co.za, by mid-1999 already offered secure cyber shopping, with a selection of over 50 shops in its directory. Another site, megashopper.co.za, also set up in mid-1999, was specific to Shoprite-Checkers stores and had same-day delivery service for orders taken before 3pm.

With its love for gadgetry and world-class shopping instincts, there's little doubt South Africans will move into e-commerce in a big way in the first years of the new millennium.

EATING

You only have to look at a cross-section of South Africans – OK, let's admit it, the middle-aged males especially – and see the extravagant bellies to know that here is a people who enjoy their food and drink. While the *boeps* (big bellies) may not weigh as heavily as in, say, the USA or Germany, South Africa has its share of enthusiastic eaters and drinkers, as also its dieters and vegetarians, and its Alcoholics Anonymous meetings.

The country produces an abundance of meat, fish, fruit and vegetables, mielie meal and bread, and dairy products, among the main food groups, and is usually self-sufficient in food, unless there is a drought year.

The country is also well known for its **food exports**, covering products familiar in the First World, like Outspan (now Capespan) oranges, Starking apples and Cape grapes, and many varieties of wine and biltong or rooibos tea for the healthy (some food terms are explained in Figure 8 and below), among others. In southern African terms, in good farming years, there is a large trade in mielie meal, which forms the basis of most cooking in black communities in the wider region.

Eating at home is what most of us do most of the time, rather than go to restaurants, as the consumer magazines would have us believe. What do South Africans eat at home, then? In busy households, where both partners go out to work – which is the norm in nearly all communities, black, white and Indian – weekday evening meals might be TV dinners, fast food takeaways or deliveries, and quick meals in the microwave.

But come weekends or public holidays, and the time is right for a *braai* or barbecue. South Africans of all communities love nothing more than gathering round a charcoal fire and making an evening of it by grilling chops, boerewors, chicken, steak and even a few potatoes.

You can expect to come across *braai* facilities at game parks, even in some city parks and motorway roadside stops, not to mention at big stadiums hosting rugby or cricket matches. Portable 'Webers', named after the best-known manufacturer of *braai* equipment, with a gas bottle and cooking stand, have made the *braai* fully mobile, so don't be surprised to find one on the beach, at the side of the road during the Comrades Marathon running race or wherever a 4×4 can go off road.

Braais are as distinctive in the South African way of life as lounging by the pool and reading the *Sunday Times*. Of course, the generally excellent and predictable climate helps (though the weather in Cape Town is as unexpected as any part of England or Germany, say). Men seem to revert to hunter or Trekker mode, at least in the serious business of fetching the meat from the butcher, lighting the fire and distributing the beer, and their female partners do a lot of the talking and entertaining. Even immigrants take on these traditional *braai* roles – just watch yourself after a few beers!

If you are having a good time, you will be having a *jol* (also known as a *jorl*), meaning merry-making, a 'thrash' or fun and games. The word also means dancing and a party, and to flirt or have fun. Add it to your vocabulary!

DRINKING

Drinking is also a hallowed part of the South African way of life. The term includes beer, wine and spirits, of course, all of which are made locally and also exported. While novelties like cider and health drinks have emerged, beer is still the main alcoholic tipple of choice, just as locally manufactured Coca-Cola is the leading soft drink by far.

Biltong: air-dried meat strips, made of many animals, from beef to kudu, crocodile to zebra. Strips are soaked in vinegar, rolled in salt and spices and suspended to dry out.

Bobotie: a Cape Malay favourite, in which spiced ground beef or lamb is topped with a savoury custard.

Boerewors: a type of farmer's sausage, with distinctive spicing.

Bunny chow: a hefty snack, consisting of a loaf of bread, scooped out and filled with curry.

Koeksister: a twisted or plaited doughnut, deep-fried and dipped into cold syrup.

Konfyt: a preserve of fruit in its own syrup, e.g. apricot, melon, orange.

Melktert: a baked custard tart, flavoured with sweet spices.

Pap: the maize-meal porridge, also called *putu*, that is the staple carbohydrate food for many black South Africans. It is often sold in the streets in bigger cities, often with *vleis* (meat, literally 'flesh') and stewed tomato and onion.

Peri-peri: a hot chilli flavouring or marinade introduced from Mozambique, and popular on seafood and chicken. Highly popular, in takeaway meals such as Nando's chicken. The first specialist chilli shop opened in 1999 in Village Walk, Sandton.

Potjiekos: a stew, cooked for hours in a three-legged iron black pot, deriving from the Trekkers of the last century.

Rooibos: also called 'bush tea', a shrub grown around Clanwilliam, which makes a stimulating health tea, without tannin or caffeine.

Soetkoekie: a traditional spiced biscuit, with cinnamon, cloves, nutmeg and ginger.

Sosaties: a kind of kebab, marinaded in spices and slow-grilled.

Waterblommetjie: a type of water lily, mainly from the Western Cape, delicious boiled, or with mutton added as a stew (*bredie*).

Fig. 8. Some South African food delights.

- You will find that brandy and coke and rum and coke are favourites in the bar and sports café, but a huge variety of wine is also enjoyed, with cider and spiced ale (Solanti's Spice was launched in mid-1999) popular among the student age group.

- South Africa is justly famous for its **fruit juices** in boxed one-litre packs (Liquifruit and Ceres sell for about R5–R6 a litre, no-name brands at supermarkets being about a rand cheaper).

- Bottled **water**, both local and imported, is also universal, though there are few parts of the country where tap water is not safe and tasty.

- South African Breweries (SAB) has an almost total monopoly of **beer** manufacture in the country, and indeed is big enough to be the fourth-largest brewer in the world. South African beer drinkers are right up there in the world league, not many bottles a year per head adrift of the Germans and Australians. If you tire of Castle, Hansa and Lion, there are local microbreweries, like Mitchell's, Knysna and Windhoek, which have a committed following, and a range of more expensive imported beers. SAB's products are technically lagers rather than beers, but with about a 5 per cent alcohol content they still pack a punch.

- **Wine** drunk with meals is increasingly the norm, although it's probably fair to say it is still more usual in white families than black or coloured – except in the grape-growing areas, of course. Up to very recent times, grape pickers were paid partly by the *dop*, that is, in liquid form. However, recent industrial relations legislation has tried to end this practice.

A book like this, on the theme of surviving and thriving in the new South Africa, could go on at length about the qualities of the country's beer and wine, as indeed its best restaurants and eating experiences, but the ground is well covered in the tourist guides and in the press and magazines. Even better, here's an area where the reader will require little encouragement to experiment and learn from friends or colleagues at work and at home.

So we won't say much more about the joys and sorrows of eating and drinking at home or out, except to note that when eating out, look to see whether a restaurant has a **drinks licence**. These licences have to be applied for by each establishment, and the process is long-winded and costly, so you cannot assume that all restaurants automatically have an alcohol licence. In the case of an unlicensed restaurant, you are encouraged to bring your own bottles, although some restaurants may still ask you to pay a 'corkage' fee.

Don't forget, too, that shops and supermarkets still have **restrictions on Sunday trading in alcohol**, one of the few instances where Sunday trading has not been fully relaxed in the last few years. Buy your bottles in the bottle store or supermarket before the weekend, and you will be fine.

One more thing: if you are going out to a *braai* or to supper at the home of a friend or business acquaintance, it is usual to take a bottle or food offering, as appropriate. It need not be a grand gift, but it will be appreciated. This holds good across the old cultural and colour divides too.

SMOKING

South Africa is a tobacco-producing country, and cigarettes and snuff are cheap, with most of the retail price of R8–R9 for a pack of 20 going in 'sin tax' to the government. In case you're interested, it'll cost you R1.80 for a small box of snuff.

New rules on smoking

Smoking in public has visibly declined in recent years, including in many company offices. This has been largely a voluntary reaction to anti-smoking legislation, which strongly discourages rather than prohibits smoking in public places, including the workplace and restaurants.

The smoking room in factories or offices and non-smoking areas in restaurants have become familiar, and it's a frequent sight to see smokers taking a break on the street outside their buildings during office hours. Aircraft flying locally are virtually all non-smoking, as are also most international flights into and out of the country.

When going to somebody's house as a guest, follow the house rule on smoking. Many hosts are no longer embarrassed to ask smokers to go outside the room, and you'd be expected to comply. However, there is no all-embracing rule to follow here.

Enter the cigar bar

There's always a counter-reaction, of course, when there's any prohibition or sanction on personal behaviour, and the 1990s saw the introduction of cigar bars in a number of upmarket shopping areas. Women have been taking up cigars, often for the first time, and there is even a factory in Krugersdorp producing Cuban cigars.

In drinking bars, pubs and sports cafés, though, as you'd expect, smoking continues as it always did – cancer scares, legislation and higher prices of cigarettes notwithstanding.

This chapter has explored aspects of South African social life at the turn of the millennium, emphasising what might be called 'normal' behaviour, which differs only slightly from what might be found in Europe or North America – the First World side of South Africa, if you will.

However, there are two facets of the South African experience – crime and HIV/Aids – which reflect terribly negatively on the country. The first is visible and much-shown, the second is a terrifying and looming presence for the near future. Posing particular threats and huge challenges, they require separate treatment, which will follow in the next chapter.

9

Crime and HIV/Aids

As it enters the post-Mandela era, South Africa is beset by many huge problems. In all the challenges of transformation, however, two harsh realities stand out. These are at the same time national crises and scourges of South African society. One is all too visible and one is so far relatively invisible; one a national disgrace and one a national tragedy in the making. **The first is crime and the second is HIV/Aids.**

- We will take an open look at both issues, which are important enough matters to influence your decision to settle in the country in the first place, and help you to weigh your personal chances of surviving them, should they come your way.

- We will suggest that while crime is the present perceived evil of society, with a reality that is almost as bad, it is HIV/Aids that poses the greater long-term threat to the lives of most South Africans.

- We will be concerned with the overall impact of crime and HIV/Aids, both in direct and indirect economic and social costs, but must also bring the issues down to personal terms: how can you as an individual 'survive and thrive' in the face of such looming threats to your life and livelihood?

CRIME

What are the facts?
While South Africa may not be the crime centre of the world, as some of the more sensational news reports suggest, it does have horrific crime figures. Parts of the country have become 'fortress South Africa', with frightened people, black and white alike, living behind high walls, protected by vicious dogs and electric fences, with armed security guards patrolling their property.

This book has no brief to wish away realities of living in contemporary South Africa, nor to make things more scary than they are. Some presentation of 'crime facts' is therefore unavoidable.

According to experts in the field, the quality of South Africa's **crime statistics**, as collected by the South African Police Service (SAPS), is above average in international terms. The police now publish data monthly, and the figures are generally considered to be transparent, without obvious cover-ups, and accurate as these things go.

- The success in reporting crime and open publication of crime figures, given South Africa's violent past and reputation, may in fact be exacerbating the problem, adding to the perception that life is more violent than previously.

- At the same time, the SAPS admits there is **chronic under-reporting of crime** to the police. For many people who have had reason to mistrust the police or find them inefficient it is just too much trouble to report petty crime at an under-resourced police station.

- The fact is that crime is known about far more than even five years ago. Some crimes to the person, like rape and domestic violence, have probably increased partly because more people are daring to report matters that were previously 'hidden' or too shameful to go to the authorities about.

So, according to the SAPS, in South Africa at the turn of the millennium:

- **Among South Africa's 43 million people there is a serious crime every 17 seconds, a murder every 30 minutes, a burglary every two minutes, and an assault or rape every three minutes.**

- **Violent acts**, including murder, assault, rape and robbery, have almost doubled since 1994, although it may be some small consolation that murder as a category has increased at a slower rate than before 1994.

- There are an estimated 4 million **illegal weapons** in the country, and most would-be criminals are armed. At the time of the 1994 election it was said a person could buy an AK47 and ammunition at Komatipoort, on the Mozambique border, for R50, and for even less in the gangland in the East Rand townships.

- **Black people are more the target than white**, both in absolute numbers and as a proportion of the population. Contrary to media coverage (and the media is still basically white-owned and white-run), which tends to show black-on-white violence, especially where the victim is high profile, the most usual victims of crime are black and most perpetrators are also black.

- More crime is committed in the (mainly black) **townships** than in the (mainly white) suburbs, both absolutely and as a proportion. This township crime is less reported in the media and has a lower conviction rate for criminals.

- The **police** are under-staffed, underpaid and under-supplied. Perceived as the enemy in apartheid society, the police have only recently started to receive sympathy and some support from the public. The SAPS is a most unsafe career, with over 1,000 policemen killed on duty since 1994; many more are murdered off duty. Frequently the motive is to obtain the constable's pistol. Most policemen who are killed or wounded are black.

- South Africa has a large and growing **drugs problem**, with evidence that it is used as a transshipment centre for hard drugs like heroin and cocaine from source areas to markets in North America and Europe. South Africa is a source of both vegetable-based drugs (like dagga, or marijuana) and synthesised drugs (like Mandrax). Drug use is an increasing problem among youth and in schools.

- Drugs and prostitution, among other activities, have been the focus of **international and local crime syndicates**. There were said to be about 350 such international syndicates operating in the country in the late 1990s. **Gang violence** is a long-term social problem in many areas in the Cape and Gauteng in particular.

- There is growing **white-collar or commercial crime**, fraud, money-laundering, computer crime and corruption among officials, both black and white.

- On the other hand, the period of the new South Africa has seen a **reduction in political violence**, train and taxi violence and random killings at shebeens (taverns) and at bus stops, which characterised the run-up to the elections of 1994.

- **Domestic violence** is recorded at unacceptably high levels, with wife (and husband) battering, child abuse and other forms of violence in the family household, not to mention familial murders (where, typically, the husband murders the children and his wife, then commits suicide).

Crime in South African life

Such bald statements of criminal statistics are mind-numbing and can be overwhelming. Clearly, each and every example of crime mentioned (and the list is far from complete) is unacceptable in any society. The average South African – and this is across all colour and socio-economic categories – fervently wishes it were not so, but relatively few actively do anything public about it, unless it be to emigrate.

There is as yet no civic culture of making things happen in the new South Africa, but a few pioneers do join the Neighbourhood Watch (and other block watch schemes), become police reservists, battle with local government officials for street lighting, and even block off suburban streets and install armed guards to protect their neighbourhood.

Crime has quickly become part of the South African reality, along with friendly *braais*, glitzy shopping malls, soccer at the FNB stadium, shack communities and driving in a 4×4 through a game park. People living in South Africa have to make their peace with the situation, each one choosing either to ignore crime and hope it will go away or take some sort of defensive steps against becoming another crime statistic.

Certainly, in both black and white households crime is more a talking point even than politics, which is saying a lot in such a politicised society. Discussions on crime almost match sport as the general preoccupation of people in all social and economic groups. Everybody knows someone who has been a crime victim.

Is crime really bad or is it media hype?

With such figures and trends, it can hardly be denied that crime in South Africa is a really bad and probably worsening fact of life. Yet the Mandela government of 1994–99, despite promises and some energy in amending the criminal justice system, did not prioritise crime in terms of providing money and resources, giving adequate pay rises to serving policemen and women, increasing police numbers (for part of the 1994–99 period there was actually a freeze on police recruitment) and improving police equipment. Many police stations still lack vehicles, telephones and even writing pads for filling in crime reports.

Summarising so far, we have already noted a triple whammy of crime perceptions:

- transparent police statistics showing more of the exact numbers of crimes and plenty of news reporting on those figures, some of it routine, some sensationalised

- a government lacking the political will to tackle the crime issue head-on or not regarding it as a priority in nation-building

- a culture or habit of much talking and complaining but little public participation in crime-fighting initiatives.

Now add the **news media** to this mix. Particularly overseas, but also within South Africa, the press, TV and radio make much of violent crime. Statistical surveys have shown that TV news coverage of South Africa abroad is almost invariably of the gloom and doom variety. It is also a matter of fact that foreign investors and tourists both avoid South Africa after incidents such as a 30-second news clip of the aftermath of a bomb that exploded at the Cape Town Waterfront or the death outside his Johannesburg home in a hijacking of the chief executive of a South Korean car assembler. The after-shots of a cash-in-transit heist, prison escape, bank robbery or shooting are highly visual in the news sense, and news editors do not hesitate to make use of dramatic footage or stills. By contrast, crimes of a domestic nature, rape or white-collar crime are harder to investigate, make for less exciting visuals and go under-reported.

In the public mind, 'increasing crime' almost always means violent crime, but that perception may not be the reality on the ground. So is the media guilty of misrepresentation by overplaying the more visual aspects of violent crime, even hyping them up, but of underplaying other equally pervasive forms of 'hidden' crime?

Such a case is sometimes made, but in general the South African media in the new open era has come through with a reputation for responsible reporting. In a time of so much crime, even 'ordinary' murders or hijackings have little news value, and news editors in the electronic and print media do try to keep the balance between providing information and slipping over into sensationalism. It has helped that the country has had no tradition of sleazy tabloid journalism.

It should also be said that South Africans' perceptions are formed just as much by conversations in the family, at work, at church or in the locker room as by media influence.

CAN I BEAT CRIME?

The only statistic that matters

Numbers are one thing, and it is easy to prove a point with the spin you choose to put on particular figures, but in looking at crime the real statistic is what happens to you personally or to your close family. To be mugged or burgled once – and some people have suffered many times – makes the impersonal numbers of direct subjective interest and may alter your whole perception. Many people who leave the country do so because of a personal experience of violent crime, or know of colleagues who were crime victims. If it is not the experience itself then it is often the fear of it that makes people say enough is enough.

What can the individual do when personally involved? Rather than offer a layperson's platitudes on how to avoid becoming a crime statistic, let us rather get the criminal viewpoint direct.

In an interesting report in *The Star* in December 1998, a number of prisoners in Pretoria Maximum Prison went public with advice, from the criminals' point of view, on how people could best avoid becoming victims of violent crime in contemporary South Africa.

Inmate Matthews Senne, 23, convicted of armed robbery and sentenced to ten years' imprisonment in 1996, joined the Criminology Society of South Africa while serving his time. He was given a project to interview fellow offenders and find out how they felt about committing crimes and what would have prevented them. The prisoners 'inside' comments were sent to the press and published. They bear some thinking about, and a few samples are given in Figure 9 below. The point of view taken is that of a teenage, black, male criminal, and a victim of any age, gender or colour.

RAPE AS A CRIME IN SOUTH AFRICA

This is not a topic that makes for easy reading, but it is important to go into a little more detail on at least one category of violent crime in South Africa today.

Rape is chosen because it is a particularly devastating assault on the person and because its sharp increase illustrates how far South African society has been dislocated, and how formerly held values of respect for the person have evaporated. It is also chosen because there are some signs that public perceptions are altering, that rape is no longer being seen as 'the woman's fault' and people are beginning to fight back.

Inside the criminal mind

Offenders are often illiterate, say the prisoners, and ill-equipped psychologically to deal with the pressures of conflict between western and African ways of doing things. They are often uneducated and lack life skills to solve personal problems.

Armed robbery

The robber coming to your house or car is probably more nervous than you, his victim. He knows you may be armed and have a secret panic button. He will probably be carrying a loaded weapon and will be prepared to use it.

- Do everything you are told to do. Don't resist or be defiant if someone points a firearm at you, however young or small he may look.

- Don't make sudden movements, and if you need to move, ask him what to do.

- Stay calm and assure him he is in charge. Convey this message in every possible way.

- Never try and run away unless you are totally sure you will succeed.

- Look for any identifying features on his face and body, and try to remember anything out of the ordinary in the appearance and behaviour of your attacker.

- Do not fight or challenge him. Taunt him and he will probably kill you.

Rape

- Avoid getting drunk in public places. Know where your wife/ daughter/girlfriend is and check on them regularly.

- Teach girls to report to a trusted person any kind of offensive touching or kissing.

Fig. 9. Crime: an inside story.

- Avoid walking at night, even in groups.

- Avoid talking to strangers or getting into an unknown car.

- Listen to your instincts, as a gut feeling is always right.

- If you are drugged or forced into a car or taken somewhere against your will, scream.

- Make a noise, draw attention to yourself and run towards other people.

- Try to learn self-defence techniques and avoid confrontation if you can by running away.

Housebreaking

- Try and leave someone to look after your house if you are absent. Work on establishing friendly relations with your neighbours.

- Make sure access to your property is not easily gained. Install burglar-proofing on all windows, including sliding doors, bathroom and toilet windows.

- Try and get to know the police in your area. Be careful and report suspicious-looking people to the police.

- Chase away anyone sitting under a tree or behind a bush near your property, and keep big, well-trained dogs.

- Develop a code or strategy you can use as a warning system with neighbours. If affordable, sign up with a neighbourhood watch and/or security company (see Chapter 4 above).

Car theft

- Install visible security devices as a deterrent against inexperienced thieves.

- Always park your car where it is visible, and never leave children waiting in it if you have to go away from the car.

Fig. 9. Cont.

Looking at the statistics

Four types of crime to the person were reported in SAPS figures for the period 1974 to 1997, namely assault, murder, rape and robbery. The figures for four key years are given in Figure 10. The table shows that incidents of **reported rape** had more than doubled from 1990 to 1994, and continued to rise after the mid-1990s. However, let's put the overall figures into a further level of contextualising:

- The number of these reported cases **referred to court** was less than half. The most recent year recorded was 1996, when of 50,481 reported rape cases only 21,863 were referred to a court.

- Of the cases referred to court only a fraction resulted in **convictions** for rape: there were 4,100 guilty verdicts in 1996.

Bear in mind these were **reported cases**. Rape is a traumatic event that victims in many cases find it impossible to go to the police about, for a variety of reasons. Most women have not even realised that rape is a criminal offence. It is very probable that thousands of rapes or near-rapes each year are **never reported**.

	Assault	Murder	Rape	Robbery
1974	138,586	8,662	14,815	37,896
1990	120,030	15,019	20,321	61,132
1994	210,250	26,832	42,429	117,323
1997	234,554	24,588	52,160	122,371

Source: SAIRR, 1997/98 Survey, page 29 (quoting SAPS figures).

Fig. 10. Reported crimes to the person in South Africa,
1974–97, selected years.

Signs of a changing attitude

This position is changing, albeit slowly and against much resistance. Social workers are saying more rape victims are feeling empowered to report the offence than ever before, which may explain part of the drastic surge in numbers. The rise in reported cases, though not yet in convictions, could also indicate a swing in mood or public opinion towards seeing rape as a crime rather than as somehow invited by the female victim. Consider these indicators of change:

- Convictions for rape were more difficult to sustain in the past because of misguided **judges' rules**, which obliged magistrates to doubt the evidence of the rape victim in a direct legal confrontation between criminal and victim. This rule has now been set aside.

- Some of the **bigger police stations** now have rape counselling services and a special room where victims (in theory at least) can receive humane treatment from women police officers trained to handle abuse cases with sensitivity.

- Pressure groups like **POWA** (People Against Women Abuse) are winning more mainstream acceptability and pushing ahead with campaigns like their One Million Signature Campaign to raise rape awareness in the community.

- Some **media** are championing the cause of rape victims, e.g. the lifestyle magazine *Marie Claire*, and using deliberately in-your-face editorial and illustrations to shock readers into taking action.

- A brave journalist, **Charlene Smith**, was raped in her Johannesburg home in early 1999 and went public on her story a few days later. She described the triple horror of the rape victim: the crime itself, the degrading treatment she received from police and law officers, and the danger of contracting HIV/Aids from the assault. Smith fought to receive the anti-Aids drug AZT as a right, and there are hopes that her high-profile victory and writing about her experiences will change official policy and allow this drug to be automatically prescribed to rape victims at the police station they report to.

- Rape counselling services are available through POWA, Life Line and Rape Crisis **telephone lines** in most big cities, and the numbers are widely advertised.

- In a well-publicised case in early 1999, **Makhaya Ntini**, a black cricketer and currently in the South African test team and due to play in the World Cup, was charged with the rape of a female student he knew. Ntini was convicted and sentenced to six years in prison. The magistrate said he was making an example of the cricketer, the product of a high-profile sports empowerment programme, to deter other men from committing the crime.

Yet such positive developments count for little until public policy is changed. The government in South Africa, as elsewhere, is rarely proactive in social and welfare matters. Government action and changes in law tend to follow widespread awareness among people (who are voters, after all) and react to mounting popular pressure for change. Even if the law is changed, popular attitudes still tend to lag behind, as many social workers know. One reported belief that seemed rooted in some black communities was that HIV/Aids could be cured by having sex with a young virgin.

It is not just the older generation whose attitudes are fixed in an ill-informed negative stereotype. There is clearly far to go when a 1999 survey of Orange Farm and Soweto youth found that 25 per cent of black boys aged between 12 and 22 said 'jack rolling' (gang rape) was 'fun' and 16 per cent thought it was 'cool'. Of girls of the same age interviewed, 43 per cent said sexual violence was very common.

CAN SOUTH AFRICA BEAT CRIME?

Crime exiles and returnees
Many people have voted with their feet. Emigrants leaving South Africa consistently cite crime and violence as the main reason for their departure. Yet it is known that 'crime exiles' often discover that their destination countries also suffer from unacceptable criminality. Figures are hard to come by, but anecdotal evidence suggests that significant numbers of emigrants do return to South Africa. Returnees tend to say they are prepared to take their chance with crime. They found they missed other lifestyle benefits and the climate of their home in South Africa.

Doing it for themselves
For most South Africans there is no opportunity to 'take the gap' or the 'chicken run', no opportunity to 'flee like cowards', as President Mandela famously said of well-heeled emigrants in 1998. South Africans who choose to stay or have no option in the matter will make a fist of it, and survive rampant crime in the same way they survived apartheid, colonialism, unemployment, failed harvests, hunger and a frontier society – by an attitude of *vasbyt* (literally, 'bite hard', meaning hold tight or hang in).

People in all communities and at all levels of wealth are starting to fight back, roused from their emotional apathy by the sheer scale and personal threat of violent crime and criminals literally getting away with murder.

- Sometimes the reactions go outside the law, towards **vigilante groups**, especially in the townships and countryside, with recurrences of kangaroo courts and instant sentences, sometimes of 'necklacing', the gruesome practice of killing someone by setting alight to a tyre around their neck.

- One well-supported if controversial anti-drugs and anti-crime group is **Pagad** (People Against Drugs and Gangsterism), founded in the Cape area in the late 1980s, by concerned, mainly Muslim community leaders. For all its detractors, Pagad has done much to publicise opposition to the crime wave.

- The **inventors** are also busy. Vehicle hijackers had better watch out if a car is fitted with the flame-throwing Blaster, which uses liquid gas ignited by a driver's pedal to scorch assailants (costs R3,900); or the Crime Blaster, which spews mustard gas from hidden jets in the dashboard (R1,200); or the Liquid Bullet, which sprays a cocktail of chili, pepper and mustard oil in an attacker's face (R2,223). All three have been declared not unlawful by the police.

- One person who has made an individual contribution is Pretoria computer boss **Christopher Riley**. His office was burgled twice in five months but Riley got nowhere in reporting stolen computer equipment to the police, despite giving them serial numbers. Even his community newspaper found his story 'unnewsworthy', and 'feeling powerless' Riley opened his own free **website** (www.crimestop.co.za). This links like-minded people across South Africa and is attracting attention overseas.

Government and business take the plunge

It is not that the government has done nothing to tackle the crime wave. However, it seems that it has not prioritised crime-fighting, anti-corruption and positive policing. It has failed to provide the massive injection of cash and resources needed to tackle the problem and is not seen to be active and caring, thus restoring the public's faith in its stewardship of law and order.

Central initiatives like the national crime prevention strategy (from 1996), legislating improvements in the criminal justice system (e.g. making bail less easy and automatic), weeding out corrupt officials, increasing criminal intelligence activities and forming new partnerships with the community (e.g. Business Against Crime, community police forums) are all being pursued.

Business Against Crime is active in Gauteng, where Soweto and Johannesburg are the worst crime spots, with measures to improve mobility of police (BMW donated many cars), open up new police stations and smaller satellite and mobile stations, assist with photocopiers, telephones and other equipment and support policies like employing street parking attendants from among the unemployed.

Given their nature, however, and fighting uphill against an inherited backlog of inefficiency and abuse, such virtuous plans will take time to show results. And immediate results are what the South African public wants and needs to see.

WHAT ABOUT GUNS?

South Africa had 3.76 million legally owned firearms in December 1997, according to the Department of Safety and Security, in the names of over two million people. Illegal firearms were thought to be in even greater numbers.

The SAPS is responsible for **gun control** and licence applications. In 1999 a stricter protocol of gun control was proposed in parliament and backed by the Cabinet. The government took the line that with the profile of gun-related crime and violence in the country, it was not possible to control illegal guns without at the same time increasing controls on legal guns and their owners. Research had shown that in the later 1990s most illegal guns were once privately owned weapons that were stolen or lost; state-owned guns were the next category and illegally imported weapons from Mozambique and other countries were the third group.

Under **new regulations**, which could become law in early 2000, gun owners would have to reapply for their licences, be restricted to one weapon each and have to pay a licence fee of R500 instead of the current R50. They would also have to undergo psychometric tests to determine their suitability to own guns.

Such radical measures were strongly opposed by interest groups, including hunters, gun and arms dealers, and sportsmen, but there is little doubt the general public would back any measure which reduced crime and the threat of violence. While some people argued that owning a gun is but one step away from vigilantism and mob justice, others took the 'American' view that gun ownership is a right, not a privilege. Here was an issue, like many others in South African life, that polarised public opinion, with middle ground hard to find.

As for whether you as an individual should own a gun, remember that there are proper channels for buying, licensing and practising with your weapon. Remember too that, while gun ownership might give you a feeling of increased safety and security, you would also become a higher-profile target.

HIV/AIDS

We said at the start of this chapter that the HIV/Aids syndrome poses the greatest single threat to South Africa's future, even more than crime. Why so? It is possible that crime, which has escalated in response to rapidly changing macroeconomic conditions, will decrease as the conditions themselves change. HIV/Aids, however, is spreading inexorably in southern Africa, leaving governments, civil society and individuals equally powerless to stem the tide.

Recognising the crisis

Aids workers say the plain fact is that South African people do not yet believe HIV/Aids is an epidemic. Why? Because they have not seen enough dead bodies. This is probably explained by the length of time it takes from contracting HIV to becoming a full-blown Aids sufferer. There is commonly said to be a seven-year window between the two stages, and HIV first became widespread in South Africa in about 1991–93. HIV sufferers, in many cases, are only becoming Aids victims as the millennium turns.

Many people who have HIV do not even know it, say the experts, and those who do often keep quiet. When HIV becomes Aids, people often get sick with illnesses like TB, malaria or pneumonia, and even doctors may fail to recognise the Aids element.

The numbers are staggering

Nobody who works in the health care sector has any doubts that the crisis is real and is now. The problem in South Africa is among the worst in the whole world.

- At a global level, at the end of 1998, 33 million people had HIV/Aids, and the figure is rising by 10 per cent a year. Half of those infected are in the 15–24 age group, and half of these are women.

- Over 83 per cent of Aids deaths are now in sub-Saharan Africa (and virtually nil now in the First World). In this sub-Saharan area one in seven infections is in southern Africa.

- It is said a quarter of South Africa's black population might die from Aids by the year 2010, and most of these will be men and women in the usually economically active age group of 18 to 30 years. The country's life expectancy figure has been dramatically downgraded in recent international social indicators.

- Already in 1997, 3 to 4 million people in South Africa were living with HIV/Aids. This was about 8 per cent of the total population.

- The figures are worse than the national average in some provinces, for example, KwaZulu-Natal (at 26 per cent). In one West Rand mining town, 50 per cent of women between 20 and 30 were already infected by the end of 1997.

- One in four South African pregnant women in mid-1999 was found to be HIV-positive; 34 per cent of children under the age of five admitted to the Chris Hani Baragwanath Hospital were HIV-positive; and 75 per cent of all child deaths under five were caused by HIV/Aids.

- 'At least' 20 per cent of the South African workforce would be infected by HIV/Aids by 2000, predicted the Department of Health in 1998.

- By 2003 there would be 590,000 Aids orphans, a figure which would grow to 1.6 million by 2008, said the Department of Social Welfare in 1998.

SOUTH AFRICA'S DEADLY SCOURGE

These are, again, mind-numbing figures. But why should South Africa have the fastest-growing HIV/Aids problem in the world? Sociologists point to the following possible reasons:

- South Africa is a uniquely unstable, stressed society in transition. In stable societies, the infection rate has been found to drop sharply and controls become effective.
- South Africa has undergone rapid urbanisation.
- Family life has been disrupted.
- Poverty is rife, with entrenched long-term unemployment.
- Traditional values and life skills are disintegrating.

Yet most of these reasons apply equally in other Third World societies undergoing rapid transformation. Is there another specific reason for South Africa to be afflicted by such a severe HIV/Aids problem?

Government drags its feet

The South African government does not have a proud record on HIV/Aids. In fact, it has played only a minor role in increasing public awareness and supplying cheap and cost-effective HIV/Aids treatment. Critics charge that it has been criminally negligent, and, given the severity of the problem, there is an argument that government inaction or inappropriate action has exacerbated South Africa's HIV/Aids problem.

- For example, in 1996 the Department of Health spent R14 million of public funds on an Aids play, *Sarafina 2*. After a public outcry the play was quickly withdrawn but the funds were not redistributed into HIV/Aids research. Dr Nkosazana Zuma, the minister, resisted all efforts to persuade her to resign, but the wrong message about state involvement in HIV/Aids had been sent, and the government had suffered a PR setback which still persists four years later.

- The same minister at least twice promoted the development of supposed anti-Aids drugs, without the normal testing protocols. When the independent medical research council opposed her policy, she disbanded the council. Again, false hope had been given to sufferers, the medical establishment had been alienated and a poor PR message had been sent out.

- By mid-1999 the government had not seen fit to authorise the drug AZT for HIV/Aids sufferers or rape victims. Compelling evidence had been presented by activists to show that mother-to-child transmission of HIV/Aids was reduced by a fairly cheap course of the drug in the last month of pregnancy. The government declared that AZT was too expensive, despite the counter-argument that costs of caring for sick and infected children were far greater.

- The HIV/Aids syndrome was not a notifiable disease at late 1999, which meant public health professionals still had no consistent recourse to rendering emergency treatment in hospitals or obtaining anti-HIV/Aids drugs; nor were there accurate national statistics.

- Although labour legislation had been passed to prevent discrimination in the workplace and elsewhere against HIV/Aids sufferers, many examples of discriminatory action were still being reported.

- While a poor neighbouring country like Uganda was able to control and even reduce its HIV/Aids statistics by constant public information campaigns about the epidemic and simple techniques to reduce its severity, such as basic health regimes and use of condoms, South Africa's government has been remarkably ineffective in following suit. The state's inertia, claim activists, is directly adding to the speed of the transmission of the HIV/Aids syndrome.

- South Africa was in a privileged position in that its HIV/Aids problem appeared much later than in neighbouring states, yet it took none of the pre-emptive measures Aids workers had been calling for from at least 1988. It was noted, on the other hand, that President Mbeki only made his first major Aids speech (as deputy president) in November 1998.

- The government has resisted calls to move beyond its feeble calls for 'use a condom' and 'reduce your number of partners' approach, which fail to meet realities on the ground.

- At the time of writing there was still no national HIV/Aids awareness policy in schools or in public broadcasting.

ECONOMIC PROGNOSIS OF SOUTH AFRICA'S HIV/AIDS EPIDEMIC

What are the likely effects on national life of this alarming situation? Here are some possible scenarios:

- **Close to a fifth of the country's economically active population was suffering from HIV/Aids at the turn of the millennium.** It is true that many HIV sufferers are fully active in the workplace and show no debilitation, but the trend to more full-blown Aids victims must impact on South Africa's productivity and gross national product generally. This will be a negative trend in a country that has been afflicted by weak productivity for many years.

- **The population pyramid as a whole will become skewed**, with a huge hole appearing in the economically active age group of both sexes (18 to 30 years), more Aids orphans and an increasingly older age group, which tends not to suffer from HIV/Aids and is getting healthier for a longer time. This may mean that older, well people will of necessity work longer and post-retirement, both to fill necessary management positions and to pay off their own hugely increased medical aid or retirement costs. It should mean that more skills will have to be imported from overseas, and especially the rest of Africa, but immigration policies would need much greater liberalisation for this to be possible.

- **Medical treatment will be dominated by HIV/Aids care**, with public hospital beds nearly exclusively devoted to the epidemic; most other medical treatment will go into the private sector, with cost implications for all wage-earners. The government focus on primary health care will be stretched to the limit.

- **Affirmative action as a government policy may not be practicable** if the HIV/Aids scenario does peak, as suggested by economic models, around 2005–10, a time when the government had hoped the economy would be largely black-run, yet the majority of victims of HIV/Aids are black.

- It is found that while larger corporations and companies often have an Aids policy and are proactive in addressing the problems of employees, **smaller businesses have often adopted a head-in-the-sand approach**, hoping the problem will disappear. Smaller business is particularly under threat from the epidemic, and the unemployed will be even worse off as the unions move to protect their members by Aids-related wage settlements.

- **Employee benefits will inevitably be hard hit**, as the epidemic moves from the HIV to the Aids phase. Aids is far more expensive in terms of medical or support treatment as the individual's health and ability to work sharply fall. Medical aid contributions must increase rapidly and death benefits may even disappear from employee rights.

A SMALL RAY OF HOPE

So the outlook on HIV/Aids in South Africa is grim, with the problem scarcely recognised by government and people in the street, and yet about to impact on the economic, social and personal life of every citizen.

Perhaps the only ray of hope is the energy and commitment of those **private sector non-government organisations** dedicated to raising awareness in the community and helping sufferers lead as normal a way of life as possible. Among such groups the following have been prominent: Aids Consortium, Aids Law Project, Centre for Applied Legal Studies at Wits University, National Association of People Living with HIV/Aids (Napwa), Metropolitan Life insurance group (which developed the first-ever life product for HIV/Aids sufferers), Aids Helpline and the National Women's Coalition. (Further details are given in the section on useful addresses.)

The South African public should support such initiatives, and above all put pressure on the central government to give priority to HIV/Aids as a national threat and potential disaster, and insist on a practical programme of action, with funding to make implementation effective.

10

Moving Around

Travelling around South Africa doesn't come much better than the scenario of driving in your convertible on a newly tarred toll road on a sunny day through the Drakensberg, or on a national road through the woods on the Garden Route. Or perhaps you are relaxing in the five-star luxury of the Blue Train on your way to the Victoria Falls.

On the other hand, you may be stuck behind a row of horn-tooting minibus taxis in the suburbs as the rain lashes Cape Town and the 'robots' are all out of action. You're trying to get to the airport, but you're going nowhere fast and your road rage is mounting.

Somewhere between the two is the reality of travelling around in modern South Africa.

THE TRANSPORT OPTIONS

Travel by road

Visitors to South Africa are often surprised by the quality and extent of the **road system**, the best by far in sub-Saharan Africa. There is a network of 84,000 km tarred national (prefixed by N), metropolitan (M) and regional (R) roads criss-crossing the country, some of them remarkable feats of engineering over difficult mountain or semi-desert terrain. These are backed up by a variety of untarred or 'dirt' roads in more inaccessible places, most of them perfectly adequate for normal vehicles. Off-road vehicles, which seem to be crowding the malls of the smart suburbs as well as the game parks, can of course create their own private highways as they go, often to the consternation of conservationists. The climate is ideal for motor bikes, scooters and pedal bikes, but, perhaps oddly, these are not found in great numbers, unlike in Europe or the USA.

Sadly, the road network, apart from the toll roads (T) added within the last 15 years or so, and which are maintained at a high level by private operators, is a declining resource. As traffic volumes increase, particularly of heavy trucks, the physical deterioration of even major highways is not being heeded. The government lacks the resources and seemingly the will to prioritise transport policy, and the backlog of necessary repairs is increasing all the time.

Still, compared to the rest of the continent, except the far north, South Africa's road network remains of a European standard. Note that:

- You do **not need additional travel permits** to drive anywhere on the roads of the new, post-homeland South Africa, apart from the obligatory car and driver's licence, as discussed below.

- You should remember to carry **cash for toll roads**, e.g. about R50 for the six-hour drive from Johannesburg to Durban (it's not easy to pay by cheque or credit card).

- Major highways and toll roads have frequent roadside **emergency telephones**, but, as we suggest elsewhere, carrying your own cellphone (mobile) is your best guarantee of getting help.

Travel by rail

Like the roads, the best of the South African rail network was laid down in colonial times, and it looks like not much has been changed since. Apart from the luxury Blue Train, which is upgraded periodically, and its rival Rovos Rail, the passenger rolling stock is generally ageing, dirty and unappealing.

Commuter services

Metrorail, a division of the state transport agency **Transnet**, is responsible for commuter rail services. Suburban and commuter rail traffic makes up the bulk of the rail system's volume, and, often unseen by the motor commuters, millions of people move to and from work daily on Metrorail's lines. The service is cheap as compared to car travel, though not as cost-effective as minibus taxis over short distances.

It is regarded as safe these days, though was decidedly risky in the 'struggle' period of the 1980s, with daily muggings and criminal activity. The shadow of those dangerous days still lingers over suburban rail commuting, and people who can afford or have access to other means of transport generally do so.

Long-distance services
Long-distance rail travel, operated by **Spoornet**, another part of Transnet, is an established tradition in southern Africa. It is also partly subsidised by government to keep fares down.

First and second class fares are available, with sleeper accommodation in both. Bedding is provided at a small extra charge: get a bedding ticket when making a reservation or on the train. Children under seven travel free, those under 12 get half-fare, and over-60s are given a 40 per cent discount.

The **cost** of long-distance rail compares well with other forms of public transport.

- Take a **journey from Johannesburg to Cape Town**. By Greyhound bus this costs about R250 single, while the train comes out at R360 for first class and R240 for second. In the cost-competitive air industry, by shopping around you could obtain a single ticket for the same route for as little as R500 on Nationwide (all costs as at early 1999). Driving in your own car, the 1,200-plus kilometres would cost well over R500 for the same journey, allowing for petrol and tolls, though you'd have the chance to stop off in the Karoo or detour by Kimberley, if that is to your taste.

- As for the **times** of these same journeys, the air trip takes about 2 hours (allow about an hour for travel to and from the airports at both ends); if you drive your own car, allow about 12–16 hours; the bus will take about 19 hours and the train a tardy 27 hours.

Travel by minibus taxi and metered taxi
When you say 'taxi' in South Africa, most people think at once of the minibus taxi commuter industry, though there is also the more universal metered variety.

Minibus taxis
The origins of the minibus or '**black taxi**', to use the familiar name, go back to apartheid, when the Group Areas Act and forced removals meant townships or ghettos of black, coloured and Indian people were deliberately set up, often in waste land far from city centres and places of work. This created a workforce of commuters, but the government provided no public transport facilities. Into the gap came the new form of taxi, particularly in the 1970s and later, when Japanese minibuses, built for 12 or 16 passengers (but often carrying well over 20), were first imported.

The system is expanding all the time, with many thousands of such taxis connecting short-haul commuters from home to work, as from Soweto to Johannesburg or Mitchells Plain to Cape Town, or much longer runs, say from Pretoria to Pietersburg or Durban to East London. For all its faults, it offers the cheapest, most market-related and frequent means of transport to a majority of black South Africans, either daily to work or back home to their families.

- Minibus taxis these days ply highly organised and competitive routes, with vehicles stopping for passengers on demand (and in practice often without warning). The routes taken are fixed, and passengers can only go where the taxi takes them.

- The fares are cheap (it costs about R5 from Johannesburg to Pretoria), and the journeys quick, sometimes even scary, in the drivers' pell-mell rush to complete as many out-and-back trips in a day as possible.

- Passengers signal for a taxi to stop by an intriguing medley of hand signs, most commonly a right index finger in the air, meaning 'to town'.

- Minibus taxis are by and large used by the black population, but many non-black students, young and some older people increasingly make use of them. A white colleague said she catches taxis if she needs a quick journey on a familiar route and she doesn't have her car.

The multimillion-rand taxi industry is nominally under Department of Transport regulation, with over a thousand distinct taxi associations registered. But the regulation is more a paper exercise than a reality on the ground, and the rich pickings have led to intermittent 'taxi wars' between rival associations operating on the most lucrative routes. These occasionally take the form of daylight shootings of drivers and sometimes passengers, at urban taxi ranks. Adding the latent violence to the often reckless driving and overloaded, poorly maintained vehicles lends the taxi industry an air of menace and danger which is at odds with its overall achievements in moving South Africans around with speed and efficiency.

Metered taxis
The metered taxi industry, by contrast, is not a flourishing sector.

Whether considering a fleet or small owner-operator, most of the cars are old, shoddy and poorly equipped.

Meter fares are high (it costs over R100 from Johannesburg International Airport to the city or Sandton, as against about R50 by airport bus or about R4 by minibus taxi), and it's often possible to bargain for prices off-meter. Hailing taxis on the streets is not the norm, and you are expected to book by phone (use the *Yellow Pages*). Don't hold your breath for exceptional or speedy service.

The industry putters on, and fills a small niche. New York or London, however, South African taxi services are not.

Travel by bus and coach

National services
There is a comprehensive national bus and coach service between South Africa's cities, offered by **private operators** such as Greyhound, Translux and Intercape. These services are generally fast, safe, reliable and reasonable in cost, with a fair degree of comfort, though the bus stations are often dilapidated and in central city locations. Bookings can be made up to a month ahead, and it's advisable to book at least a week in advance (as it is with the trains).

Local services
City and suburban bus services, by contrast, are generally poor, especially in Johannesburg (which must have one of the worst public transport systems of any large city in the world). Usually run by the municipality, these bus services focus on major routes and peak times for **commuters and schoolchildren**. Outside these times, say 6.30 to 8.30am and 2.00 to 3.00pm (for the schools) and 4.30 to 6.00pm (for commuters), you're pretty much on your own.

The buses are usually driver-only and they appreciate correct bus fares, though it's usually a battle to find a bus timetable or fare table even in larger bus stations. You can obtain weekly and monthly tickets, which give a reasonable discount.

Travel by air
South Africa has a state-owned airline, South African Airways, which was partially privatised in mid-1999 by the sale of a 30 per cent equity stake to Swissair, and a variety of smaller commercial airlines operating both passenger and freight services. The competition is intense, often to the benefit of the consumer, and shopping around through a travel agent is recommended. The main airlines are SAA,

BA Comair and Nationwide, with one of the newer private and empowerment lines, Sun Air, closing towards the end of 1999.

Air services connect the main cities and tourist locations, with aircraft ranging from big jumbos to older propeller-driven craft in the smaller centres. Most international airlines now operate to Johannesburg, with an increasing number to Cape Town too. Indeed, several airlines, including BA and Virgin, would like to operate extra flights direct to Cape Town from the UK, but their approaches for an additional flight licence are rebuffed at regular intervals by the Department of Civil Aviation, i.e. the government.

The Airports Company of South Africa is responsible for running most of the country's **airports**, and has embarked on an ambitious upgrading and expansion of facilities, especially at Johannesburg, Durban and Cape Town international airports. Partly in anticipation of and also as a contributor to the international tourist boom to South Africa, the improved service of the leading airports is also a boon to domestic travellers who long endured sloppy standards. However, until the building work at the major airports is completed, officially by 2001, travellers will have to be patient with provisional parking and check-in delays.

Durban, by the way, is considering moving its airport to a new site at La Mercy, north of the city, but such a move is some years away.

Travel by water
South Africa has little by way of water transport, with few canals and no tradition of river travel. Sea transport is more or less reserved for cargo, although an increasing number of luxury passenger cruise ships offer the Cape Town to Durban trip and other ports along the coast.

Travel by foot and hitch-hiking
It is often forgotten by the motorised traveller that in Third World and rural southern Africa most journeys are made by foot, whether to and from work or socially. There are a huge number of **pedestrians**, most of whom have had no education in road safety, and far too many are killed or injured on the roads each year. Drivers must stay alert for people rushing across even major roads without warning.

Hitch-hiking is officially forbidden on the national roads and motorways, but there is little supervision and you still come across people thumbing lifts. Strangely, there still appears to be a colour code in offering rides, with black people usually stopping for black hitch-hikers and white for white. In country areas, you are often expected to pay a small amount for a lift.

In an atmosphere of rampant crime, violence and hijacking, there's understandably much caution, both by drivers in offering lifts and by hikers in taking them. Travel in pairs rather than alone and be very circumspect. The best advice is to resort to hitch-hiking only if there's really no alternative.

OWNING AND DRIVING YOUR OWN CAR

Against a background of generally poor public transport, South Africa has a high proportion of private car owners. The country supports a highly competitive motor manufacturing industry and a large second-hand vehicle sector.

The competition in selling new cars works to the advantage of consumers, who can often negotiate extra discounts, particularly for cash deals, but it is likely the manufacturers will go through a period of mergers and rationalisation. The buyer has the choice of over a hundred models, most of them made locally.

The national 'vehicle park' is ageing all the time, and the age of an average vehicle is currently over 10 years. With rusting and corrosion prevalent only at the coast, it is not unusual to see 30-year-old Beetles or ancient American Chevrolets or Valiants on the highveld, still in good working order.

Buying a car

Most **new-car buying** is done through manufacturers' agents. Prices are listed regularly in the press (e.g. in *Motoring*, a Thursday supplement to *The Star* in Johannesburg). If you are a non-South African, you should take along your passport, work permit, driving licence (overseas and international driving permit), insurance certificate and bank-guaranteed cheque.

- An **international driving permit** can be obtained in your country of origin from a recognised organisation like the AA or RAC in Britain, and is valid for 36 months. Non-residents can also use their own national licences in South Africa, provided they carry two passport-size photographs with their signature.

Buying a **second-hand car** can be done through the classified pages of the newspapers, the increasing number of cheap all-advertisement papers, like *Junk Mail*, or through regular auction sales, a method that is becoming very popular. Reputable auctioneers advertise in the *Yellow Pages* and offer full service records and even warranties in some cases. Alternatively, online buying for used cars is now available to those with Internet access. The biggest second-hand sales operation is claimed by McCarthy Motors, using a toll-free phone number. Most towns have a street or area devoted to second-hand cars (e.g. Jules Street in Johannesburg). The Motor City franchise, with integrated services for purchase and repairs, is also found in most of the bigger centres.

- One term newcomers to South Africa should be aware of is '*voetstoots*' (Afrikaans for 'as it stands'), meaning a sale without a warranty or guarantee. It is equivalent to saying 'what you see is what you get'.

- South Africa has no annual vehicle test analogous to the British MoT, but at the point of sale for both new and second-hand vehicles there must be a **roadworthy certificate**, obtained from a certified motor trader. The roadworthy test covers very basic functions such as braking, steering, electrics and lights, plus general bodywork.

Licensing requirements

There are two separate steps to be taken before you can legally run a car in South Africa. You have to license the car and license yourself as a driver. In smaller centres the licensing department may be the same office for both functions, but in larger cities you could find yourself going to different places. Both are run by the municipality concerned.

- The **passenger car licence** currently costs R108, but more for trucks and lorries. You will obtain a motor vehicle licence and clearing certificate (MVL1) on payment of the fee. The document lists the vehicle details and supplies a round disc, which goes on the windscreen. It is valid for a year. Reminders are sent, provided your address details are current.

- The **driver's licence** (new-style with barcode) presently costs R75 and is valid for five years. In a two-stage process, you have to complete an eyesight test at the testing centre and give your fingerprints on a first visit. Some weeks later you are summoned back to the centre to collect the small, credit-card-sized document.

- **Older licences** remain valid, but the government is trying to effect a changeover to the new system by the early 2000s, at least in theory.

- For **new drivers,** getting a new licence is a matter of taking the learner's test, consisting of a written text on the highway code. A learner's is valid for 18 months and enables you to drive when accompanied by a licensed driver.

- The **driving test** or K53 is in three parts, done consecutively on the same day: a pre-trip inspection of the car, a yard test of driving skills and a road test.

- The law in South Africa states that licensed drivers must **carry their licence** with them at all times, although a notarised photocopy is also acceptable.

- **Driving schools** are listed in the *Yellow Pages* under 'Driving Instruction'. Cost is at least R75 for an hour, and instructors recommend at least six lessons for adequate coaching on passing the K53 test.

- Newcomers to South Africa can get copies of the *Highway Code* from most CNAs, along with useful illustrated **books** on the learner's and K53 tests, both of which contain pictures of the internationally compatible road signs in common use.

Help on the road

Membership of the **AA** is well worth taking out (current cost for one year is R284). Benefits include emergency rescue, travel, technical and roadworthy and legal services, along with travel information and free maps for members.

The AA supplies **international driving permits** for R28.50 to members or non-members. Take two small photographs and your licence along to an AA office, and the licence can be provided on the spot.

Some new cars come with **warning triangle** supplied, but it would be prudent to purchase one, at a supermarket or from an AA office, if your car lacks this useful aid.

On most motorways and national roads and toll roads there are free telephones by the highway every few kilometres, but carrying your own **cellphone** (mobile) remains the most reliable self-help tactic drivers can adopt. A word of caution, however: keep portable cellphones out of sight and not on the passenger seat, to deter would-be thieves.

Hiring a vehicle

All the leading international car hire services are represented in South Africa, at airports, ports and some of the larger railway stations and hotels. The usual minimum age for hiring is 21. Tariffs vary widely and a kilometre charge is levied.

You can also hire caravans, campers and 4 × 4s at some outlets. Note that Hertz is incorporated into Imperial in South Africa.

RULES OF THE ROAD

With thousands of kilometres of wide-open and still mainly good roads and a generally sunny climate, you might expect South Africa to be a driving Nirvana. Yet the country has a notoriously **bad accident record**, with between 8,000 and 10,000 road fatalities a year over the past few years. Many of these deaths are caused by or involve pedestrians, as mentioned above. The figure is slowly falling, but only marginally, despite more visible safety campaigns by the government. The Christmas (i.e. summer) holiday period is particularly dangerous, with around a thousand people, often whole families, perishing from mid-December, when most offices, factories and schools close down, to early January.

The cause of the roads carnage is partly inadequately tested vehicles; partly it is lack of highway patrols and a police presence on the roads; and partly it must be the sheer **bad driving habits** of many South Africans. Many drivers, often among the minibus taxis, are unlicensed or buy forged licences, and drive as though they have never heard of the highway code or road rules. Even if you have lived in South Africa for many years, it pays to drive defensively.

● One of the worst problems is **flouting of lane discipline**. South Africans drive on the left, as in the UK or Australia, and expect to give way to the right (though at four-way stops it's usually the car which arrives first which crosses first). However, whereas in the UK, say, on a three-lane highway the outside lane is for overtaking, the middle one for quicker drivers and the inside for slow traffic and trucks, on South Africa's roads the rule is 'go for the gap'. Frequently drivers move abruptly into another lane without signalling; and minibus taxis are renowned for stopping without warning, as passengers ask to alight. Even more than in the UK, in South Africa **you must keep looking in your rear-view mirror**.

- Another problem is **speeding**. The general speed limits are 120 kph (74 mph) on motorways, 100 kph (62 mph) on rural roads and 60 kph (37 mph) in built-up areas. These tend to be used as lower limits rather than higher by many drivers. The municipal traffic departments appear to focus most of their efforts on speeding, rather than on enforcing good driving habits, but even so the great length of the national highway system, prevalence of powerful cars, the large numbers of vehicles and small numbers of patrol officers mean the problem is always running out of control, with pitifully few convictions.

- Watch out for the so-called '**traffic-calming**' zones in cities, which often seem to have the opposite effect. Ditto with the many '**mini-circles**' in built up areas. Both are poorly indicated, and if you are not vigilant your suspension can suffer a nasty accident as you speed over these 'bumps'.

- Many accidents are caused at **traffic lights**, known throughout South Africa as 'robots'. The sequence is red-green-amber-red, but many drivers seem to ignore the meanings of the lights and accelerate to beat them.

- **Zebra crossings** do exist in many cities, but are rarely observed by drivers. The only such crossing, for example, in Johannesburg which ever seems to command respect is at the Rosebank Mall where shopping centres on both sides of the road emit a constant stream of shoppers who by force of numbers stop the cars.

- A further annoyance and a dangerous practice is **tail-gating**, or driving too close to vehicles ahead as a tactic to persuade them to pull over. It is illegal, but nobody ever seems to be prosecuted for the offence.

- Another alarming problem is **drink and drive** accidents. There is a breathalyser system in place but it is barely enforced and operates on a minute scale. The process of driver education is rudimentary and even though some beer companies do promote anti-drink and drive campaigns over Christmas, their efforts are unrewarded, as far as reducing the scale of accidents caused by excessive drinking is concerned.

- **Seat belts** are nominally compulsory, for driver and front-seat passenger, but again there is a huge gap between the law and its enforcement. Children in the lap are supposed to be carried on back seats, but there is as yet no compulsion for rear-seat belts to be worn.

OTHER ASPECTS OF DRIVING

Reporting an accident

There is an obligation to report automobile accidents to the police, within three days or so of occurrence. Your goal in reporting an incident, however, is less to get some sort of legal case going and press for judgment than it is to obtain a **police case number**. Without a case number you have no hope of interesting your insurance company in the accident, even if you have taken out comprehensive insurance. With it, the legal process of seeking recourse can get under way, even if you only have third party insurance.

Fuel

Newer cars run on unleaded petrol (91 octane inland, about 95 at the coast), which is 4c or 5c cheaper per litre than leaded (93 octane inland). Diesel is cheaper still. Relative costs at the time of writing are diesel R2.50 a litre, unleaded R2.60 and leaded R2.65.

- Note that leaded fuel will be available in South Africa after 1 January 2000, unlike the UK, which moved to an unleaded-only regime at that date.

Petrol stations on motorways are open 24 hours a day, but in cities and smaller places you may find opening times from 6am to 6pm only, with Sunday closing. Increasingly, shops at petrol stations offer daily necessities, like milk and bread, as well as the usual sweets, cigarettes and newspapers.

It is actually a pleasure of driving in South Africa to fill up at a good service station. There is a large and helpful population of male and female petrol attendants, who will routinely clean your windscreen as they fill your tank. They will generally offer to check oil and water and tyre pressure too. A normal tip is about 50c up to a rand for special service.

Hijacking and car theft

Hijacking and theft are a national menace. Police figures for 1997, the most recent data to hand, indicate about 100,000 reported cases of car theft; of these nearly 13,000 were hijackings. Over half of thefts and hijackings occurred in Gauteng. Against such alarming figures, the private car owner has to be defensive:

- Keep briefcases or handbags off the front seat (in fact, driving with all valuables in the boot is recommended).

- Do not open windows in built-up areas, even on hot days, to avoid snatch thieves.

- Fit a gear lock or manual steering lock (e.g. Gorilla).

- You may even decide to go to the expense of fitting a global positioning satellite system (e.g. Tracker) for vehicle recovery.

Special care is needed in city centres and at night. Parking is a time of vulnerability, and drivers are at risk as they leave or return home and halt to allow electric gates to open or close.

Police advice for hijacking protocol is to be very compliant and hand over anything the assailants demand. If you are a gun carrier, make no effort to shoot back. Although there are instances reported in the press where a driver has shot his attackers and survived, many more people have been killed precisely for their guns.

Residents and new immigrants alike must learn to live with the ever-present risk of hijack or theft while driving. It makes little difference whether you own a BMW or minibus (favourite targets), or an old banger, because there could always be someone who has nothing and is prepared to do anything to take what is yours.

The circle of supply and demand is as yet unbroken: given the poor public transport system, especially in Johannesburg, driving your own car in urban (and rural) South Africa is unavoidable; but given the profitability and relative impunity of car crime there will be syndicates and individual criminals who keep up the supply of stolen vehicles.

How will the circle be broken? Far more than an isolated and individual response, meaningful change requires two forces to come together: police action at all levels in catching the car criminals and achieving successful prosecutions, and the public saying enough is enough.

11

Making the Most of Your Free Time

If you have read this book from the beginning to here, nearly at the end, you may still be saying 'but where is the real South Africa?' You mean you didn't find it in the chapters covering *braais* and shopping, or even minibus taxis and crime? Well, this is your last chance. We're going to look at leisure rather than work, boiling these down to sport and wildlife, rugby and the Kruger Park, hobbies, the arts, and a bit on holidays and tourism. Perhaps the true spirit of South Africa is to be found in what South Africans do in their spare time?

A SPORTING OBSESSION

Rugby

Although it is not the nation's most popular sport (try soccer), rugby is what most people in the wider world associates with South Africa. The game's crowning moment was the **1995 Rugby World Cup,** held in South Africa for the first time, which the Springboks won at Ellis Park, Johannesburg. Joel Stransky's last-minute drop kick put paid to the All Blacks, who were better on the day but somehow could not match the passion or the sheer need of the Springboks to win.

If that kick was the crowning moment, the defining moment came a few minutes later at the celebrations on the pitch. President Nelson Mandela, in a masterpiece of PR (which he apparently orchestrated himself), donned a number 6 green and gold jersey, and hoisted the cup alongside the captain, François Pienaar, the winning team's number 6. Pienaar caught the mood exactly when he said the outcome wasn't a victory for the 65,000 wildly cheering spectators in the stadium but a win for all 43 million South Africans.

If you want a moment when white South Africa, in one of its most hallowed places of sporting worship, grew to love its Madiba, and when he in turn instinctively knew how to rebuild a million old and broken bridges between black and white, here it was. The nation went mad, and it was the 1994 election days all over again, as a strong and warm surge of national pride flowed around the country.

Black and coloured players
Despite impressions, rugby never had been an exclusively white or Afrikaner game. The Eastern Cape, for instance, has a century-old rugby tradition, in schools and clubs, of mixed players and supporters. However, few of the players from the area made it to the provincial team or into the Springboks. Even now, at the start of the new millennium, there have only ever been a handful of black Springboks – probably fewer than a 15-man rugby team.

Something happened in 1995 to bring rugby into the national, rather than merely the white, consciousness, and that meant over and above success or failure on the field the game was now on the political agenda. Change has been thrust on South African rugby, as on all national institutions and cultures (and surely this is both). The question of quotas of 'players of colour', or affirmative action in sport, became more insistent as the Springboks rebuilt in 1999, prior to the World Cup in Wales.

Sports administrators found it easy to talk of the necessity of having at least two or three black players in all teams, from school level to the Boks. The Bok coach, Nick Mallett, got into deep water for defying this sentiment by saying the national team must be chosen exclusively on merit. The black players in his squad came out behind Mallett, agreeing that merit was the only criterion they would recognise. The question became a fascinating microcosm of the bigger issues of national transformation and affirmative action.

Meanwhile, at school, club and provincial level the game expanded, and the Currie Cup (July to September), Vodacom Cup (February to May), Super 12 (also February to May) received more sponsorship, TV exposure and bigger gates in 1999 than ever.

Then, printed in a story tucked away on the sports pages in early August 1999 was a sign of hope that while the national team was enduring a series of crises both on and off the field prior to the World Cup, the under-21s were on top of the world. The 'Baby Boks' won an eight-team contest in Argentina, beating New Zealand in the final, as if to echo François Pienaar's team in 1995. And the under-21s had at least six black or coloured members in the squad on merit.

Soccer
The national game is surely soccer. Bafana Bafana, the national

team, became African champions, winning the African Nations Cup in 1996, to scenes of noisy celebration at the FNB stadium, near Soweto – even noisier, more colourful and equally as passionate as those a year earlier down the road at Ellis Park. And, yes, President Mandela was also there, taking the opportunity to do a bit more 'nation-building', as he always termed it.

Top clubs like Kaiser Chiefs, Orlando Pirates, Mamelodi Sundowns and Manning Rangers are known far beyond South Africa's borders. Elite teams in the 18-club PSL, the country's top league, command a fervent following, with regular crowds of 50,000 and more (with white supporters increasingly going to matches), and weekly TV broadcasts of top games.

The big soccer issue as 2000 approached was the bid by South Africa to host the **2006 Soccer World Cup**. The winning bid would be known in March 2000, and South Africa was well in the running, with Fifa, the world body controlling soccer, openly saying it was Africa's turn to host the cup. Consultants Kessel Feinstein estimated that should the World Cup come to South Africa it would mean some R30 billion being pumped into the economy, 2 per cent coming off the unemployment rate and 2 per cent added to gross domestic product (GDP). The sports tourism industry, which already comprised about 1.9 per cent of GDP, would escalate.

The chief executive of the 2006 bid company, Danny Jordaan, had an interesting angle in an early 1999 interview when asked the obvious question about South Africa's terrible crime record. He said three-fifths of the crime was confined to specific locations, like squatter camps and townships, where it posed no threat to foreign visitors. Take these away, and South Africa's crime figures were no worse than in other candidate countries like England, Brazil and Germany. Whether such an approach would convince the world soccer authorities in favour of South Africa would be known as this book was printed.

Cricket

The South African eleven, called by a new bland name of the 'Proteas' but still popularly known as the Springboks, has had a magnificent few years in the 1990s as a one-day outfit and to some extent as a test team. Although it has stumbled in knock-out competitions, such as the 1999 World Cup in England, when it lost bizarrely in the tied semi-final to eventual champions Australia, the team has earned its reputation for disciplined effort and all-round fighting spirit. Jonty Rhodes, Alan Donald and Hansie Cronje are world-famous names in the sport, matching giants of the past like Barry Richards and Graeme Pollock.

The profile of the game in national life has been high, with considerable developmental work to take cricket to a grass roots level. Initiatives like Baker's mini-cricket and action cricket (a streamlined game played in gyms), deep-pocketed sponsorship of the provincial game and massive TV coverage have stimulated new audiences, including many women and children, to attend games and say, in the words of the cricket anthem, 'we don't like cricket, we love it!'

At the same time as huge and painstaking efforts are being made to broaden the game's support structure, like rugby, cricket has experienced difficulties in the wider cultural and political spheres as the pace of transformation is criticised as too slow and not apparent at the highest levels.

- South Africans are passionate about their teams, in whatever sport, and it's perhaps not cynical to observe that as long as the team is winning, these broader and more reflective matters are put on the back burner, lost in the emotion of winning. By the same token, when the team starts losing, the captain and coach come under the whip and the game is branded as suspect – because the teams are not representative enough, and deserve to fail, or simply because the coach or manager have 'lost it'.

- It's a tension that exists throughout South African society in transition, and many players and administrators do fall victim to top-level pressures which may have little to do with the sport as sport. The experience is not new, but magnified as the monetary rewards get bigger and the newsworthiness of sport increases.

Golf

Bobby Locke and Gary Player between them put South African golf on the map, a tradition which Ernie Els and others are continuing in the present day. There are many magnificent golf courses, all around the country, with a summer professional golf circuit.

Among the well-known **tournaments** are the Million Dollar Challenge in Sun City in December (16 invited world-class players), the Alfred Dunhill PGA Championship at Houghton in January, the SA Open, Players' Championship and SA Masters in January and February (rotating venues). All receive extensive TV coverage.

Golf is both a sport and a place to do business, in South Africa as everywhere else. Club memberships tend to be in the R2,000 to R5,000 bracket, with green and caddy fees on top. It's not expensive by, say, Japanese standards, and you will often see business executives golfers on the golf course or driving range mid-week, enjoying the good weather and well-constructed kikuyu grass courses, as they talk over new deals in their foursome.

There are more and more non-white players on the courses, as membership exclusions have been dropped and as more black role models among the players appear on TV golf. Tiger Woods, not surprisingly, is a firm favourite when he visits to play in the Million Dollar. A local player to watch is Soweto's Bafana Hlophe.

Athletics

South Africa was well enough developed in athletics infrastructure to host the All-Africa Games in September 1999 (Johannesburg) and in 1998 the World Cross-Country Championships (Stellenbosch), as well as other international athletics meetings.

World sprint champions like Marion Jones have discovered Johannesburg as a training venue, where the altitude, good weather and cheap rand combine to make an ideal camp in the US winter, along with meetings like the ABSA series in January and February, and Engen grand prix in March.

South Africa has a healthy athletics tradition, with as always a few superstars leading the way, like Zola Budd (Pieterse), Elana Meyer, and a clutch of under-2 hours 8 minutes black marathon runners, led by Gert Thys who in 1999 recorded the third-fastest marathon to date (2 hours 6 minutes and a few seconds). The first black South African to bring home an Olympic gold medal was Josiah Thugwane, who won a close Olympic men's marathon in 1996.

Field events are making a comeback, including the javelin, high jump, hurdles and shot put, where the country has had international winners in recent times.

Road running

Even more characteristically South African is road running. The years of sporting isolation, along with more TV coverage and approachable local stars like Bruce Fordyce and Alan Robb, made the **Comrades** ultramarathon from the late 1970s a national sporting spectacle unequalled anywhere else.

The Comrades is held on 16 June, Youth Day, and is run on the road between Durban and Pietermaritzburg, a distance of around 88 km. The 'up' run is to Pietermaritzburg and the 'down' to Durban, but whichever way the race goes there are formidable hills through the KwaZulu-Natal midlands. The winner will come in in about 5½ hours, the top 10 men and women earn a gold medal (real gold), all finishers under 7½ hours get a silver medal and finishers before the 11-hour cut-off receive a bronze medal. While most competitors are South African, an increasing number of foreign runners, male and female, take part in what is an unofficial world championship of ultramarathon running.

What is amazing is the number of people competing: over 13,000 runners enter the race, and over 85 per cent of them finish in time. The event is screened live on SABC for many hours between the 6am start and 5pm finish, and it is a national talking point. Up to a million spectators and well-wishers line the route, and many volunteer to stand at water points to hand the runners water, Coca-Cola, potatoes, bananas and other sustenance.

Another internationally acclaimed road race is the **Two Oceans** race, held on Easter Saturday in Cape Town. The 56 km route includes some of the most scenic hills and roads of the Cape Peninsula and the race is superbly organised.

Otherwise each province has regular weekly races at distances from 5 km to 100 miles. Sporting clubs nearly all have running sections, and road running remains a popular pastime in all age groups and areas.

Cycling
Cycling also has its fanatical followers, and here the **Argus** 110 km race in Cape Town in March deserves a mention. This race attracts upwards of 30,000 cyclists a year, from the élite riders who finish the course in three hours or so to recreational riders who might take eight. The **Highveld** 94.7 km race around Johannesburg later in the year also draws in thousands of keen riders.

In both races the organisation is superb and, as with Comrades and the Two Oceans, the inspiring thing is the number of ordinary people who take part, do their best, enjoy the challenge and have no thought of monetary gain. If it is the professionals who attract the TV sponsorship and compete for big money, it is the run-of-the-mill competitors and supporters who give these events their backbone and spirit.

Canoeing
Canoeing is much the same as running and cycling in attracting all-

comers. The big race each year is the Duzi, held in late January over three days, in KwaZulu-Natal along the Umzimduzi river. Whether one-man canoe or two, the skill of this endurance race is knowing when to paddle and when to port (run with the canoe on your head – yes, it's true!). Even such a challenge attracts hundreds of competitors, and from Christmas onwards every dam (lake) in the country has its Duzi trainers. Seeing cars with a roof rack for a lightweight canoe is second nature in Johannesburg at this time of year.

Endurance events
These include duathlon and triathlon events (various combinations of canoeing or swimming, cycling and running), the Midmar Mile swim (which also pulls in thousands of competitors) and walking races (like the Big Walk and Gandhi Memorial events).

Other sports
Our overview of sporting South Africa would not be complete without mention of:

- **aerial sports** (most of the country is ideal for hang gliding, gliding, light aircraft, hot air ballooning and the like)
- **basketball** (a new but rapidly growing sport, in both conventional and wheelchair forms)
- **bowls** (in which South Africa has a number of world champions)
- **boxing** (ditto)
- **horse racing** (the big event each year is the Rothmans July, held on the first Saturday of the month at Greyville, Durban)
- **martial arts** (high standards have been achieved, with a number of world champions)
- **polo**
- **sailing**
- **squash** (many gyms have attached courts, and it remains a popular sport for the energetic)
- **surfing** (the Gunston 500 in Durban is on the world surfing calendar, as is Jeffrey's Bay in the Cape)
- **swimming** (the role model is Penny Heyns, a double Olympic gold medallist at Atlanta in 1996 and breaker of three world records in one week in July 1999)
- **tennis** (not as high profile as formerly, but in Amanda Coetzer the country has a regular top 10 female player)
- **10 pin bowling**
- **volleyball**.

We should not forget here South Africa's only claim to originating a sporting activity, namely **jukskei**. Deriving from a recreation of the Voortrekkers, the modern game consists of throwing pegs (or 'skey') at a stake planted in a sand pit from a set distance. Truth to say, it is a minority sport even in its own country, and rarely receives TV or newspaper coverage.

In **motor sport** there is a South African motor cycling grand prix (in Welkom in October) but the Formula One car grand prix has yet to return to Kyalami, in Midrand, where it was a regular item on the race calendar in the 1980s. AA Kyalami is used most weekends for saloon, sports and other formula car races. Go-karting has its adherents around the country, as does drag racing.

AN OBSESSION WITH FITNESS

Health clubs

Coming back to indoor pursuits, we should note the trends in training in gyms. In fact, there aren't many private gyms left, and you now go to a health club. The big name is the **Health & Racquet Club**, which has dozens of clubs around South Africa, and a few overseas, in the UK and Germany, for example.

The **Old Edwardians Club** in Johannesburg is the largest in the group, and its membership in 1999 was a staggering 38,000. This figure includes dependants, and members with reciprocal status at several clubs. The active membership at Old Eds is put at 15,000, with a daily access of about a quarter of that total. That's a lot of people at peak times (before work and early evenings), with classes like aerobics and spinning often overflowing. Old-fashioned body-builders vie for equipment with weight-conscious twentysomethings of both sexes, and there are always people in the swimming pool and on the squash courts. Personal trainers are on hand for those people who want one-to-one guidance.

Membership of these health clubs is open to all, and you find a cross-section of South African languages and backgrounds. Big money is involved all right: the Sandton Health & Racquet club (35,000 members) was renovated at a cost of some R12 million in late 1999.

It has been over a decade since the Health & Racquet group began its expansion, buying up older gyms and constructing purpose-built and fully equipped sports centres, and each year the end of the bubble has been predicted. However, by careful siting of the facilities and controlled management, the group has confounded its critics and gone from strength to strength. The group is part of the JSE-listed company LeisureNet.

The South African man and woman in the street clearly wants to get into shape in a gym, as well as take part in organised sport, and there's no reason to think the fitness trend will disappear soon. Turn on the TV before work in the mornings and you'll see how South Africa chooses to start the day: with magazine programmes and fitness demonstrations.

Sporting clubs

Sporting clubs, by contrast, have been around for ages – even a young city like Johannesburg, which began life in about 1884, has a number of centenarians, such as the Wanderers and Pirates clubs. Big towns have a multiplicity of such clubs and most small towns have one.

Hosting sections including bowls, soccer, rugby, cricket, running and squash, among others. These clubs are a vital sporting link for the enthusiast used to good facilities in school (and in former days the armed forces) who wants to continue with a favourite sport, at a competitive or more social level.

Frequently struggling to make ends meet, these clubs were as recently as early 1999 threatened by local government with paying replacement value rentals to the councils. Located in some of the older and more desirable areas, many hallowed clubs would have no chance to pay the sort of market-related rentals their areas now command, and it seemed for a while that a tradition of South African life would disappear, leaving a huge hole in its sporting infrastructure. However, furious reaction from club officials and members seemed to do the trick, and the government put the proposal on ice, although the threat remains.

INDULGING A NEED TO GAMBLE

It may not be sport or health, but South Africans do love to have a flutter now and then. In apartheid days, the Transvaal-based gambler would go to **Sun City**, because it was in Bophutatswana, which, so the pretence went, was an independent state and could license forms of entertainment, including gambling, which were not allowed in good, moral South Africa. Other gambling destinations were the Transkei, Swaziland and Mozambique, the latter until the civil war began in 1974.

Of course, **betting on the horses** took place whether it was legal or not, but dog racing has never really caught on. Nowadays the Tote is online, or available for telephone bets, and there is on-course betting at the dozen or so horse racing venues around the country.

If going to the races is not the drawcard it once was, a great many ordinary people do visit **gaming complexes** and play the one-armed bandits or try their luck in the casino.

Government control and legislation

The new South Africa has approached the gambling question thoroughly and systematically, recognising the need to balance the financial benefits to the investment groups involved with the interests of communities where casinos are to be sited. Issues of job creation, empowerment, tax revenue for the government, crime and security have been debated at length, along with the morality of gambling in the first place.

The **National Gambling Act** was passed in 1996, coming into effect in 1997, and gaming complexes were selected from many bidders by a national panel. Each province was allocated a number of casino licences (Gauteng, for example, had six), and temporary facilities began opening about the end of 1998. One result of the new Act was the closure of many hundreds of illegal back-street casinos across the country, which emerged from nowhere as the liberalisation of gambling law was being debated.

As the new millennium came in, the country had a well-organised and seemingly crime-free gambling industry, with new, well-designed and secure complexes opening up. On larger or smaller scale, they all offer non-stop gambling with big cash prizes (there are frequent million-rand jackpots at some casinos), restaurants and fast food outlets, movies, live entertainment, hotels and in some cases conference centres.

The lottery

In mid-1999 a **national lottery operator** was appointed, the winning group being Uthingo Management Services, a black empowerment consortium. Uthingo had as one partner the Camelot Group, which had raised over R60 billion for charities in the UK in four years. The lottery itself is due to begin in March 2000.

Annual sales for the SA lottery are projected at R6 billion, with over 20,000 new jobs created and R100 million donated to charities in the lottery's first year.

ENJOYING THE ARTS AND MUSIC

Arts for the majority

The arts have an established if precarious place in national life. Why precarious? Because there is little state money to be had, few resources and scant sponsorship to support live theatre, say, or museums and libraries in smaller towns or townships.

There's more than money involved here. The cultural institutions for the arts are often derived from the old South Africa and reflect a dated, imperialist, pro-white time which has little relevance in the new South Africa. As in health, education, housing, welfare and other aspects of social life, there has been a radical change in policy and philosophy since the early 1990s.

The relevant ministry, the Department of Arts, Culture, Science and Technology, openly states its priority as promoting historically 'disadvantaged' forms of art and culture and making these accessible to as many South Africans as possible. The available finance will thus be allocated primarily towards community-based arts projects and hardly at all to the older cultural institutions and 'classical' art forms, such as the performing arts and orchestras.

Looking for sponsors

The result has been consternation among the old-style institutions and the enforced need to find commercial sources of support, often in association with the private sector. **Business Arts South Africa**, founded in 1997, is one such initiative, stating its aim as developing partnerships between the two sectors, with advisory support and sponsorships; over 80 such partnerships were active in late 1999. The group also planned to lobby the tax authorities for help in recognising arts as a legitimate marketing expense, but nothing more had been heard of this worthy plan by the time of publication.

Major companies these days do have social responsibility programmes as part of their annual budgets, and when money is not being put into education or housing benefits for staff, it is often directed into sporting sponsorship. The arts may not rate highly as a revenue producer, but some companies do take the long view and maintain cultural programmes extending over many years.

An outstanding festival

One such programme, which has been running for over 25 years, is the **Standard Bank National Arts Festival**, held each July for two weeks in Grahamstown. The range of events is huge, with a mainstream and a fringe festival, including drama, dance, jazz, comedy, ballet, classical music, rave and pop, and one of the most popular flea markets in the country. The whole town is taken over by the festival and every spare room used for either accommodation or performances.

The festival is big and bold and brave, but makes little monetary return for the sponsor. Although the performances and venues are completely mixed, and have been so from the 'bad old days', the festival organisers are still accused of being Eurocentric in their programming. It is another case of a continuing tension between what is financially viable and culturally desirable for a range of involved parties.

Other festivals of note include the **Klein Karoo National Arts Festival**, an annual, mainly Afrikaans event; the **Johannesburg Biennale** (running for three months every two years); and pop/rock festivals at **Rustler's Valley** in the Free State over the Easter weekend and at **Oppikoppi**, north of Pretoria, for four days in August.

How an orchestra survived

One cultural institution, the **National Symphony Orchestra**, had survived, at least at the time of writing, the loss of its R15 million annual subsidy by the SABC, in 1997. In 1998 it became a section 21 (i.e. 'not for gain') organisation.

By making its plight public and inviting support and identification from the ordinary citizen as well as business sponsors, by going into the townships and offering free concerts at places where nothing could be afforded, the NSO won its reprieve. In the process it created a new following among music lovers who would never think of going to a symphony concert in the conventional sense.

Perhaps the NSO solution offers a model of the way ahead for other cash-strapped and officially unsupported cultural institutions if they are to survive in the new South Africa. Clearly, the days of Johannesburg spending R130 million on building its Civic Theatre in the 1990s and the State Theatre in Pretoria commanding unlimited funds from its political masters in earlier decades are past.

The artistic struggle continues

Even world-famous theatres that came through the apartheid era, like the Market Theatre in Johannesburg and the Baxter Theatre and The Nico in Cape Town, remain in struggle mode. This time, however, it is not so much the political content of the plays as the declining box office that constitutes the challenge. Reduced to essentials, in a market-related environment, if there is a demand for a theatre, a music festival, a ballet, an opera or a rock concert, there will be a supplier.

There is no dearth of local artists, whether it is the Soweto String Quartet and kwaito stars TKZee, or Mimi Coertze and Just Jinger – not to mention the international stars who visit the country, from the Three Tenors to Roberta Flack. We should perhaps celebrate the diversity and opportunity for such artists to perform rather than bemoan the passing of what cannot be seen as other than minority art forms.

A lively youth culture
Let us close this section by referring to the booming youth entertainment industry. Youths in South Africa do seem to have more disposable income than before, and they do not hesitate to spend on clothes, music, clubbing and 'hanging out', just like their peers in the north.

Radio stations, youth magazines, clubs, clothes and shoe manufacturers feed this growing market. If youth, both black and white, choose to wear Nikes, Tommy Hilfiger, Kangol and Polo (at the risk of these names seeming passé by the time we go to print), and to speak in fake American accents, and if they decided en masse that voting in the 1999 elections was not for them, there's nothing the adult world can do about it.

Rave, comedy and night clubs come and go, and if you want to know who is hot, better ask a teenager and follow their advice. Most towns have an active social scene for the young (and for gays and lesbians if we want to identify another subculture). If all else fails, there's always the mall or the McDonald's to be seen in.

HOBBIES AND NON-SPORTING LEISURE
Making contact and networking
The interesting thing about South Africa is that if you look hard enough and make an initial contact you can always find somebody or a group of people who do what you do. This applies whether it's a minority religion, an unusual martial art or anything else from amateur dramatics to zen meditation. They are all in the country somewhere.

We don't have the space to look at individual leisure activities, and you might anyway enjoy the challenge of finding fellow enthusiasts for yourself. But we can at least look at a couple of popular leisure activities – choosing gardening and bird watching – and offer some general ideas on how to make contact with the peer group of your choice.

- If the number is in the *Yellow Pages*, you can call **INFO** at 10 11 8 from anywhere in the country. The service applies to business numbers especially but is always worth a try for other numbers.

- **Cafés** (in the South African sense of corner shops) sometimes have notice-boards for small advertisements, and the café owner knows the neighbourhood – so ask him! Some places have Internet cafés. The same goes for smaller post offices.

- The big **newspapers** all have leisure sections, and the Friday editions cover weekend activities, events and the arts pretty well. You can often find things in the **classified** advertisements section, and there are magazines like *Junk Mail* which consist only of advertisements.

- *Hello Johannesburg, Cape Town* and *Durban* are monthly publications which list mainly leisure events, and other magazines, for example, *SA Citylife*, which is subtitled 'South Africa's entertainment and information guide', go some way to filling the need for a local version of *Time Out*, the magazine guide that makes living in London so much easier.

However, the real task is to get into the right network. If you have a child at school, you have a good channel to other parents and all their networks. The same goes for colleagues at work, in the country club, at the health club, church or temple, the *braai* or sports bar and other social meeting places. There is no single hey presto! website which will connect you to the group you want to join, but you will find South Africans by and large friendly and open if you want them to help by introducing you into their network. As we say in other chapters too, make your breakthrough contact and a world opens up.

Let's turn to a hobby, or for some people a passion, you can do alone or with others, in a flat, on a plot in the country or in suburbia. Along with fishing or soccer it has a claim to being the country's most popular leisure activity. And there is an economic twist to the story too.

Digging in for a long stay

Gardening is a quieter pastime than some we discuss, but it has never been as widespread. The country is blessed with a variety of climates and soils, and a huge number of native species of plants and trees. It is hardly surprising that it has a long history of exporting plants to the rest of the world, and winning prizes almost routinely at the Chelsea Flower Show.

- If you want ideas for your own garden, patio or even balcony, try one of the many garden centres in both city and countryside, or visit the botanical gardens such as those in Pretoria, Johannes-burg (actually in Roodepoort) and Durban, and the head-quarters of the National Botanical Institute at the world-famous Kirstenbosch in Cape Town.

- *SA Gardening* (circulation 31,000 at December 1998) is an excellent glossy monthly magazine for the would-be gardener; a subscription makes a lovely gift to friends or families overseas. Ditto its competitor, *SA Garden & Home* (90,000), and the related homes and gardens magazines, like *SA Garden and Home*, *Condé Nast House and Garden South Africa* and *SA Home Owner*.

One interesting development being discussed at Kirstenbosch is collecting and hybridising local species for international sale, and an agreement was signed with a US company in 1999 to start the process. The Kirstenbosch name on a plant would be a sure selling point. This could be one effort to reverse the usual First World exploitation of natural resources, plants and animals alike, suffered in South Africa as elsewhere. As it is, South Africa loses tons of irreplaceable cycad species and aloes among others each year to smuggling. A special department of the SA Police Service investigates such activities.

On a commercial note, some people are now asking why it is that vast numbers of proteas are farmed in Hawaii and arum lilies in New Zealand, for example, when the plants grow wild in South Africa. South Africa, such critics note, has a few world-class advantages, and these must be marketed in a 'new economy' where global competitive advantage is recognised and rewarded by tax benefits and other forms of financial support.

- For information on Kirstenbosch, phone 021 761 4916 or go to www.nbi.ac.za.

This one's for the birds

This book isn't the place to examine the many opportunities South Africa presents to study wildlife, from insects to mammals, including freshwater and sea fish, in a natural setting. Go to any game reserve or wildlife park, and you'll see a mind-numbing variety of species, whether it is butterflies or a hunt for the Big Five.

One feature where South Africa is world-class in opportunities to see a vast range of species is in **birdlife**. Not only are there about 900 species represented in the area, but what might be called the ornithological infrastructure is well developed. There are many protected habitats, numerous bird societies, tours, excellent textbooks (including the well-known illustrated books by Newman, Lockwood and Maclean, the last in revising *Roberts' Birds of Southern Africa*) and high-profile conservation campaigns, e.g. to save the Red Vulture.

- See vultures 30 minutes from Johannesburg in the 'vultures restaurant' at the Rhino and Lion Nature Reserve, Kromdraai, near the Sterkfontein Caves.

Well-heeled foreign ornithologists are said to spend up to R25 million in the country each year, but it is local 'twitchers', as the passionate birders are sometimes called, who are making birdwatching a fast-growing hobby and even changing the fortunes of some small towns. **Wakkerstroom** was a dying *dorp* in Mpumalanga, but it had a wetland. Since birders discovered its White-winged flufftail, Rudd's lark, Bald ibis and Blue korhaan, and many other unusual species, local property prices have gone through the roof. People from the nearby township, Esizameleni, have been trained as bird guides, and the town is back on at least the twitchers' map, as long as it keeps its wetland in its present state.

You can say the same for bird-rich wetlands at Rietfontein on the Vaal river and Memel in the Free State, while the African penguin colony near Simon's Town in the Western Cape pulls in many visitors each year.

- For more details contact BirdLife South Africa (Tel: 011 888 4147).

TAKING A HOLIDAY

Plenty of days to enjoy

The new South Africa recognises 12 current public holidays. These were decided on by the Mandela government following extensive consultation with interest groups, and are shown in Figure 11.

New Year's Day	1 January
Human Rights Day	21 March
Good Friday	March/April
Family Day	the old Easter Monday, March/April
Freedom Day	27 April
Workers' Day	1 May
Youth Day	16 June
National Women's Day	9 August
Heritage Day	24 September
Day of Reconciliation	16 December
Christmas Day	25 December
Day of Goodwill	26 December

If any of these days falls on a Sunday, the following day is recognised as a holiday.

Fig. 11. Public holidays in South Africa.

Many people in the country complain of the days lost to productive activity by what they feel is a plethora of time off, but actually South Africa is no different from other countries. Switzerland, for example, has 15 public holidays; South Africa's neighbours Namibia and Botswana have 14 each and Zimbabwe has 12. The USA has 10 federal holidays, and England and Wales have six bank holidays plus other religious holidays.

Being a multicultural society, South Africa also has Jewish, Hindu and Muslim holidays. Offices, factories and schools, for example, may be affected if staff or students take time off for their own religious celebrations in addition to the statutory holidays.

How do you use these holidays?

Since you are now a South African resident, or planning to become one, we will not discuss the usual tourist holidays you would take as a visitor. This is not to say that going to the Kruger Park, up Table Mountain and the Cape Winelands tour or Durban's beaches are not wonderful things to do. They are, and you should not deprive yourself of any chance to enjoy them.

As a resident, however, you will have more freedom to try other things. This is why we have mentioned various sporting events, gardening and birding activities as examples of alternative ways to use your leisure. Clearly it's a good idea to combine things which various family members would like to do: so if dad is cycling in the Argus, mum and the kids can visit Cape Point or Stellenbosch, and everybody can end the day at the I-Max cinema and eat at Nando's in the Waterfront.

Here are a dozen ideas to consider:

- The **South African War of 1899–1902** is the subject of a rolling programme of activities, including re-enactments of battles, tours of the battlefields, parades, military balls, cultural festivals, exhibitions and sporting events. Contact Ladysmith 1999/2000 Commemoration Project on telephone 0361 22992 or on website: www.battlefields.co.za/centenary. Professional tours of the Battlefields Route can also be found at Tel: 082 802 1643 or email at route@battlefields.org.za.

- Travel the southern African countryside on a **Harley-Davidson** with Wild Hog Tours & Safaris (small groups only, all equipment supplied). The American legend meets wild Africa and it's to be had at Tel: 011 462 2016.

- If the first two ideas are just a bit noisy, the **Buddhist Retreat Centre** at Ixopo in the Natal Midlands is intended for relaxation and meditation. There a programme of conducted retreats or make your own peace. Tel/fax: 039 834 1863 or email at brcixopo@futurenet.co.za. Timeshare also available.

- Another quiet way to spend your time could be creative writing: find a **local writing group** through Writers' World via Options Publishing. Tel: 021 852 4728 or email at optpub@iafrica.com.

- Fancy a **working holiday**? Sattvic Farm near Tzaneen in the Northern Province is an organic vegetable farm, with hiking and sailing on hand. Tel: 0152 3073920.

- Just so that you know and can decide to go there or, perhaps, take efforts to avoid it, **top resort in Africa in 1999** was officially the Palace of the Lost City, at Sun City, as voted by the *Condé Nast Traveler*, published in New York.

- At another end of the holiday spectrum, **Jimmy's Face to Face Tours** have been officially taking visitors on a trip through Soweto for some 15 years, but unofficially for far longer. The three-hour visit costs R150 at the time of writing. Tel: 011 331

6109. Jimmy says he shows the good, the bad and the ugly.

- If you get up a head of steam from travelling on old-style **coal-fired railway engines**, two experiences to savour are the Outeniqua Choo Tjoe, which travels the 100 km from George to Knysna and back in a morning. Tel: 0441 738202, and the Apple Express, a narrow gauge train which runs from Port Elizabeth to Thornhill. Tel: 041 507 2333.

- **Disabled travellers** have a helping hand in Disabled Adventure Tours, contactable in Cape Town. Tel: 021 557 4496.

- If you're the **mountaineering** type, the way to find fellow climbers is to ring the mountain clubs at the universities: try Wits, University of Cape Town (UCT) and University of Natal, Durban.

- There are over 700 **outdoor camp sites**, run mainly by the government's Overaai Resorts, Tel: 012 346 2277 and the private Club Caravelle, Tel: 011 622 4628. These organisations will help you with caravaning and caravan hire.

- If the notion of southern Africa as the cradle of humankind appeals to you, there's many a cave site to visit, including such hallowed ground for the **palaeotourist** as Sterkfontein and Swaartkrans, west of Johannesburg, Giants Castle in the Drakensberg and Klasies River near Port Elizabeth. Excellent books exist cataloguing the many rock art sites. Pursue through the local office of the tourist board, the museums (e.g. the South African Museum) or through the anthropology department at Wits University or UCT.

Glossary

Note that a selection of food and cooking terms is listed on p. 168 above.

Amandla. Freedom.
Apartheid. Literally 'state of being apart', the National Party policy of racial segregation.
Apteek. Pharmacy.
Asseblief. Please.
Babelas. Hung over.
Bad. Bath.
Baie dankie. Thanks very much.
Bakkie. Light delivery truck.
Bantustans. Homelands.
Bel. Phone, ring.
Berg. Mountain.
Bioscope. Cinema.
Boep. Belly, beer gut.
Bonsella. Gift.
Bottle store. Shop selling alcohol.
Bundu. Bush, country.
Buppie. Black yuppie.
Burg. Town.
By us. As in 'stay by us', with us.
Café. Corner shop.
Checkers. Plastic bag, as from supermarket group of this name.
Combi. Closed-in passenger van or minibus taxi.
Comma. Decimal comma, as in decimal point.
Dagga. Cannabis.
Diens. Service.
Donga. Gully created by soil erosion.
Dop. Tot of spirits.
Dorf. Stupid.

Dorp. Small town.

Dumela. Good morning (Sesotho).

Dutchman. Afrikaner.

Dwaal. Not 'with it', dozy.

Ekskuus. Pardon me.

Fanagalo. Mixed language used on the mines.

Fundi. Expert.

Gatvol. Literally 'gut full', cheesed off.

Gebou. Building.

Gesondheid. Health.

Goeiemore, goeienaand. Good morning, good evening.

Hamba kahle. Go well, goodbye (Siswati and general use).

Haw haw. Insect.

Homelands. Reserves for black people in apartheid era, now reabsorbed into the Republic.

Howzit? How are things?

Indaba. Gathering of Zulu chiefs, now any political meeting.

Izit? Really?

Ja-nee. Yes, no, maybe.

Jol. Party, fun.

Just now. In a while, soon.

Kantoor. Office.

Kerk. Church.

Klar. Clear, as in 'finish and klar', meaning 'completely finished'.

Koppie. Hill.

Kraal. Cattle or sheep pen.

Kunjani? How are you? (Siswati and general use.)

Kwaito. Black urban pop music, fusing many styles.

Kwela. Township jazz, using penny whistle.

Laager. Circle of wagons, protection.

Laan. Road.

Larney. Posh, smart.

Late. Deceased, as in 'my father is late'.

Lekker. Nice, good.

Links. Left.

Location. Old name for township.

Marabi. Township jazz.

Mfecane. Literally 'crushing', as in Shaka Zulu's conquests.

Molo. Good morning (Xhosa).

More. Morning, tomorrow.

Mpaqanga. Township jive.

Muti. Medicine, mainly herbal.

Niks. Nothing.
Now now. Very soon.
Oke. Fellow, guy.
Ou. Fellow, guy.
Pad. Road.
Padkos. Literally 'food for the road', packed lunch.
Poskantoor. Post office.
Regs. Right.
Robot. Traffic light.
Rondavel. Circular hut.
Rooibos. Literally 'red bush', herbal tea.
Ry. To drive.
Rylaan. Avenue.
Sangoma. Traditional healer.
Sawubona. Good morning (Siswati).
Shame. Oh, sorry, or Isn't it sweet?
Shebeen. Township tavern.
Sis. I'm disgusted.
Skakel. Ring up, dial.
Skelm. Rogue.
Slegs. Only (in road signs).
Spruit. Stream.
Stoep. Verandah.
Straat. Street.
Takkie. Sneaker.
Te koop. For sale.
Tot siens. Goodbye.
Toyi-toyi. Triumphant dance, often in political or strike context.
Tsotsi. Gangster, also their slang.
Ubuntu. Humanity, tolerance.
Vaalies. Visitors from (former) Transvaal, usually at seaside.
Vasbyt. Keep trying, hold on.
Veld. Grassland.
Voetsak. Go away!
Weg. Road.
Winkel. Shop.
Yebo. Yes, good morning (Zulu and general use).

Useful Addresses

Note that telephone dialling codes are given in parenthesis for non-South African numbers but not for South Africa numbers. This is to remind readers of the need to be sure how much of the prefix code you need when making local or international calls (see also note at the end of the Preface).

EMBASSIES AND CONSULATES

South African embassies overseas

Australia: Rhodes Place, Yarralumla, Canberra, ACT 2600. Tel: (02) 6273 2424; Fax: (02) 6273 2669.

UK: South Africa House, Trafalgar Square, London WC2N 5DP Tel: (020) 7930 4488; Fax: (020) 7839 1419.

USA: 3051 Massachusetts Avenue NW, Washington, DC 20008. Tel: (202) 232 4400; Fax: (202) 265 1607 or Suite 300, 50 North La Cienega Boulevard, Beverly Hills, CA 90211. Tel: (213) 657 9200; Fax: (213) 657 9125.

Zimbabwe: Temple Bar House, Baker Avenue, Harare. Tel: (04) 75 3147.

Overseas embassies in South Africa

Australia: 292 Orient Street, Arcadia, Pretoria 0083. Tel: 012 342 3740; Fax: 012 342 4222.

UK: Liberty Life Place, Block B, first floor, Glyn between Pretorius & Schoeman Streets, Hatfield, Pretoria 0083. Tel: 012 483 1400; Fax: 012 483 1444 (passport), 012 483 1433 (visa). Note that the **passport section** is open to the public from 8.30am to 1.30pm, Monday to Friday; phone queries are taken from 8.30am to 1.30pm only. The **visa section** is open to the public from 8.15am to 12pm, Monday to Friday. Also consult the website at www.britain.org.ca. If you have a touch-tone phone facility, visa and passport forms can be sent through the fax-on-demand service on 082 232 5643.

UK consulate-general: Dunkeld Corner, 275 Jan Smuts Avenue, Dunkeld West, Johannesburg 2196. Tel: 011 327 0015; Fax: 011 327 0156. Check here for branch offices in Cape Town and Durban.

USA: 7877 Pretorius Street, Arcadia, Pretoria 0083. Tel: 012 342 1048; Fax: 012 342 2244.

Zimbabwe: 17th floor, Anderson Street, Johannesburg 2001. Tel: 011 838 5620.

TOURIST OFFICES

The **South Africa Tourist Corporation (Satour)** is the main government tourism organisation. It prints brochures and maps, and lists accommodation options, so might be useful to you for orientation on a first trip to South Africa.

Satour head office in South Africa is at 442 Rigel Avenue South, Erasmusrand, Pretoria 0181. Tel: 012 347 0600; Fax: 012 454 889; website: www.africa.com/satour/index/htm. The main cities have local offices, as given in the telephone book.

Among the Satour offices overseas are:

Australia: Level 6, 285 Clarence Street, Sydney, NSW 2000. Tel: (02) 9261 3424; Fax: (020) 9261 3414.

UK: 5–6 Alt Grove, Wimbledon, London SW19 4DZ. Tel: (020) 8944 8080; Fax: (020) 8944 6705.

USA: 500 Fifth Avenue, 20th Floor, New York, NY 10110. Tel: (212) 730 2929 or (800) 822 5368; Fax: (212) 764 1980; Suite 1524, 9841 Airport Boulevard, Los Angeles, CA 90045. Tel: (310) 641 8444 or (1 800) 782 9772; Fax: (310) 641 5812.

Zimbabwe: Offices 9 & 10, Mon Repos Building, Newlands Shopping Centre, Harare. Tel: (04) 70 7766; Fax: (04) 78 6489.

FRIENDSHIP CLUBS

These private clubs offer discounts on air fares between the UK and South Africa and some car rentals, and limited help with accommodation and travel insurance. The main value of joining could be to increase your networking options as a new arrival (whether in the UK or South Africa).

Friends of the Lion, the 'family reunion specialists', operate out of Johannesburg (head office at Friendship House, corner Oxford and Anerley Road, Parktown 2193, Tel: 011 486 2000), Durban Tel: 031 202 7444 and Cape Town Tel: 021 419 6075. In the UK they are known as **Friends of the Springbok** (at Friendship House, 49–51 Gresham Road, Staines, Middlesex TW18 2BD. Tel: (01784) 465511).

In the UK, the **South Africa Society** describes itself as 'the number one club for South Africans and friends of southern Africa'. Contact at Citibox 80, 2 Old Brompton Road, London SW7 3DQ. Joining fee is £20 a year. Tel: (01883) 626156. The website is: www.southafrica.demon.co.uk.

SOUTH AFRICAN WEBSITES OF INTEREST

A word of caution about the list that follows: websites can change very quickly. This is one of their strengths, of course, but you may find that by the time this book is published even these well-established sites have changed their names or otherwise moved on. With this proviso in mind, try:

South Africa.net at www.southafrica.net (a search engine for sites specific to South Africa); **Aardvark** at www.aardvark.co.za (ditto); **Ananzi** at www.ananzi.co.net (ditto); **Zebra** at www.zebra.co.za (ditto).

Among South African business websites, **South Africa Online** at www.saol.co.za/index.html is a general index for links to South Africa-specific business sites; also useful are **Nedlac** (National Economic Development and Labour Council) at www.nedlac.org.za and **SANGONeT's Open Government page** (NGO listings) at wn.apc.org/environment/envhome.html.

AddressNet is a search engine for South African email addresses, at www.addressnet.co.za.

Among newspaper sites **Mail & Guardian On-line** at www.mg.co.za/mg (the site for the *Mail & Guardian* weekly paper, perhaps the best site for the latest information on the country); **Sunday Times** at www.suntimes.co.za (good for up-to-date stories on personal finance, social security matters, the law and consumer affairs).

The **South African government** has a patchy presence on the web. The Department of Labour, for example, has a site at www.gcis.gov.za/gov/labour/index/htm, which lists the Department's provincial offices and labour offices in each town. The Department of Home Affairs, however, appeared not to have a site accessible to the public at the time of writing.

Sites for the **UK and US governments** offer safety information for overseas tourists or business people, and this may help you in respect of visiting South Africa. The UK Foreign and Commonwealth Office is at www.fco.gov.uk or Tel: (020) 7238 4503, and the US State Department is at www.travel.state.gov or Tel: (202) 647 5225.

The **Internet Service Providers Assocation of SA** can be contacted by email at info@ispa.org.za and the website is www.ispa.org.za.

HUMAN RESOURCES AND LABOUR

See the comprehensive list of contacts given in Chapter 5 above. Note in addition:

Department of Labour head office, 215 Schoeman Street, Pretoria 0001 Tel: 012 309 4000; Fax: 012 323 5449; email: jerry@labourhq.pwv.gov.za.

Commission for Conciliation, Mediation and Arbitration (CCMA) head office Tel: 011 377 6600; Fax: 011 834 7352; email: ho@ccma.org.za.

Congress of South Africa Trades Unions (Cosatu) Tel: 011 339 4911; Fax: 011 339 5080; email: samwu@wn.apc.org.

South African Institute of Management Tel: 011 339 2364; Fax: 011 403 1441; email: saim@netactive.co.za.

Institute of People Management SA Tel: 011 482 4970; Fax: 011 482 5542/3; email: toba@pixie.co.za.

Andrew Levy & Associates (labour consultants and research) Tel: 011 784 9200; Fax: 011 784 9209; email: alagen@bizweb.co.za.

HELP IN TIMES OF EMERGENCY

Crime and violence have become urgent realities of everyday life in contemporary South Africa. Unfortunately, however, help for victims is not dealt with in a co-ordinated way, and there is no single number (like a 911 system as in the USA) to call if you are in a personal crisis. The following numbers are no more than a start.

Life Line runs a crisis telephone counselling service. The national office is at Tel: 011 880 9676; Fax: 011 447 4048. Among other cities already linked are: Cape Town, Tel: 021 461 1111; Durban Tel: 031 23 2323; East London Tel: 0431 220 000; Johannesburg Tel: 011 728 1347; Port Elizabeth Tel: 041 55 5581; and Pretoria Tel: 012 460 666.

Rape Crisis has branches in a number of cities, including Cape Town Tel: 021 47 9762, Pietermaritzburg Tel: 0331 45 6279 and Port Elizabeth Tel: 041 54 3804.

The **Aids Consortium** (an umbrella for 85 organisations) is head-quartered in Johannesburg, Tel: 011 403 0265/0390; the **National Association of People Living with HIV/Aids (Napwa)** is on Tel: 011 403 8113; and the **Aids Helpline** is on toll-free 0800 012 322.

Crime Stop is for people to report crime incidents to the police under conditions of anonymity, at toll-free 0800 11 12 13. Some of the newspapers run **crime-watch** columns, to report both crime activity and police successes (*The Star*, for example, can be telephoned at 011 633 9111 or emailed at crime@star.co.za). The monthly magazine *City Life* runs a useful page of **emergency numbers** (email: donald@citylife.com).

South African Police Services are found in the back of the telephone book under Government Departments, Police Service (SA) section.

Trauma centres offering counselling for crime and violence victims can be contacted in Cape Town, Tel: 021 23 0613 and Durban Tel: 031 305 3497. The Centre for the Study of Violence and Reconciliation is a source of information on all aspects of crime. It is based in Johannesburg. Tel: 011 403 5650; Fax: 011 339 6785.

An all-round telephone emergency and advice service in the Johannesburg area is the **702 helpline** offered by Radio 702. Tel: 011 884 8448, weekdays 10am to 5pm.

BUSINESS CONTACTS

Among foreign chambers of commerce in South Africa are:

American Chamber of Commerce in SA Tel: 011 788 0265; Fax: 011

880 1632; email: amcham@mail-jhb.printlink.co.za.

South African Britain Trade Association Tel: 011 482 4807; Fax: 011 327 0185; email: sabrita@iafrica.com.

Among local umbrella business organisations in South Africa are:

Cape Chamber of Commerce and Industry Tel: 021 418 4300; Fax: 021 418 1800; email: cci@cis.co.za.

Johannesburg Chamber of Commerce and Industry Tel: 011 726 5300; Fax: 011 482 2000; email: jcci@ciz.co.za.

National African Federation of Chambers of Commerce (Nafcoc) Tel: 011 336 0321; Fax: 011 336 0420.

South African Chamber of Business Tel: 011 482 2524; Fax: 011 358 9773/4; email: sacob@cis.co.za.

The Registrar of Companies and Close Corporations Tel: 012 319 9111.

For small business contacts, see Chapter 5.

BANKS

ABSA: action line Tel: 0800 123 456; lost or stolen cards Tel: 0800 111 155; communications centre Tel: 0800 414 141; home loans Tel: 0800 118 007; Bankfin Tel: 0860 000 002.

First National Bank (FNB): customer care Tel: 0800 111 722; lost cards Tel: 0800 110 132; home loans Tel: 0860 334 455; card division Tel: 011 52 5678; WesBank Tel: 0800 137 137.

NBS: inquiries Tel: 0860 331 133; info centre Tel: 0860 333 111.

Nedcor: lost, stolen or returned cards for Nedbank, Permanent or Peoples Bank Tel: 0800 110 929; Visa or Mastercard Tel: 0800 117 871; card division Tel: 0800 116 662; electronic banking Tel: 0860 115 060; cellular help line Tel: 0800 114 990; home loans Tel: 011 710 3000/4444; client care Tel: 0800 110 180.

Standard: hotline for stolen cards Tel: 0800 020 600; Diners Club inquiries Tel: 0800 112 017; home loans Tel: 0860 123 001; Stannic customer services Tel: 0860 123 002.

Banking ombudsman (only to be contacted after having complained to your bank) Tel: 011 838 0035; Fax: 011 838 0043.

RETIREMENT

SA Council for the Aged Tel: 021 24 6270; Fax: 021 23 2168; email: saca@iafrica.com.

SA Association of Retired Persons Tel: 021 592 1279/1289.

The British government office dealing with overseas national insurance contributions is the **NI Contributions Office**, International Services, Newcastle upon Tyne NE99 1ZZ, UK. Tel: (from UK) 06452 57877, Tel: (from RSA) 0944 191 2257877. Until 1998 the office was known as The Contributions Agency.

INSURANCE

The Insurance Institute of SA Tel: 011 834 6062; Fax: 011 834 2732; email: iisa@iafrica.com; website: www.iisa.co.za.

The Life Offices Association Tel: 021 419 3063; Fax: 021 419 3887; email: loa@loa.co.za.

Institute of Retirement Funds of SA Tel: 011 403 2286; Fax: 011 403 1410; email: irfsa@global.co.za.

The SA Insurance Association Tel: 011 403 8150; Fax: 011 403 2273.

Life insurance ombudsman (if disputes with life and long-term insurers cannot be resolved) Tel: 021 461 5010; Fax: 021 465 3769.

Short-term insurance ombudsman (ditto) Tel: 011 339 6525; Fax: 011 339 7065.

PROPERTY

For problems with builders of a new property, check if they are registered with the **National Home Buildings Registration Council** (they should be). Tel: 011 886 3636; Fax: 011 789 2902.

For problems with estate agents, the national body is the **Estate Agency Affairs Board**. Tel: 011 883 7700; Fax: 011 883 5655; email: eab@eaab.org.za; website: www.eaab.org.za.

The **Sectional Title Help Line** is a free advice service for sectional title holders. Tel:/Fax: 011 393 2671; email: bobgauld@pixie.co.za.

The **Landlord/Tenant Dispute Resolution Board** for landlord/tenant problems. Tel: 011 355 4000/4006; Fax: 011 838 8971.

CARS

The **Automobile Association** offers members technical and legal advice and aid. For breakdowns, Tel: 0800 010 101 or 011 799 1500; legal: 011 799 1300/1305; technical: 011 799 1963/4.

The **Vehicle Security Association (Vesa)** oversees the quality of security systems like gearlocks and alarm systems; most insurance companies insist on Vesa-approved systems. Tel: 011 315 3588; Fax: 011 315 3617; email: vesa@vesa.co.za; website: www.security.co.za.

The **Motor Industry Federation (MIF)** approves member garages, and keeps an eye on standards of new and second-hand car sales and car repairs. MIF has offices in the major cities. Head office, Tel: 011 789 2542; Fax: 011 789 4525.

Driving licence: for problems with the new credit card format, Tel: 012 309 3722 or 012 309 3759.

The **car manufacturers** all have help lines, some toll-free and some not. Look in your telephone book.

CREDIT RATINGS

With a high level of debt defaults and liquidations, credit ratings can be a hazard for South African citizens. To check your own credit rating or seek advice, try one of the two leading bureaux: **Experian** Tel: 089 110 5665 or **ITC** (via agents Compu-Pay) Tel: 011 488 2911 or 011 484 0308.

If there are still problems, write to the **Credit Bureau Association** at PO Box 57039, Arcadia, Pretoria 0007.

HEALTH

The **Interim National Medical and Dental Council of SA** (which is due to be renamed the Health Professions Council of SA) is the national body which hears complaints about doctors and dentists.

Tel: 012 328 6680; Fax: 012 328 5120.

The **medical ombudsman** investigates complaints about charges or treatments by doctors. Tel: 0800 119 820.

The **dental ombudsman** performs a similar function in the case of dentists. Tel: 0800 113 334.

For complaints about medical schemes, contact the **Registrar of Medical Schemes**. Tel: 012 312 0000; Fax: 012 326 4344 or 012 325 5978.

PENSIONS

Problems with government pensions should be referred to the local welfare department (address in phone book). The **National Department of Welfare** has a toll-free number at 0800 601 011.

The **Pension Funds Adjudicator** is contactable at Tel: 021 454 041; Fax: 021 454 046.

If you still have problems with the state pension the next port of call is the **Public Protector**, Tel: 0800 112 040 or 012 322 2916; Fax: 012 322 5093. This office investigates complaints by the public against any government department or state-owned company, including Telkom, the Post Office, Transnet, government or regional hospitals, the SA Revenue Service, most universities and technikons and Satour.

POST OFFICE

Toll-free numbers exist for complaints about postal crime. Tel: 0800 033 554; speed services 0800 023 133; for track, trace and general complaints 0800 111 502.

TELKOM

The toll-free number for ordering a new telephone service or getting information is 10219; service faults 10212; account enquiries 10210. Ask for the regional executive if your problem is not being attended to.

TAXES

The local office of the **SA Revenue Service (SARS)** should be able to resolve most tax problems; if not, go higher to the regional manager (there are five of these countrywide), then the SARS communication and client service. Tel: 012 422 4000. SARS has a website at www.sars.gov.za.

Further Reading

The A to Z of Careers in South Africa (Don Nelson, Cape Town, 1998).

The A to Z of Work and Study Opportunities in South Africa (3rd edn, Don Nelson, Cape Town, 1997).

Analysing Company Information: A Book for Trade Unions, Trade Union Research Project (TURP, Johannesburg, 1998).

Anatomy of a Miracle: The End of Apartheid and the Birth of the New South Africa, Patti Waldmeir (Penguin, London, 1998).

The ANC and the Liberation Struggle: A Critical Political Biography, Dale McKinley (Pluto Press, London, 1997).

The Atlas of Apartheid, A. J. Christopher (Witwatersrand University Press, Johannesburg, 1994).

The Best IT Companies in South Africa (Zebra, Rivonia, 1999).

Business Blue-Book of South Africa 1999 (National Publishing, Cape Town, 1999). Annual updates, in print over 60 years.

Country of My Skull, Antjie Krog (Random House, Johannesburg, 1998). A poet attends the TRC hearings.

A Dictionary of South African English on Historical Principles: South African Words and their Origins, Oxford University Press/The Dictionary Unit for South African English (Oxford University Press, New York, 1996).

Doing Business in South Africa, eds Jonathan Reuvid and Ian Priestner (4th edn, Kogan Page, London, 1999).

Everyman's Guide to the South African Economy, Andre Roux (Zebra, Halfway House, 1997).

Everyone's Guide to Stock Market Profits in South Africa, Bernard Joffe (Zebra, Halfway House, 1998).

The 50 Most Promising Companies in South Africa, Corporate Research Foundation (Zebra, Halfway House, 1998).

'Five Years into Freedom', article by Nadine Gordimer, *Sunday Times*, 27 June 1999.

The 49 Best Companies to Work For in South Africa, Corporate Research Foundation (Zebra, Halfway House, 1998).

Giving People with Disabilities the Opportunity to Enjoy Our National Heritage, Rob and Julia Filmer (Eco Access Guide, Johannesburg, 1999; Tel: 011 477 3676; Fax: 011 477 3675; website: www.link.co.za/ecoace).

Indaba, My Children, Credo Mutwa (Hahn & Averill, London, 1994).

Last Days in Cloud Cuckooland: Dispatches from White Africa, Graham Boynton (Jonathan Ball Publishers, Johannesburg, 1997).

The Life and Times of Thabo Mbeki, Adrian Hadland and Jovial Rantao (Struik, Cape Town, 1999).

Long Walk to Freedom, Nelson Mandela (Random House, Johannesburg, 1994). Abbreviated and illustrated editions also available.

Mail & Guardian A–Z of South African Politics: The Essential Handbook, eds. Philip van Niekerk and Barbara Ludman (Penguin, Johannesburg, 1999).

Managing Your Finances after Retirement, H. B. Falkena and C. W. Luus (4th edn, ABSA Bank/Southern Book Publishers, Halfway House, 1998).

Mandela: The Authorised Biography, Anthony Sampson (Jonathan Ball/HarperCollins, Johannesburg, 1999).

The Mind of South Africa, Allister Sparks (Knopf, New York, 1990).

One Miracle is Not Enough, Rex van Schalkwyk (Bellwether Publications, Johannesburg, 1998).

Retirement: The Amazing and Scary Truth, Bruce Cameron and Magnus Heystek (Worth Publishing, Fourways, 1998).

Sing the Beloved Country: The Struggle for the New South Africa, Peter Hain (Pluto Press, London, 1996).

South Africa at a Glance (4th edn, Editors Inc, Johannesburg, 1999).

South Africa Business Guidebook: The Essential Guide to Doing Business in SA (WriteStuff Publishing, Joahnnesburg, 1998).

South Africa Handbook 1999, S. Ballard (3rd edn, Footprint Handbooks, London, 1998).

South Africa Survey 1998/99, SA Institute of Race Relations (SAIRR, Johannesburg, 1999). The long-established survey, updated annually.

South African Politics since 1994, Tom Lodge (David Philip, Cape Town, 1999).

South Africa's Future: From Crisis to Prosperity, Anthony Ginsberg (Pan Macmillan, Basingstoke, 1998).

South from the Limpopo, Dervla Murphy (Flamingo, London, 1998).

Soweto: A History, Philip Bonner and Lauren Segal (African Book Centre, London, 1998).

Starting Your Own Business in South Africa, Guy Macleod (9th edn, Oxford University Press, Cape Town, 1999).

The Structure of the South African Economy, J. du Toit (ABSA Bank/Southern Book Publishers, Halfway House, 1998).

Successful Small Business Management in South Africa, Collin Wright (6th edn, Struik, Cape Town, 1995).

Tomorrow is Another Country: The Inside Story of South Africa's Negotiated Revolution, Allister Sparks (Arrow Books, London, 1995).

Tourism Talk: Tourism Statistics (5th edn, Grant Thornton Kessel Feinstein, Johannesburg, 1998).

Traveller's Survival Kit, South Africa, J. & D. Penrith (Vacation Work, London, 1997).

The Truth about the Truth Commission, Anthea Jefferey (SAIRR, Johannesburg, 1999).

Twentieth-Century South Africa, William Beinart (Oxford University Press, Cape Town, 1994).

'Unity's Rainbow', article in *Time* by Peter Hawthorne, part of a special report on South Africa, 24 May 1999.

With Criminal Intent: The Changing Face of Crime in South Africa, Rob Marsh (Ampersand Press, Johannesburg, 1999).

You're the Boss! How to Grow Rich by Working for Yourself, Mike Lipkin and Eric Parker (Deloitte & Touche, Johannesburg, 1999).

Newspapers and magazines

Dailies: *Beeld, Business Day, Business Report, Cape Times, The Citizen, The Mercury, Sowetan, The Star.*

Weeklies: *Financial Mail, International Express* (Southern Africa edition), *Mail & Guardian, Sunday Independent, Sunday Times.*

Lifestyle: *Cosmopolitan* (SA edition), *Ebony SA, Fair Lady, Marie Claire* (SA edition), *Men's Health* (SA edition), *Personality, You.*

Index